German Theater before 1750

The German Library: Volume 8
Volkmar Sander, General Editor

GERMAN THEATER
BEFORE 1750

Edited by Gerald Gillespie
Foreword by Martin Esslin

CONTINUUM · NEW YORK

1992
The Continuum Publishing Company
370 Lexington Avenue, New York, NY 10017

The German Library
is published in cooperation with Deutsches Haus,
New York University.
This volume has been supported by a grant
from the Marie Baier Foundation.

Printed in the United States of America

Library of Congress Cataloging-in-Publication Data

German theater before 1750 / edited by Gerald Gillespie ; foreword by
Martin Esslin.
    p.   cm. — (The German library ; v. 8)
   ISBN 0-8264-0702-1 (cloth) — ISBN 0-8264-0703-X (pbk.)
   1. German drama—Translations into English.   2. English drama—
—Translations from German.   I. Gillespie, Gerald Ernest Paul, 1933–
. II. Series.
PT1258.G48   1991
832.008—dc20

                                     91-15686
                                         CIP

Contents

Foreword: Martin Esslin   vii

Introduction: Gerald Gillespie   xi

HROTSVITHA OF GANDERSHEIM
Dulcitius   3
Translated by Katharina Wilson

HANS SACHS
Fool Surgery   13
Translated by Martin W. Walsh

PAUL REBHUN
Susanna   27
Translated by M. John Hanak

ANDREAS GRYPHIUS
Leo Armenius   99
Translated by Janifer G. Stackhouse

DANIEL CASPER VON LOHENSTEIN
Sophonisba   139
Translated by M. John Hanak

JOHANN ELIAS SCHLEGEL
The Dumb Beauty   215
Translated by André Lefevere

Foreword

Hans Sachs (1494–1576), who described himself, in an oft-quoted rhyme, as a "shoe- / maker and poet too," and one of whose Shrovetide plays is included in this volume, is the hero of Wagner's *Mastersingers of Nuremberg* (1868). There he represents the most genuinely poetical among the guild of amateur poets and composers, whose practice of their art is ridiculed by Wagner as hidebound by mechanical and arbitrary rules and conventions. Sachs is the only one who senses that the young knight, Walter von Stolzing, is a genuine poet whose genius is spontaneous and free from these shackles.

One of the main themes of the opera is the great divide between the literature of the epoch before the rise of the eighteenth-century classics and early nineteenth-century romantics and that of the previous two centuries, which was, like the work of the mastersingers, felt to be clumsy, quaint, and slightly comic. In the consciousness of most Germans (and even more so of the outside world insofar as it takes any interest in German literature at all) German drama tended to start with the Enlightenment, the great rivals Johann Christoph Gottsched (1700–66) and Gotthold Ephraim Lessing (1729–81) who opened the way towards the rise of the great German classical drama of Goethe and Schiller and the reentry of Germany into the circle of the major national literatures of Europe to rival the France of Corneille, Racine, and Molière, the England of Shakespeare and Ben Jonson, the Spain of Calderón and Lope de Vega.

What lay between the Middle Ages and their great Middle High German troubadours and epic poets (on whom Wagner drew for the material of so many operas—*Lohengrin, Tannhäuser, Tristan, The Ring, Parsifal*) appeared to the post-Enlightenment generations as, with very few exceptions, second-rate, barbaric, and as far as drama was concerned, unperformable. Had not, in the seventeenth century, the German language and German art lost its foothold even in most princely courts, where French was spoken and Italian operas formed the staple entertainment?

In his great programmatic pronouncement at the end of the *Mastersingers* Wagner makes Hans Sachs himself warn, with the infallible prophetic power of a later epoch's hindsight, that there will soon be a time when "in false Frenchified majesty no prince will understand his own people any more and Frenchified fog and Frenchified frivolity will be planted in our German lands." Here Hans Sachs speaks for the mastersingers—"do not despise the masters," he tells Walter, because, imperfect as they might be, they represent the continuity of German art. Yet it is equally significant that Wagner's true poet, Walter von Stolzing, himself derives his poetry from having read an old book by Walther von der Vogelweide, the greatest of Middle High German minnesingers.

Thus Wagner's work, one of the most significant creations of German theater of its century, represents the self-contradictory paradox in the attitude of his generation of late romantics: if the German art of the fourteenth to seventeenth centuries was quaint and uncouth, yet it was still German and could become the soil from which a new great German literature could spring.

It was only in the first half of the twentieth century that the literature of this despised, and almost repressed, period of German culture was gradually rediscovered: a modernist poet like Hugo von Hofmannsthal was deeply moved by the sublime simplicity of late medieval mystery and morality plays and re-created one of them in his *Everyman;* and the expressionists found affinities both with the drastic directness, bluntness, and "naïveté" of the Nuremberg artisan poets and the ornate and stately pathos, mingled with the most brutal cruelty, of such Jesuit playwrights as Bidermann or the Silesian Protestant dramatists, Gryphius and Lohenstein.

Walter Benjamin, one of the most important critics of the twenties and thirties, in his treatise on the *Origins of the German Trauerspiel,* used the Silesian school as the basis of a most illuminating distinction between classical concepts of "tragedy" and the baroque "Trauerspiel" (play of mourning), which lacks the element of genuine moral conflict and becomes a stately ritual of mourning, an allegory of the inherent sadness of the human condition. He linked this literature with the baroque preoccupation with melancholy (as exemplified in Robert Burton's great *Anatomy of Melancholy,* 1621). For Benjamin the overelaboration and "bombast" of these baroque dramatists seemed by no means a handicap, and he saw that in baroque works "the authority of a pronouncement does not depend on its immediate comprehensibility, that indeed it can even be enhanced by its opacity"—an insight pointing towards surrealism in the early twentieth century and towards poststructuralist stylistic doctrines of our own time.

Benjamin's generation was in revolt against the oppressive prominence of the "classics" of German drama (Goethe, Schiller, Heinrich von Kleist, Friedrich Hebbel, Franz Grillparzer) both in the German repertoire and in the intellectual furniture in the minds of the *Bildungsbürger,* the educated and philistine bourgeoisie. Hence their desire to go back to the wild and perhaps crude forms of theater the Enlightenment reformers had suppressed and discredited. If Gottsched had tried to banish improvisation and obscene unscripted ribaldry from the German stage by the ceremonial burning of the "Hanswurst" in 1737, the opposition against the academically respectable and "cleaned-up" drama of the German Stadttheater tried to rekindle the old traditions of the popular forms derived from the strolling English companies of the early seventeenth century, the commedia dell'arte influences that had shaped German popular theater from Italy, and the mystery and artisan drama of earlier times. Much of this tradition had survived in the Austro-Bavarian folk-theater centered in Vienna, in the dialect and peasant troupes of rural areas, and in the puppet theater (from which, after all, Goethe had derived the idea for his *Faust*).

Walter Benjamin's close friend Bertolt Brecht became one of the protagonists of this movement away from the "respectable" drama taught in the schools; he abominated Schiller, despised Goethe, and violently objected to Wagner. The Munich folk comedian Karl Valentin, the clowns and barkers at fairgrounds, the Viennese folk drama of Ferdinand Raimund and Johann Nestroy with its liberal use of "couplets," refrain-songs addressed directly to the audience, and the Bavarian dialect play *(Volksstück)* became his models for an attempt to link up with the hitherto despised crude, inelegant, and "uneducated" tradition.

Brecht today is one of the dominant influences on German dramatic writing as well as the style of production and performance; on the directors who, while still performing Goethe and Schiller, are bent on "deconstructing" them and play them "critically." Here too the hitherto suppressed traditions reemerge onto the surface. If a playwright like Franz Xaver Krötz returns to the rudeness and directness of artisan and peasant theater, others like Peter Handke in plays like *Über die Dörfer* and *Spiel vom Fragen* echo the immensely long and "undramatic" speeches of the Silesian baroque, while a radical innovator like the later Heiner Müller experiments in dumb show, ritual, allegory, and static recitation.

Walter Benjamin considered the Baroque Trauerspiel to be essentially closet drama, for reading rather than performance, although the works were presented by the pupils of the grammar schools of Breslau in their time. Yet in the postmodern atmosphere of today efforts to reintroduce Gryphius and Lohenstein have been made in the German theater, albeit in heavily edited versions that tend to omit the choral-balletic interludes *(Reyen)*. Whether they succeed in reestablishing these plays as an essential ingredient of the German "classical" repertoire remains to be seen; yet the impact of these plays as poetry and their influence on contemporary creative work are stronger than ever, and hand in hand with their reemergence into the limelight of literary and academic interest, the baroque playwrights in new editions have closed the hiatus that so long bisected Germany's literary and theatrical history.

MARTIN ESSLIN

Introduction

From the eleventh to the thirteenth centuries German writers rivaled the Provençal and French in the creation of heroic epics, courtly romances, and poetry of exceptional beauty. Another striking parallel with the Romanic world was the absence of a high drama cultivated in the international German language of the Middle Ages. The early story of drama in the German-speaking lands is one of several rebeginnings. It is also a story set forth in two languages, Latin and German.

Although a genuine classical revival first took place at the end of the fifteenth century, Terence, Plautus, and Seneca were known throughout the Middle Ages. When in 1494 Conrad Celtis rediscovered the Latin works by the Saxon canoness Hrotsvitha from the late tenth century, his fellow German humanists, eager to vie with their Romanic neighbors, were thrilled over this evidence of their own nation's cultural roots. Hrotsvitha adapted Terentian comedy form to dramatize spiritual conflict and the triumph of Christian values. The swift action, lively dialogue, and rhetorical sophistication of her plays in rhymed rhythmic prose supported the Augustinian worldview. Her *Dulcitius,* with which our volume begins, serves to represent the brilliance of the Ottonian period and the abiding appeal of the martyr drama. This was one tradition that the great Protestant playwrights of the baroque would readily coopt for their own purposes.

Outside intellectual centers like the imperial convent of Gandersheim where Hrotsvitha composed in elegant Latin, there were both religious and secular forms of theater in German well before the Renaissance.

As in England and France, miracle, mystery, and morality plays in the vernacular were popular in medieval Germany. The mystery plays derived from the celebration of sacred moments in the ritual calendar, especially the liturgical ceremonies of Christmas, Easter, and other major feasts. Originally couched in Latin, these works eventually expanded beyond the confines of the church and became an important element of town life. Although still written and directed by members of the clergy, the parts were acted in German by local citizens. Even if the physical stage were laid out on ground level, imaginatively the action opened onto the two other levels, Heaven and Hell. Sometimes the three cosmological strata were expressed by the theater scaffolding, with earth and its human actors in the actual middle, Heaven above, and Hell underneath the stage. That was the implicit situation of humankind in the didactic genre of the morality plays like the influential Dutch *Homunculus* or English *Everyman*. The Cologne printer Jasper von Gennep's translation of 1536 helped assure *Everyman*'s lasting popularity in German. Miracle plays ordinarily celebrated one or more legends associated with a saint, the Virgin Mary being by far the favorite subject.

But a tendency toward narrative expansion appeared around the fourteenth century. Religious plays began assuming epic proportions, covering the entire range of salvational history. Passion plays might actually deal with everything from the creation and fall of man, to the figures of the Old Testament and notable heathens, the story of Christ, the collapse of pagan antiquity, the struggle with the Antichrist, and the last Judgment. We see this sweep, analogous to the pictorial wealth of a great cathedral, in the anonymous Hessian work *Redemption* (earliest MS 1337). Easter plays proper were concentrated more specifically on Christ's life, crucifixion, and resurrection. Typically they, too, were staged in the actual town square and could last several days. As the scene shifted from location to location, the attending citizens alternated between being actors and spectators, and could enjoy copious subplots and small details. The plays ranged through a wide repertory of subgeneric moments and rhetorical modes. In some larger cities like Vienna, teachers and students of the university's faculty of arts were involved in such productions, and they enjoyed aristocratic patronage. But there were also complaints about unseemly worldly elements in such plays.

It is interesting that comedy evolved naturally from all three types—the miracle, morality, and mystery play. Once they left the confines of the church, religious plays were pulled toward the culture of the folk at large. The devils furnished a major internal source of comedy with their ridiculous looks and antics. Diverting entertainment was ordinarily the purpose of the interludes breaking up the serious action; these often contained music (and were the nucleus of the later *Singspiel* or sung intermezzo). Farce invaded from the secular world, as successors to the ancient Roman mimes, jugglers, and strolling players found gainful employment at religious festivals or students took over their techniques. The *Schwank* or farcical jest, like the French *sottise,* remained popular. The ritual fool figures, who originated in the pagan nature festivals of Europe, most notably Shrovetide (entering Lent) and Twelfth Night (Christmas to kalends of January), provided staple clowns. In the mid–sixteenth century, the diverse roles of the Italian commedia dell'arte began to be appreciated in the large cities of the German South and West. A celebration exploiting commedia motifs is recorded in Munich in 1568. The commedia entered by way of the sophisticated Renaissance courts, but its clowns never displaced the native favorites such as Hanswurst (Jack Pudding) on the marketplace.

The seasonal outbreaks of folly were an opportunity for members of the lower clergy and burghers not only to celebrate but also to exercise the traditional license to mock and critique the authorities and social phenomena. In the carnivalesque setting powerful surges of crude realism could occur. The Shrovetide plays of the late Middle Ages reflect regional and class variations. In the Low German areas they were cultivated by the bourgeois patriciate and urban nobles and had a strong didactic streak. In the Alpine region they were attached to the oldest folk usages, native tales, and grotesque figures. In southern cities like Nuremberg companies of mummers, largely artisans, put on endless revues of traditional fools, carried out pranks, and enacted allegories and mock trials. Their repertory included pre-Christian ritual activities such as dancing, parades, and combats, but also materials of classical learning and medieval lore. The Nuremberg poet Hans Rosenplüt made the Shrovetide play into a vehicle for contemporary social and political satire on such topics as the ills of the church, the threat posed to burgher and peasants by the nobles, and the failure of the Holy Roman Empire in the face of the Turkish menace.

The effects of the Renaissance and Reformation on drama in the sixteenth century were profound. The new universities were less inhibited than the schools, and humanist comedies copying Roman models began to reach performance in the 1480s and 1490s. Jacob Wimpfeling's *Stylpho* (1480), a Terentian satire on the greed of the clergy, anticipated sentiments in the famous confrontation between Renaissance adherents and opponents sparked by the *Letters of Obscure Men*. This international debate of the second decade of the sixteenth century swirled around the humanist Hebrew expert Johannes Reuchlin, whose earlier play *Henno* (1497) cheerfully attacked academic ignorance and charlatanism in pure Latin iambics, while introducing the neoclassical five-act structure. Sebastian Brant and his student Jakob Locher published a Terence edition in 1499, but Brant's *Mirror of Virtue* (1512) adopted the German language to reach the broad public, following the trend set by the mystery plays. Erasmus's edition of Seneca came out in 1516. By 1518, Thomas Naogeorgus translated all of Sophocles into Latin. The presentation of Aristophanes' *Pluto* in Greek in Zurich in 1531 was accompanied by the reformer Huldrych Zwingli's music. One of the most remarkable centers of renewal was the academy theater of the Protestant gymnasium at Strassburg headed by Johannes Sturm (1538–81). Students were instructed in Aristotelian and Horatian poetics, the works of Plautus, Terence, Sophocles, Euripides, and put on neo-Latin dramas, often with biblical themes. The academy continued into the seventeenth century under Kasper Bülow (1585–1627), its repertory augmented by new plays influenced by Seneca.

It was crucial that Martin Luther encouraged Protestants to cultivate the drama both in Latin and German as a means to educate youth and build the intellectual cadres required for the transformation of society. One of the effects of the Reformation was a rapprochement of the learned and popular theater. Another was the weakening of the mysteries and their retreat into the Catholic territories. Although the mysteries became firmly implanted in the South by the Thirty Years' War, in Catholic cities like Munich they were modified to purge vulgar or corrupting elements. This met the heightened intellectual standards of the Counter-Reformation. Officially supported theater became a battleground of beliefs. When the Counter-Reformation eventually gained control over the school stages in many universities and reused the old plays, it assimilated many techniques of humanist theater and introduced currents from Spanish drama. I shall return to this significant new opening to European drama in connection with the emergence of a high drama in the baroque period.

It is noteworthy that although Protestants rejected the mysteries with the cult of the saints, they clung to the native tradition of Shrovetide plays. As successor to the Nuremberg mastersinger Hans Folz, Hans Sachs united in his comedies the traditions of the popular and university theaters. While drawing on all newer sources of erudition, he kept the peppery diction and predominantly iambic, four-beat line *(Knittelvers)* of the Shrovetide genre. *Knittelvers* resembles its next of kin, the four-beat "doggerel" of older English plays. Both were displaced by the end of the sixteenth century through the introduction of Italian and French prosody. Sachs's *Fool Surgery* of 1557, reproduced in this volume, represents the lasting hold of the thematics of folly in the Renaissance period. The Nuremberg poet also tried his hand at introducing tragedy in German, for example, writing a *Lucretia* (1527) and *Virginia* (1530), stories well-suited for raising burgher consciousness.

The boisterousness of the Shrovetide genre appears in many partisan plays by religious propagandists. This is more evident in southern and Swiss authors. For example, in Niclaus Manuel's *Pardon Peddler* (1525), the indulgence seller who is tormented, despoiled, and driven out by undeceived villagers fills the role of the fool as criminal scapegoat. The Protestant humanist Thomas Naogeorgus's *Pammachius* (1538, originally composed in Latin), is a broader attack on the contemporary Catholic church and papacy transposed onto the reign of the emperor Julian. Naogeorgus coopts the framework of salvational history from the older passion plays for his own purposes. The work opens with Christ, Peter, and Paul reviewing the historical situation, Satan himself and allegorical figures intervene in the action, prophetic reference is made to Luther, and at the end the audience is told directly that the drama, that is, the struggle against Catholicism, will and must continue. The Rhineland author Burkard Waldis's *Prodigal Son* (1527) marks the start of Protestant "biblical" drama proper. The entire action centers around this favorite parable that is understood as validating the Lutheran doctrine of salvation by faith rather than good works, and Waldis adapts the classical chorus to function as the communal voice. Similarly, the Old Testament story in the play *Susanna* by the Austrian Paul Rebhun, who became a member of the Saxon school of writers, is transparently interpretable as upholding Lutheran tenets of inward trust and morality. By her perseverance the pious wife pictures the model citizen and believer, while with his fresh voice of truth the young prophet Daniel (Luther) exposes the corrupt authority of merely outward law in the Elders (the old Catholic order of Europe). The wrongly accused woman who is vindicated also was a popular theme of the humanist novella.

Rebhun's *Susanna* was successful when rewritten in "doggerel" three years after tepid reception of the experimental verse forms used in its first performance (1535). Rebhun anticipated the modern course both of German prosody and of dramatic structure, but his innovation—the version reproduced in this volume—was precociously in advance of its public. The division into acts and scenes, and the pattern of rising action toward the climax and falling action toward the catastrophe, reflected (Italian) Renaissance practice; closure of each act by a chorus, an attempt to imitate ancient drama, strengthened the clear construction. Most remarkable was Rebhun's skillful adaptation of Romanic line forms and meters. He frequently used three-, four-, and five-beat iambic verses, the latter the earliest analogy to English blank verse, and four-, five-, and six-beat trochees. The longer lines are reserved for important scenes and moments of solemnity, as in court, but hexameter and anapest are avoided in dialogue. Somewhat as in later Spanish Golden Age drama, the specific verse form establishes the ground tone of each scene. The choruses employ complicated strophic forms and attain genuine lyrical heights. Martin Optiz would recapitulate this breakthrough of Renaissance standards at the boundary of baroque style in the third decade of the seventeenth century.

The multiple foci of drama in the later sixteenth century included all the above-named and some newer developments. The high tradition of humanist drama in Latin was well represented by Nicodemus Frischlin's works such as the symbolic comedy *Priscianus vapulans* (1578), and the narrative dialogues *Dido* (1581) and *Venus* (1584). His *Julius redivivus* (1585), featuring the hero Arminius, was notable as a panegyric to German nationalism; while his *Rebecca* (1576) and *Susanna* (1577) built on the new biblical school drama. The literary reputation of the mastersingers began to decline as the newer learned class trained by humanists assumed increasing importance. Troupes of English "comedians," that is, Elizabethan players who performed in Denmark and Holland, began to tour German cities, too, in the 1580s and 1590s. Jakob Ayrer (d. 1605) continued the Nuremberg Shrovetide play but also cultivated the more refined *Singspiel* (musical) influenced by the English strollers. The English introduced the taste for mixed genres and for such favorite clowns as Jack Pudding *(Hanswurst)* and Pickeled Hering *(Pickelhäring)*. For example, Duke Heinrich Julius of Brunswick invited the company of Thomas Sacheville for a sojourn in 1592; their influence can be seen in the duke's own comedy of character, *Vincentius Ladislaus*. Eventually, German actors replaced the foreign, and the serious plot materials of the English comedians, later termed *Haupt-und Staatsaktionen* (chief and state actions), devolved into the general repertory of wandering troupes. The taste for violence and gruesomeness fed by the "English" players had its more elegant parallel in the Senecanism of the Strassburg academy theater. When Johannes Paul Crusius returned from Paris to assume the directorship in 1611, his emphasis was on dividing each piece into a main and several subplots; this permitted combining popular scenes, operatic elements, and horrific moments. The juxtaposition of Renaissance impulses with newer popular modes appears in the efforts of Landgrave Moritz of Hesse who in 1604 built Germany's first standing theater, the Ottoneum, in "the old Roman style." On the one hand, he was influenced by the English comedians and created many plays on biblical themes. On the other hand, he admired Ariosto, promoted the study and translation of Italian, and invited Castiglione as a teacher.

The international Jesuit theater was one of the most important forces helping consolidate Renaissance awareness of drama by the seventeenth century. Its roots in Germany went back to the performance of the festival play *Samson* in Munich in 1568 for the wedding of Duke Wilhelm V. The theory and practice of the Bohemian German Jakob Pontanus at the end of the sixteenth century blended Italian ideas, accepted a general Aristotelian definition of tragedy, stressed the educative, rhetorical function of schooling in drama, and contributed to the rebirth of humanist cultivation of Latin for high literary art. The Italian Jesuit Alexander Donatus emphasized the keeping of the unities, correct delineation of character, and the use of music for accompanying effect. The most lasting influence on seventeenth-century Jesuit dramaturgy from Jakob Gretser, over Jakob Bidermann, to Nikolaus Avancini came from the Lowlander Jakob Masen who embraced the Aristotelian concept of catharsis, approximated the French classical direction, and insisted on verisimilitude in characterization, but favored the Spanish principle of making the viewer aware of the illusion on stage and using surprise. The goal of such baroque theater of the world was the artistic transfiguration of reality.

The first significant embodiment of the thematics of the theater of the world, Jakob Bidermann's *Cenodoxus* (ca. 1602 in Latin), typifies the new surge of creativity at the baroque threshold. Expressly subtitled *comico-tragoedia,* Bidermann's fusion of genres, ordinarily separated in Renaissance neoclassical poetics, yielded a construct well suited for attacking the vainglory of humanism. While the scholar Cenodoxus's admirers are dazzled by the deceptive exemplary action, the outer audience appreciates with increasing dismay this show by a self-disciplined actor who rounds out the hollow role of heroic intellect in a perfect Stoic death. His entire existence, we realize, is in effect only a play within a play, but he has become beholden to his own illusory "image" before a public whose applause he craves. The ironic spectacle begins with humor that contains the elements of disaster and ends with the consequences that emerge from the deceptive levity of existence. Bidermann holds in reserve, for the end of act 5, St. Bruno's striking withdrawal to found the Carthusian Order as a contrast to the prolix, deception passion of Cenodoxus. The outer audience directly witnesses the arguments in the trial of Cenodoxus above before heaven's tribunal, completing the dramatic conflict already fought on the temporal plane. Bruno thus functions as the ideal spectator-player below on the world stage, unlike the prideful, empty, condemned darling of this world's elite.

Conversion is the subject of Bidermann's *Philemon martyr* (ca. 1615). Because Philemon possesses an imaginative flexibility that permits his heart to be stirred and become a vessel for divine inspiration, the proletarian wastrel, a mere pagan actor, is led onto a new pathway. The Christian community faces a real test when the imperial decree arrives commanding public obeisance to Jupiter. Overpowered by fear, their leader Apollonius hires the eager Philemon to impersonate him at the loyalty rite. An angel intercepts Philemon busy considering his role, and the actor rationalizes that it is again only another "dream." There ensues a comic confusion, as the Christians lose confidence in the "true" identity of Apollonius because of his apparent disloyalty. But meanwhile, tutored by angels, Philemon practices ecstatic monologues and, interrogated in the guise of Apollonius, upsets the governor with his subtle play with the secret of his emerging *real* identity. The governor is so vexed that he wants to send for the actor Philemon who, with his wit, may chase away his bad humor. A swift-moving further series of ironic confusions of identity ultimately leads to mutual recognition uniting a small brotherly community. Through exchange of costume, symbolic self-loss, each has found himself. At the end, as the angels celebrate, we learn the city is swinging to Christianity, the whole social body discovering its heart beneath the mask. The Bavarian Jesuit Bidermann's play of the actor of himself anticipates and shares the baroque archetype of the "actor" that we find in such celebrated plays as Lope de Vega's *Lo Fingido Verdadero* (1618) and Jean Rotrou's *Le véritable Saint Genest* (1647).

The four major historical plays of the Silesian Lutheran poet, Andreas Gryphius, are imbued with this spirit and reflect, among other things, thoughtful reaction to the work of Joost van den Vondel in Holland and Pierre Corneille in France. Gryphius points proudly to the originality and modernity of his own art, since as he claims it does not derive from Sophocles or Seneca. He insists on his historical accuracy, even though he changes or mutes elements to generalize the religious faith of his protagonists. His early *Leo Armenius* (1650)—selections of which are reproduced in this volume—develops the exhaustion of the Byzantine ruler leading to the catastrophe during midnight mass at Christmas, so that his assassination acquires figural meaning. Having risen to power by craft and violence, Leo is wearied under the burden of his sacred office but unable to act decisively against a suspect newer usurper, his ruthless friend Balbus. Act 3 brings us fully into the treacherous and nightmarish aspect of existence. As the highest earthly representative of a divine order, the monarch's role, in Gryphius's view, conveys the entire predicament of human nature. Leo, as wakeful king, must perform for the body politic a tyrannical duty analogous to the function of reason in the flesh. Like the soul of man, he may never really rest in resisting engulfment by the powers of darkness. Many intensely lyrical and emblematic dreams and dreamlike moments reveal the inherent tension between Leo's ideal role and his actual limitation by circumstances. The final act, devoted to Queen Theodosia's eloquent madness in grief, forms a drama in itself—a not untypical feature in Silesian dramaturgy. Her craving for retribution and glorious insistence upon her own rank and identity express the audience's pent-up indignation over a callous triumph of evil, that is, the frustration of the German mind before the spectacle of rampant injustice and fraud during the Thirty Years' War, for which Gryphius blames the German princes in his introduction.

Wholly unambivalent is the sublime feminine martyr in Gryphius's intensely lyrical *Catharina von Georgien* (1657). This once most active political heroine, entrapped while trying to negotiate with the shah, now has only spiritual weapons at her disposal. Catharina names "reason" and "conscience" as her guides, and the dominant theme throughout is the defense of "freedom," not just her own, but that of an entire people and their church. Through a series of emblematic dreams, "freedom" further acquires the ultimate sense of release from the prison house of life and the travails of history. After her execution, her image appears in regal beauty in the miraculous apotheosis of act 5 to announce the collapse of the Persian dominion; as in Calderón's *Príncipe constante,* we are vouchsafed an immediate confirmation of her potent sainthood and of promised justice. Gryphius offers a powerful contrasting portrait of the all-too-human shah, totally consumed and crushed by her light, inexorably mortified by his own crime—for modern audiences the really tragic figure. He vacillates under perplexing domestic and foreign pressures until he precipitates the martyrdom and damages his own majesty.

Gryphius's most complex historical play, *Carolus Stuardus* (1657; 1663), was conceived in immediate horror over the infamy of regicide that could only portend dire national retribution. Hence, upon the restoration of the monarchy in England, Gryphius rewrote in the aftermath of the crime to incorporate the apparent confirmations of divine Providence. In version two, he projects the further course of events—terrible civil war, overthrow of the Commonwealth, dishonoring of the Cromwellians—in the vision of Poleh, which, coming just before Charles's brilliant final speech on the scaffold, provides a triumphant backdrop. Gryphius depicts Charles, completely enmeshed in the drama of history, as the conscious figural representative of the principle of order, the high victim in a tragic frenzy with ritualistic meaning. Viewing his royal office as sacred despite personal sins, he accepts dying on behalf of his people's and the church's welfare, refuses to betray the divine trust that fell upon his shoulders with the mantle of authority. The play is, in one respect, a long courageous divestiture, a meditation on a mysterious role beneath the mortal costume. In another respect, because Gryphius faithfully represents the political arguments of the Protestant radicals and moderates, the play embodies a profound conflict of rival visions of terrestrial order.

Gryphius's late play *Papinianus* (1659) completes the secularization of the political martyrdom by removing the issues to ancient times. Papinianus's great opening monologue not only characterizes his life and ideals, but completely analyzes the historical situation in Rome and the impending test of his integrity in serving "holy justice," the fundamental law above even the prince. In an imposing scene in act 4, Papinianus's honors are stripped from him, and this literal divestiture foreshadows the stripping away of physical life, his reduction to pure mind in God's tiring room. The final chorus is funereal hymning as in an oratorio. But far more fascinating today is the intrepid Machiavellian Laetus who plans to replace the discredited emperor in a coup d'état if he makes the final mistake of eliminating Papinianus. Suddenly outcalculated by the vengeful dowager empress, Laetus stands on the razor's edge and slips to horrible death through minor indecision. But he expires with libertarian defiance, like the staunchest martyr, a magnificent criminal who believes only in himself and the requirements of a role he has chosen to enact.

One generation younger is Silesia's other major dramatist, Daniel Casper von Lohenstein, who in the words of Kurt von Faber du Faur "combined the unrestrained temperament of an ecstatic with the iron-clad industry of a scholar— . . . qualities . . . which predestined him for the role of a champion of High Baroque." Lohenstein's drama settings—the cities and courts of Cyrtha, Alexandria, Rome, and Istanbul—draw our attention to crises that occur under unique historical circumstances and are depicted with an operatic intensity and lavishness. His spectacles of strong-willed response to particular challenges, and often of failure against invincible historical odds, furnish examples for the ironic study of man as a role-playing creature. "Is not the work of nature itself a constant play?" Lohenstein asks in his introduction to *Sophonisbe,* the play that is reproduced minus its choruses in this volume. Man is born into nature's on-flowing script:

But above all is Man a play of time.
Fortune plays with him, and he with everything.

Lohenstein's African tragedies *Sophonisbe* and *Cleopatra* exhibit the fall of unique, exotic, irrational complexes—entire cultures—before the triumphant advance of Rome in real history. Their queens embody the spell of these doomed nations and perish with them, while the Roman conquerors exemplify ambivalently the masculine principle of adamant political reason, *raison d'état*. The Romans are depicted, in their pristine phase of development, as conscious of a historical mandate and confidently attuned to the drift of fate. The ethic of a Scipio or Augustus, masterminds who manipulate people and events, is on a different plane because they aspire to become earthly divinities through the greatness of their conceptions and accomplishments.

More spellbinding yet are the complex characters of the threatened queens. Cleopatra discovers with bitter irony the role for which, as an unconscious actress of herself, she has literally rehearsed in her faked burial with the design to precipitate Antony's suicide. Sophonisbe grows progressively aware of her many intertwining roles and tragic commitment as queen, mother, lover, priestess of a doomed cult and land. In her vision of the course of human history before her death in act 5, she fully identifies with her ancestress and archetype Dido and is granted mysterious foreknowledge of the ultimate collapse of inimical Rome. In the play *Agrippina,* Lohenstein's portrait of Nero lapsing into homicidal paranoia is worthy to stand with that by Racine in *Britannicus*. Lohenstein's tribute to the queen mother's dark glory and his staging of her desperate seduction attempt and the grim matricide attain a daring we associate with a Webster or Ford in Britain. In the drama *Ibrahim Sultan,* Lohenstein secretly is rivaling the French tragedian Tristan L'Hermite in gazing into the abysses of the soul. But Lohenstein recasts Tristan's passionate "daughter of the Mufti" in Ambre as a Lucretia who shames the Turkish nobles into rebellion, while the nature of the Turkish state remains fundamentally unaltered. Lohenstein's title heroine of the play *Epicharis,* in contrast, outshines her namesake in Tristan's *La Mort de Sénèque*. In Lohenstein's rival version, Epicharis's political vision and physical courage are sublime. In the depicted testing of a variegated humanity at a nadir in the historical process, Lohenstein contrasts the individual weaknesses and collective corruption with her resolution. This collective unmasking, disillusionment, and degrading of humankind constitutes a complex, awesome analysis of the reasons for the race's general enslavement, without denying the validity of the exceptional person.

To understand this shift of perspective with far-reaching consequences for the German tradition of a world theater, one would need to consider Lohenstein's encyclopedic rationalism as a larger system. The approaching frontier of baroque and Enlightenment interpretations of life in terms of theatricality can be drawn by citing two plays by Christian Weise: the tragedy *Masaniello* (1682) and the comedy *The Netherlandic Peasant* (1685). The progression of the tragedy of the Neapolitan rebel Masaniello is expressed in the many symbolic shifts of ceremony and costume, and his sinister entrapment by his own attirement reveals the corruption of power that deflects from the original purpose of reform. The haunting visionary qualities of *Masaniello* melt away under the beams of reason when in *The Netherlandic Peasant* Weise writes yet another version of that favorite baroque story of the drunk who, as a joke, is first treated as a visiting prince and then laid back in the gutter in his old clothes, so that he holds the experience in the palace to have been a wonderful dream. We are guided by the wise chamberlain Robert to harbor no illusions about our own hidden passions, but also to draw generous conclusions about the natural honesty of the peasant, an example of common sense beneficial to higher minds.

Gryphius and Lohenstein established the German hexameter as the principal dramatic verse form and it retained its preeminence as the equivalent to the French alexandrine well into the early eighteenth century. As the prestige of French neoclassical drama increased, German playwrights began to follow the Gallic example more subserviently. They abandoned the chorus, which had been standard in the Silesian high baroque. They tended to reduce the number of characters, the sweep of plot, and the range of motives and language. The leading proponent of a neoclassical theater reform in Germany, the francophile Johann Christoph Gottsched, sought to purify and regularize dramatic genres. His reconstitution of the older humanist hierarchical order of forms spoke to the new moral and rationalist enthusiasms of the rising bourgeoisie. He denounced Lohenstein for his dark insights, rhetorical excess, and plot complexity; rejected any mixture of tragic and comic elements;

wanted to replace the improbabilities of opera with more seemly pastoral plays; and tried to create a socially proper comedy, literally banishing Hanswurst ceremonially from the Leipzig stage in the 1730s. The idea that drama constituted a "rational illusion" was central in Gottsched's prosaic poetics. He saw artistic creation as the application of the appropriate stylistic means and story form to clothe a "fable" or philosophic lesson. His own practical involvement in the theater, his encouragement of translations and rewritings, as well as the successive editions of his influential treatise *A Critical Poetics for the Germans* (1730), made him the most significant representative of the early Enlightenment. When Lessing attacked the dominance of French models in the 1760s, he aimed some of his sharpest shafts at Gottsched. However, even without Lessing's forceful advocacy of a change of course, Gottsched's arid rationalism could not survive in the new climate that Johann Gottfried Herder's organic view of history and language fostered.

An early countertrend appeared in the works of the anglophile Swiss authors Johann Jakob Bodmer and Johann Jakob Breitinger. In their weekly *Discourses of the Painters* (1721–23) and joint treatise *On the Influence and Use of the Imagination* (1727), they heaped scorn on what they saw as the perversity and bombast of baroque drama and advocated a principle of imitation that embraced natural wonder. Bodmer's 1732 prose translation of Milton's *Paradise Lost,* and later treatises praising it as a licit model of grandiloquence and example of the natural sublime and poetic wonder, sparked off a lasting feud with Gottsched, who rightly suspected that this was a bypass that reconnected with baroque literature. Bodmer also reopened the gates to Christian mythology as an important source of poetic materials. The entrance of Milton into the German literary world under the combined banner of religion and poetry helped stimulate receptivity for the more problematic secular works of Shakespeare. Together these great English poets tended at first to displace not the French, but the German, writers of the seventeenth century; by the time Lessing used Shakespeare as a counterexample to Corneille and Racine, especially Lohenstein was eclipsed in public memory. Yet significant dramatists of the early decades of the eighteenth century recognized the epochal connection. Johann Elias Schlegel's essay *A Comparison of Shakespeare and Andreas Gryph* (1741), treating mainly *Julius Caesar* and *Leo Armenius,* asserted that it was the portrayal of great characters that carried tragedy. Schlegel sensed that, despite their historically determined differences, ancient drama and British drama were related through their inner principle.

Gottsched's *Dying Cato* (1731) epitomizes neoclassical density of form, observance of the unities, and propriety of language in the rationalist mode. Though Schlegel himself came from Gottsched's circle, his last tragedy *Canut* (1746) reveals important new impulses. By its choice of a national subject matter (intended for the theater in Copenhagen), the play's orientation is expressly English, rather than French. The villain Ulfo evidences more than Senecan traits; he has absorbed coloration from Richard III. Moreover, Schlegel's hero king embodies the ideal of feeling and humane rulership. The Shakespearean touches in diction, the Nordic setting, and the expression of powerful individuality foreshadow Storm and Stress.

On the threshold of the baroque period, German comedy still retained much from its vital native traditions but also showed the growing importance of newer foreign models. The publication of a large German anthology of *English Comedies and Tragedies* (1620) demonstrated that these popular materials were too well entrenched to be dislodged by Martin Opitz's plea for neoclassical "rules" in his famous *German Poetics* (1624). Duke Heinrich Julius's already-mentioned *Vincentius Ladislaus* (1594) drew on the Elizabethan stage and Italian commedia as well as German humanist comedy. Ludwig Hollonius's comedy *Sommnium Vitae Humanae* (The dream of human life) (1605) exploited the king-for-a-day and topsy-turvy-world topoi that figured prominently in the disillusionistic drama of the international Jesuit theater as well as in Shakespeare, Lope de Vega, and Calderón. This general background still informed Christian Weise's above-noted satire *The Netherlandic Peasant,* although its naturalism and orientation to burgher norms unmistakably foreshadowed the Enlightenment. Christian Reuter's *The Respectable Woman of Plissine* (1695) squarely engaged the ordinary burgher world; its central figure, the slovenly widow Schlampampe, gave the language a new term. Weise's satire on small-town politics and society in *The Harassed Latinist* (1693), which borrowed the motif of the hoaxed beauties from Molière's *Les Précieuses ridicules* (1659), corroborates the rising importance of the French theater for German playwrights going into the eighteenth century.

The comedy of types and baroque complexity peaked with Gryphius in the decades of the 1650s and 1660s. His allusion-laden *Peter Squenz* (1657) reworked the idea of an amateur production of Pyramus and Thisbe before an inner sophisticated court audience, taken from Shakespeare's *A Midsummer Night's Dream* (likely through a derivative text of the itinerant players). In Gryphius's satire, the bumbling mastersingers are shown as hopelessly outmoded and are relegated to the folk according to the norms of elegant literature. His double comedy after the Italian model, *The Beloved Thornrose* and *The Enamored Ghost* (1660), could be divided into separate performances or woven together with a resolving episode of judgments and marriages that reaffirmed social order from top to bottom. *Thornrose* borrowed freely from the Dutch author Vondel's peasants love comedy *The Leeuvendalers,* and *Ghost* from the French author Philippe Quinault's *Le phantome amoureux;* together they exhibited the whole social range of speech from dialect to preciosity. Just a few years later Gryphius's *Horribilicribrifax* (1663) outbid all prior German comedy with its linguistic brilliance, targeting the widespread contemporary use and abuse of foreign tongues and habits peculiar to the demimonde among other things. This playful demonstration of the universe of human language matched his social and generic tour of the human estate. The baroque comedy of types and the principle of colorful comedic "confusion" that is pleasurably unraveled reached a culmination in Gryphius's ingenious interlacing of multiple subplots—the schemes and rivalry of two preposterous con men, the fortunes of virtuous well-born lovers as against social climbers, and the marginal existences of a bemused pedant and lusty gypsy procuress.

The eventual break between Gottsched and the playwright Johann Ulrich König is illustrative of the division in approaches to comedy that occurred in the first half of the eighteenth century. Gottsched at first hailed König as a "German Molière" for his *The Land of Upside Down* (1725), a purified version of the "magical" utopia, a standard genre of Italian commedia already popular in France. The immediate antecedent in German was Weise's play with the same title in 1683. Although using the familiar clowns such as Harlequin and Scaramouche, König toned down baroque rhetoric, adhered to good taste, and attempted to speak to all social classes. This work was destined to serve as one source for the fantastic comedy by the same name in which Ludwig Tieck departed in seminal new directions as a practitioner of Romantic irony at the end of the century. But before midcentury Gottsched turned against both the erudite Italian Renaissance comedy, such as Machiavelli's *The Mandrake*, and the commedia dell'arte. The fixed types of the latter he rejected as irrational, violating the requirements of verisimilitude. By keeping alive the public's love of clowns, the commedia also impeded the triumph of good taste. Gottsched led a crusade against folk taste because he wanted a moral and edifying drama that was oriented to the life situations of the core classes of the Enlightenment, the bourgeoisie and lower nobility. A compromise approach was the attempt by Johann Christian Krüger, taking a cue from Pierre Marivaux and others, to sentimentalize the Harlequin figure as an embodiment of the natural human heart.

The codes of neoclassicist rationalism and of sentimentalism informed most early eighteenth-century comedies that had literary pretensions. Encouraging his circle to expand the repertory by translation, through his publication *The German Stage* (1740–45), Gottsched promoted especially French satirists (e.g., Philippe Destouches, Charles Rivière Dufresny, Saint-Evremond, Molière, but not their plays influenced by Italian theater), also the Danish author Ludvig Holberg (whose Italianate streak was overlooked), and the English author Joseph Addison. The action in rationalist comedy involved the exposure of criminals or social vices and the enlightenment of protagonists with respect to their weaknesses. Gottsched's wife Luise Adelgunde Victoire, one of the most productive translator-playwrights, furnished a master example of this genre with her *False Devotion in a Herringbone Frock; or, The Would-be Lady Doctor* (1736), transposing a French satire of the Jansenists to pillory the German Pietists. The satiric strain was often mixed with, and gradually ceded by midcentury to, the sentimental strain that in contrast favored emphasizing admirable character, virtuous love, and poetic justice. The new literature of "feeling" cultivated a pleasurable sense of the possibility of human happiness with honor and reaffirmed theodicy. This genre in which beautiful sentiments triumph over adversity or misunderstanding reached its high point in Christian Fürchtegott Gellert's *The Tender Sisters* (1747).

Like Gottsched, Johann Elias Schlegel first moved away from the fixed types of Italian comedy toward a drama based on individual character, and also sought to bridge the satiric and sentimental strains. But in emphasizing the aesthetic dimensions of feeling over moral considerations, he reflected the philosophic current of "eudaemonism," the German analogue to British and French "hedonism," as well as the educational optimism of the Enlightenment. Schlegel recognized the social nature of comedy and the need to tailor character according to national traits as well. His one-act play *The Dumb Beauty* (1747), which appears in this volume, exploits the means of both the contemporary satirical and sentimental comedy, but adroitly avoids heavy-handed moralizing or contrasts of vice and virtue. With its playful poetic spirit and graceful eloquence, *The Dumb Beauty,* tested a new realm of humor where human inadequacy is an accepted reality. Lessing justifiably celebrated it as "our best original work written in verse." It was in large measure because German drama had come of age by the time of Schlegel that the critic-playwright Lessing could inspire and lead a qualitative surge of independent creativity that eventually would be crowned by Goethe and Schiller in the second half of the century.

For readers of English, the German drama for all purposes starts with Lessing. This is hardly surprising in view of the fact that, aside from Sachs's Shrovetide plays, the dearth of translations of German dramatic works from the sixteenth and seventeenth centuries—the important Renaissance era of a rebirth of theater—has impeded any reception outside of the ranks of Germanists. The present volume seeks to make a start at remedying the situation by bridging this gap with an illustrative selection that, it is hoped, will stimulate further efforts. Whereas a series of outstanding German translators worked throughout the eighteenth century mastering the difficulties presented by Shakespeare and enshrining his plays in the German repertory by the start of the Romantic period, there is no reciprocal tradition of translating the major German playwrights of the baroque age and early Enlightenment into English. Thus the editor is grateful to the translators for having the courage to enter into print as pioneers whose generous chief aim is to be superseded and supplemented. Garland Publishing Inc. has kindly granted permission to reprint Katharina Wilson's translation of the medieval work *Dulcitius*. Special thanks are owed to Giles R. Hoyt who read parts of the *Sophonisba* and offered advice on the perplexing choices faced in dealing with older German diction and prosody. The editor was pleased to collaborate on the *Susanna* and *Sophonisba*, but it was M. John Hanak who had the tenacity to imitate the original meters and line forms for the historical record in this first effort and any measure of success with these plays is due to his energies.

G. G.

German Theater before 1750

Hrotsvitha of Gandersheim

DULCITIUS

Dulcitius; or,
The Martyrdom of the Holy Virgins,
Agape, Chionia, and Hirena

The martyrdom of the holy virgins Agape, Chionia, and Hirena whom, in the silence of night, Governor Dulcitius secretly visited, desiring to delight in their embrace. But as soon as he entered, / he became demented / and kissed and hugged the pots and the pans, mistaking them for the girls until his face and his clothes were soiled with disgusting black dirt. Afterward Count Sissinus, acting on orders, / was given the girls so he might put them to tortures. / He, too, was deluded miraculously / but finally ordered that Agape and Chionia be burnt and Hirena be slain by an arrow. /

DIOCLETIAN: The renown of your free and noble descent / and the brightness of your beauty demand / that you be married to one of the foremost men of my court. This will be done according to our command if you deny Christ and comply by bringing offerings to our gods.

AGAPE: Be free of care, / don't trouble yourself to prepare our wedding / because we cannot be compelled under any duress / to betray Christ's holy name, which we must confess, / nor to stain our virginity.

DIOCLETIAN: What madness possesses you? What rage drives you three? /

AGAPE: What signs of our madness do you see? /

DIOCLETIAN: An obvious and great display. /

AGAPE: In what way? /

DIOCLETIAN: Chiefly in that renouncing the practices of ancient religion / you follow the useless, newfangled ways of the Christian superstition. /

AGAPE: Heedlessly you offend the majesty of the omnipotent God. That is dangerous . . .

DIOCLETIAN: Dangerous to whom?

AGAPE: To you and to the state you rule. /

DIOCLETIAN: She is mad; remove the fool! /

CHIONIA: My sister is not mad; she rightly reprehended your folly.

DIOCLETIAN: She rages even more madly; remove her from our sight and arraign the third girl. /

HIRENA: You will find the third, too, a rebel / and resisting you forever. /

DIOCLETIAN: Hirena, although you are younger in birth, / be greater in worth! /

HIRENA: Show me, I pray, how?

DIOCLETIAN: Bow your neck to the gods, set an example for your sisters, and be the cause for their freedom!

HIRENA: Let those worship idols, Sire, / who wish to incur God's ire. / But I won't defile my head, anointed with royal unguent by debasing myself at the idols' feet.

DIOCLETIAN: The worship of gods brings no dishonor / but great honor. /

HIRENA: And what dishonor is more disgraceful, / what disgrace is any more shameful / than when a slave is venerated as a master?

DIOCLETIAN: I don't ask you to worship slaves / but the mighty gods of princes and greats. /

HIRENA: Is he not anyone's slave / who, for a price, is up for sale? /

DIOCLETIAN: For her speech so brazen, / to the tortures she must be taken. /

HIRENA: This is just what we hope for, this is what we desire, / that for the love of Christ through tortures we may expire. /

DIOCLETIAN: Let these insolent girls / who defy our decrees and words / be put in chains and kept in the squalor of prison until Governor Dulcitius can examine them.

* * *

DULCITIUS: Bring forth, soldiers, the girls whom you hold sequestered. /

SOLDIERS: Here they are whom you requested. /

DULCITIUS: Wonderful, indeed, how beautiful, how graceful, how admirable these little girls are!

SOLDIERS: Yes, they are perfectly lovely.

DULCITIUS: I am captivated by their beauty.

SOLDIERS: That is understandable.

DULCITIUS: To draw them to my love, I am eager. /
SOLDIERS: Your success will be meager. /
DULCITIUS: Why?
SOLDIERS: Because they are firm in faith.
DULCITIUS: What if I sway them by flattery? /
SOLDIERS: They will despise it utterly. /
DULCITIUS: What if with tortures I frighten them? /
SOLDIERS: Little will it matter to them. /
DULCITIUS: Then what should be done, I wonder? /
SOLDIERS: Carefully you should ponder. /
DULCITIUS: Place them under guard in the inner room of the pantry, where they keep the servants' pots. /
SOLDIERS: Why in that particular spot? /
DULCITIUS: So that I may visit them often at my leisure. /
SOLDIERS: At your pleasure. /

* * *

DULCITIUS: What do the captives do at this time of night? /
SOLDIERS: Hymns they recite. /
DULCITIUS: Let us go near. /
SOLDIERS: From afar we hear their tinkling little voices clear. /
DULCITIUS: Stand guard before the door with your lantern / but I will enter / and satisfy myself in their longed-for embrace. /
SOLDIERS: Enter. We will guard this place. /

* * *

AGAPE: What is that noise outside the door? /
HIRENA: That wretched Dulcitius coming to the fore. /
CHIONIA: May God protect us!
AGAPE: Amen.
CHIONIA: What is the meaning of this clash of the pots, and the pans?
HIRENA: I will check. / Come here, please, and look through the crack! /
AGAPE: What is going on?
HIRENA: Look, the fool, the madman base, / he thinks he is enjoying our embrace. /
AGAPE: What is he doing?
HIRENA: Into his lap he pulls the utensils, / he embraces the pots and pans, giving them tender kisses. /

CHIONIA: Ridiculous!

HIRENA: His face, his hands, his clothes are so soiled, so filthy, that with all the soot that clings to him, he looks like an Ethiopian.

AGAPE: It is only right that he should appear in body the way he is in his mind: possessed by the Devil.

HIRENA: Wait! He prepares to leave. Let us watch how he is greeted, / and how he is treated / by the soldiers who wait for him.

*   *   *

SOLDIERS: Who is coming out? / A demon without doubt. / Or rather, the Devil himself is he; / let us flee! /

DULCITIUS: Soldiers, where are you taking yourselves in flight? / Stay! Wait! Escort me home with your light! /

SOLDIERS: The voice is our master's tone / but the look the Devil's own. / Let us not stay! / Let us run away, the apparition will slay us! /

DULCITIUS: I will go to the palace and complain, / and reveal to the whole court the insults I had to sustain. /

*   *   *

DULCITIUS: Guards, let me into the palace; / I must have a private audience. /

Guards: Who is this vile and detestable monster covered in torn and despicable rags? Let us beat him, / from the steps let us sweep him; / he must not be allowed to enter.

DULCITIUS: Alas, alas, what has happened? Am I not dressed in splendid garments? Don't I look neat and clean? / Yet anyone who looks at my mien / loathes me as a foul monster. To my wife I shall return, / and from her learn / what has happened. But there is my spouse, / with disheveled hair she leaves the house, / and the whole household follows her in tears.

*   *   *

WIFE: Alas, alas, my Lord Dulcitius, what has happened to you? / You are not sane; the Christians have made a laughingstock out of you. /

DULCITIUS: Now I know at last. I owe this mockery to their witchcraft.

WIFE: What upsets me so, what makes me more sad, is that you were ignorant of all that happened to you.

DULCITIUS: I command that those insolent girls be led forth, / and that they be publicly stripped of all their clothes, / so that they experience similar mockery in retaliation for ours.

SOLDIERS: We labor in vain; / we sweat without gain. / Behold, their garments stick to their virginal bodies like skin, / and he who urged us to strip them snores in his seat, / and he cannot be awakened from his sleep. / Let us go to the Emperor and report what has happened.

* * *

DIOCLETIAN: It grieves me very much / to hear that Governor Dulcitius has been so greatly deluded, / so greatly insulted, / so utterly humiliated. / But these vile young women shall not boast with impunity of having made a mockery of our gods and those who worship them. I shall direct Count Sissinus to take due vengeance.

* * *

SISSINUS: Soldiers, where are those insolent girls who are to be tortured?

SOLDIERS: They are kept in prison.

SISSINUS: Leave Hirena there, / bring the others here. /

SOLDIERS: Why do you except the one?

SISSINUS: Sparing her youth. Perchance, she may be converted easier, if she is not intimidated by her sisters' presence. /

SOLDIERS: That makes sense. /

* * *

SOLDIERS: Here are the girls whose presence you requested.

SISSINUS: Agape and Chionia, give heed, / and to my council accede! /

AGAPE: We will not give heed. /

SISSINUS: Bring offerings to the gods.

AGAPE: We bring offerings of praise forever / to the true Father eternal, / and to His Son coeternal, / and also to the Holy Spirit.

SISSINUS: This is not what I bid, / but on pain of penalty prohibit. /

AGAPE: You cannot prohibit it; neither shall we ever sacrifice to demons.

SISSINUS: Cease this hardness of heart, and make your offerings. But if you persist, / then I shall insist / that you be killed according to the Emperor's orders.

CHIONIA: It is only proper; that you should obey the orders of your Emperor, whose decrees we disdain, as you know. For if you wait and try to spare us, then you could be rightfully killed.

SISSINUS: Soldiers, do not delay, / take these blaspheming girls away, / and throw them alive into the flames.

SOLDIERS: We shall instantly build the pyre you asked for, and we will cast these girls into the raging fire, and thus we'll put an end to these insults at last. /

AGAPE: O Lord, nothing is impossible for Thee; / even the fire forgets its nature and obeys Thee; / but we are weary of delay; / therefore, dissolve the earthly bonds that hold our souls, we pray, / so that as our earthly bodies die, / our souls may sing your praise in Heaven.

SOLDIERS: Oh, marvel, oh stupendous miracle! Behold their souls are no longer bound to their bodies, / yet no traces of injury can be found; neither their hair, nor their clothes are burnt by the fire, / and their bodies are not at all harmed by the pyre. /

SISSINUS: Bring forth Hirena.

* * *

SOLDIERS: Here she is.

SISSINUS: Hirena, tremble at the deaths of your sisters and fear to perish according to their example.

HIRENA: I hope to follow their example and expire, / so with them in heaven eternal joy I may acquire. /

SISSINUS: Give in, give in to my persuasion. /

HIRENA: I will never yield to evil persuasion. /

SISSINUS: If you don't yield, I shall not give you a quick and easy death, but multiply your sufferings.

HIRENA: The more cruelly I'll be tortured, / the more gloriously I'll be exalted. /

SISSINUS: You fear no tortures, no pain? / What you abhor, I shall ordain. /

HIRENA: Whatever punishment you design, / I will escape with help Divine. /

SISSINUS: To a brothel you will be consigned, / where your body will be shamefully defiled. /

HIRENA: It is better that the body be dirtied with any stain than that the soul be polluted with idolatry.

SISSINUS: If you are so polluted in the company of harlots, you can no longer be counted among the virginal choir.

HIRENA: Lust deserves punishment, but forced compliance the crown; neither is one considered guilty, / unless the soul consents freely. /

SISSINUS: In vain have I spared her, in vain have I pitied her youth.

SOLDIERS: We knew this before; / for on no possible score / can she be moved to adore our gods, nor can she be broken by terror.

SISSINUS: I shall spare her no longer. /

SOLDIERS: Rightly you ponder. /

SISSINUS: Seize her without mercy, / drag her with cruelty, / and take her in dishonor to the brothel.

HIRENA: They will not do it. /

SISSINUS: Who can prohibit it? /

HIRENA: He whose foresight rules the world. /

SISSINUS: I shall see . . . /

HIRENA: Sooner than you wish, it will be. /

SISSINUS: Soldiers, be not afraid / of what this blaspheming girl has said. /

SOLDIERS: We are not afraid, / but are eager to do what you bade. /

* * *

SISSINUS: Who are those approaching? How similar they are to the men / to whom we gave Hirena just then. / They are the same. Why are you returning so fast? / Why so out of breath, I ask? /

SOLDIERS: You are the one for whom we look. /

SISSINUS: Where is she whom you just took? /

SOLDIERS: On the peak of the mountain.

SISSINUS: Which one?

SOLDIERS: The one close by.

SISSINUS: Oh you idiots, dull and blind. / You have completely lost your mind! /

SOLDIERS: Why do you accuse us, / why do you abuse us, / why do you threaten us with menacing voice and face?

SISSINUS: May the gods destroy you!

SOLDIERS: What have we committed? What harm have we done? How have we transgressed against your orders?

SISSINUS: Have I not given the orders that you should take that rebel against the gods to a brothel?

SOLDIERS: Yes, so you did command, / and we were eager to fulfill your demand, / but two strangers intercepted us / saying that you sent them to us / to lead Hirena to the mountain's peak.

SISSINUS: That's new to me. /

SOLDIERS: We can see. /

SISSINUS: What were they like? /

SOLDIERS: Splendidly dressed and an awe-inspiring sight. /

SISSINUS: Did you follow? /

SOLDIERS: We did so. /

SISSINUS: What did they do? /

SOLDIERS: They placed themselves on Hirena's left and right, / and told us to be forthright / and not to hide from you what happened.

SISSINUS: I see a sole recourse, / that I should mount my horse / and seek out those who so freely made sport with us.

*   *   *

SISSINUS: Hmm, I don't know what to do. I am bewildered by the witchcraft of these Christians. I keep going around the mountain and keep finding this track / but I neither know how to proceed nor how to find my way back. /

SOLDIERS: We are all deluded by some intrigue; / we are afflicted with a great fatigue; / if you allow this insane person to stay alive, / then neither you nor we shall survive. /

SISSINUS: Anyone among you, / I don't care which, / string a bow, and shoot an arrow, and kill that witch! /

SOLDIERS: Rightly so. /

HIRENA: Wretched Sissinus, blush for shame, and proclaim your miserable defeat because without the help of weapons, you cannot overcome a tender little virgin as your foe. /

SISSINUS: Whatever the shame that may be mine, I will bear it more easily now because I know for certain that you will die.

HIRENA: This is the greatest joy I can conceive, / but for you this is a cause to grieve, / because you shall be damned in Tartarus for your cruelty, / while I shall receive the martyr's palm and the crown of virginity; / thus I will enter the heavenly bridal chamber of the Eternal King, to whom are all honor and glory in all eternity. /

Translated by Katharina Wilson

Hans Sachs

FOOL SURGERY

T*he doctor enters with his boy and speaks:*

DOCTOR: Good evening! I have come on out here
    As I've heard there were sick folk about here,
    Some folk in these infected parts
    Who'd like to consult my healing arts.

                      (No response.)

    Now, if they be here, either man or frau,
    They should show themselves to me right now;
    Whether they've gangrene, or the stones,
    Whooping cough, rheumatic bones,
    Fevers, or drank too much schnapps,
    Got stomach cramps from shooting craps,
    Suffer love's pains, or jealous compulsions,
    Have rotten teeth, runs, or other convulsions,
    Whatever disease it may happen to be,
    I shall heal it through my artistry—
    For a small remuneration—
    For I am a doctor of highest station,
    As you can see, under letter and seal.

He shows his sealed diploma.
The boy looks up and down.

BOY: Master, we took a wrong turn, I feel.
    I don't see any sick folks here.
    Just look at this crowd, it's perfectly clear,
    All merry, fresh, healthy, and free,
    They have no need for your remedy.
    (Aside) I don't want to appear too cynic,

But this is a half-assed traveling clinic.
We need a better booking agent.

The doctor bows.

DOCTOR: Ladies and gentlemen, please be patient.
We've obviously mistaken the place.
Don't take it ill, no great disgrace,
Your kind indulgences we bid . . .

> *(Loud bellows offstage.)*

A large-bellied sick man comes in, supported on two crutches.

BOY: Now, here's a likely invalid!
SICK MAN: O, Master Doctor, are you the one
Whose fame's been trumpeted so long,
Who helps each one in wondrous wise?
I've come to you to seek advice,
Since my paunch so huge is blown
Like some woman pregnant grown.
Something stirs there night and day.
Dear Doctor, what is it? Can you say
Whether it's dropsy or—I'm loath
To say it—some foul hideous *growth?*
O, see if you can help me, please,
And by your healing arts bring ease.
Your cures have never gone amiss.
DOCTOR: Have you caught your morning's piss?
Then give it here and let me see it.

The sick man hands him a urine sample.

SICK MAN: Indeed, dear sir, amen, so be it.
Here, take and examine, you or your fellow.

The doctor examines the urine sample.

DOCTOR: Friend, your piss is cloudy and yellow.
Truly, the problem's in your craw.

The sick man holds his belly.

SICK MAN: Something inside does nibble and gnaw,
And my belly's hard like rigor mortis.

DOCTOR: If we're to help, *you* must support us.
  To ward off death, you must with speed
  Drink a small potion—it's all you'll need—
  Which I myself will now prepare.
SICK MAN: Certainly, Doctor, never a care.
  I've often drained the pitchers all
  And stumbled home along the wall.
  Would I turn down a little drink?
DOCTOR: You've got the wrong idea. Just think,
  By swilling so for days on end
  You've made your belly so distend
  That all inside's a mixed-up rout.
  That's why I've got to *flush you out.*

The sick man sits himself down.

SICK MAN: Well, sir, if all is as you say,
  Better tell these folks to clear away,
  For like a carcass it will stink.
BOY: Remember, first down our little drink
  And that'll leave your guts quite free.
SICK MAN: What sort of "little drink" will it be?
  Is it wine, or mead, or lager beer?
  Dear sir, I wish I had it here
  Because, just now, I've got the thirst.
DOCTOR: First you must eat a large *Blutwurst,*
  Then afterwards you take the dram—
  A quart of buttermilk warmed in a pan
  With a quart thereto of summer beer.
  And drink it twice a day, you hear?
  That'll purge the old reticulum.
SICK MAN: But Doctor, I've eaten two hundred plum
  And drank your beer-and-buttermilk too,
  But it made in my tummy such a stew!
  It rumbled with such terrible howls
  Sweeping through all my tender bowels,
  Sent me, maybe, twelve times to the pot
  And tore my tripes like I don't know what!
  But there's been no sure recovery.
DOCTOR: Boy, I must repeat uroscopy.
  I'll reexamine this disease.

He looks again at the sample.

> Should I speak of a wonder, few'd believe—
> This man is stuffed chock full of *Fools!*
> BOY: Strike the iron, friend, before it cools.

(Brandishing a knife.)

> We must perform—Foolectomy!
> SICK MAN: I don't know if I quite agree.
> The Doctor, he's not spoken truly.
> How can these Fools have crept into me?
> A poor sick man would like to know.
> DOCTOR: But I shall prove it to you though.
> Here, drink your urine sample down
> While it's still warm—don't fuss and frown—
> So that the fools will set up a pother
> And scramble like ants all over each other.

The sick man drinks the urine.

> SICK MAN: O, Doctor now I feel it truly—
> Fools are in there through and through me.
> And they've set such a croaking up
> Just like a frog pond in my crop.
> It's the worms, the worms, I fear.
> DOCTOR: Look in this mirror, just look here.
> Will you now believe your true physician?

The sick man looks in the mirror and feels his ass's ears.

> SICK MAN: Only now do I see my true condition.
> O, please help me, come what may!
> BOY: If we operate on you today,
> In the Doctor you must place all trust.
> Foolotomy indeed is dangerous,
> So prepare and think on—Death.
> SICK MAN: Under the knife? What, my last breath?
> If I should croak my wife would dance!
> Risk death? Never! Not a chance!
> BOY: Friend, if you just let things lie
> So that these Fools can multiply,
> Too soon they would your belly split.
> SICK MAN: I'd sooner the Devil on me shit!

But since it can't be any other way,
I pray, commence and cut away . . .
But first I beg you, tell to me,
How costly is Fool Surgery?
DOCTOR: I shall operate upon you gratis
To prove to you how great my art is.
You strike me as a welfare case.
Come now, Boy. Let's start apace.

The boy lays out his things.

BOY: Master, here's all the stuff together:
Scalpels, sponges, straps of leather,
Forceps, tinctures, precious balm . . .
SICK MAN: Doc, so's I shouldn't come to harm,
Before we're off, please, just one drink . . .
DOCTOR: Boy, careful now, when I tip the wink
Sneak this towel around his gullet,
Then I'll begin. You just pull it.

The boy binds the sick man down by his throat with the hand towel.

BOY: So fare thee well! Now we can start!
Bite your teeth and bite them hard
And that'll put you more at ease.
DOCTOR: Hold out the basin. Scalpel, please.

He cuts.

SICK MAN: Stop, stop, God's life, you're hurting me!
BOY: We told you that before, you see,
It's not going to be as easy as pie.
You want them Fools to suck you dry?

The doctor plunges the forceps into his belly and pulls out the first fool.

DOCTOR: Would you look, lad, at this idiot!
What a swollen head it's got.
SICK MAN: Already I feel a bit relieved.
DOCTOR: That I can full well believe.
This Fool has puffed you up inside.
He's schooled you in the sin of Pride,

Blown you up with too much leisure,
Made you vain beyond all measure,
Uppish, stubborn, flashy, bored,
Bragging, wasteful as a lord.
It would have been miraculous
If he hadn't torn apart your guts.
BOY: Master, you better look inside
And see if more Fools there reside.
Methinks his belly hasn't shrunk.

Doctor examines inside the belly.

DOCTOR: Indeed, yes, there is another hunk.
                                    (He tugs at another fool.)
Hold on, dear man, this one I've got . . .
SICK MAN: Owww, you hurt my little pot!
BOY: God's bones, keep still, and don't you squawk . . .
                                    (The fool is extracted.)
Look, what a sharp, four-cornered gawk!
Didn't he make your insides squeeze?
SICK MAN: Ahh, that has brought some little ease.
But now I'd really like to figure out
What this cubic Fool is all about.

The doctor lifts up the fool in the forceps.

DOCTOR: This is the Fool of insatiable Greed
Who's oppressed you long indeed
With wholesale buying, drudging, slaving,
Running about, scrimping, saving,
Gathering all in one big heap,
That someone else'll get dirt cheap
And laugh at you. What worse woe?
Let's hope they're no more Fools to go.

The sick man grabs his sides.

SICK MAN: There's yet another, chewing away
Whom I have carried many a day.
BOY: Listen, it gnaws just like a mouse.

The doctor probes inside and yanks out another.

DOCTOR: See, I've ripped him from his house!

SICK MAN: O, Doctor, who is this same fellow
  So thin and meager, pale and yellow?
DOCTOR: Behold, this is the *envious* Fool
  Who made you mistrustful, distant, cool.
  Neighbors' ill luck gave you much joy,
  You stooped to every unfair ploy,
  Your friend's good fortune made you smart,
  And thus you gnawed at your own heart.
  I'm really surprized this yellow mole
  Hasn't gobbled your heart up whole.
SICK MAN. Herr Doctor, that is perfectly true.
  For years he did my insides chew.
BOY: Friend, you'd better check it double—
  Any more Fools to give you trouble?
  Your belly's still got quite a puff.

The sick man grabs himself.

SICK MAN: There's another treats me awfully rough.
  What Fool could he be there within, sir?
  O, don't delay, apply your pincer.

The doctor grips and pulls.

  O, the pain! Let this one stay behind . . .

The doctor extracts the fool.

DOCTOR: Silence! You'd soon lose your mind.
  Look, how did you spawn this twisted mess?
  This is the Fool of Unchasteness
  Who vexed you with wooing, dancing, flirting,
  Coyness, the heart's romantic hurting . . .
  You think your amours so closely veiled
  That gossips haven't the town regaled?
  If I hadn't cut this Fool from you,
  You'd suffer far more pain and rue.
SICK MAN: Like a gypsy you appear to me;
  You know all secrets dear to me.
  Ouch! There's another stuck within.
  Sir, see if you can locate him.

The doctor tugs on the forceps.

DOCTOR: God's life, this Fool is slippery!
  He tries to squirm away from me.
  I'll have to try and yank him back . . .
SICK MAN: O, my sacroiliac!
  Leave it, Doctor, it can wait.

The doctor holds up the fool.

DOCTOR: It's already consumed your whole estate,
  For this is the Fool of Gluttony,
  Who's dwelt much, much too long with thee
  And made you excessive in food and drink,
  Lusting for delicates; made you stink.
  He sickened your body, dulled your mind,
  In pocket left not one penny behind,
  While he raised your paunch—and compost pile.
  Why would you want a thing so vile?
SICK MAN: O, of this Fool I repent me sore.
BOY: Do you think you haven't any more?
SICK MAN: All are out now, I trust, dear friend.
  Sew me up. I'll homeward wend.

The boy listens.

BOY: I think I hear another snarling.
  Doctor, don't forget this darling.
  Our patient's strong and still can bear it.
  Rip out this Fool and never spare it!

The doctor tugs with the forceps.

DOCTOR: Hold on, I'll break this one off too.
  Achhhh, the forceps it's strung right through!
  Boy, help me now to grip them tight,
  And we'll extract this Fool all right.
                          (Business with prodding.)
SICK MAN: Pain, o the pain! He stings my flanks!
  O, pull him *out* and win my thanks!
DOCTOR *(extracting the fool):*
  Hold still! Be of good cheer; fear not.
  This is the crazy Wrathful Sot,
  Who made your grudge the smallest slights
  And got you into brawls and fights.

In company you would raise a din
Till bruises covered all your skin.
What do you want with this harsh gnome?
SICK MAN: Dear Doctor, let me trot on home.
You've got them all. Please stitch me up.
BOY: Are you at peace now in your gut?
There's no more, then, that give you pain?
SICK MAN: One in the back now smarts amain!
He seems as big as a slab of wood.
O, yank him out, high time you should.

The doctor grabs on.

DOCTOR: So hold fast now. Try and be brave.
How he defends himself, the knave!

He extracts the fool.

BOY: Look there, how he hangs his head.
DOCTOR: This is the laziest lump of lead,
Who made you worthless, full of Sloth,
Full sleepy, with a dreary pall,
Fed up and soon bored with all.
Had I not ripped him out of thee
He'd have brought you soon to beggary.
My good man, now tell me true,
Do you feel any more of these Fools in you?
SICK MAN: Fools rumble in my guts no more,
But my belly's as big and hard as before.
What it all means is a mystery . . .

The doctor holds the belly.

DOCTOR: Be of good cheer, and let me see—
Inside you still's the Ninny Nest!
Be brave, hold on, it's for the best
To suffer one more harsh purgation.
I proceed to the Nest's evacuation!
SICK MAN: O, for a little juice of the vine!
My strength's departed—prithee, wine!
Here in a freezing sweat I sit.
I don't know how I'll go on with it!
O, leave the Nest there, it'll mend . . .

BOY: My friend, you do not comprehend.
  If we don't cut the Nest, indeed,
  Young Fools again you soon would breed
  So, "out of the frying pan, into the fire."
SICK MAN: Just don't fillet my guts entire.
  I'm willing to endure this penance
  If you get the Nest and all its tenants.

The doctor grapples with the forceps.

DOCTOR: Hold tight, hold tight, dear man, hold on!
    (*He slowly removes a large misshapen wad full of slimy
                    creatures.*)
  The thing's so gross, misshapen, raw,
  Attached to the lining of your maw.
  Look how the lumpish thing can squirm!
  Yuk, what a wild and nasty worm!
  Look how it crawls with teaming schools
  Of wiggling squiggling embryo Fools!
  All these, too, would've come to term.
SICK MAN: What Fools could they be then, in germ?
BOY: Various species: corrupted judges,
  Black magicians, alchemical drudges,
  Financiers, flimflams, assorted trickers,
  Liars and scoffers, fat ass-lickers,
  Quacks and hacks, the moody, the rude,
  The rough, the clownish, the horny and crude,
  The ingrate, the coxcomb, the senile and potty,
  The braggart, the whiner, the snooty and snotty,
  The malcontent, and the worrywart,
  The welcher and others of that sort,
  Jealous husbands who lock up their wives,
  The swift to censure other folks' lives,
  Gamblers, anglers, hunters of fame
  Who waste their means for a dish of game,
  Summa summarum, as they were hailed
  By Sebastian Brant and so have sailed
  In his immortal *Ship of Fools.*
DOCTOR: To preserve us from such corpuscules,
  This verminous heap at once deliver
  Into the nearby Pegnitz River,

The deeper the better and let it soak.
(Hands Nest to boy.)
SICK MAN: Sew up my wound, please, 'fore I croak!
Methinks the worst is now quite past.
DOCTOR: Hold still now, I'll stitch you fast.
(Business of sewing him up.)
So, there! Now hop up merrily.
You don't need crutches, so I see.
SICK MAN: Dear sir, I feel so clean and sound,
For joy I'll hop and dance around.
(He gambols, then pauses.)
But how did these Fools first incubate;
Was it something I drank or something I ate?
I'll watch out how I stuff my craw.
DOCTOR: Know you not the old, old saw:
"When everyone likes his own ways best,
Then is the land by Fools oppressed."
Your Fools sprang from one primary cause:
You made your lusts your only laws;
To your weak will you gave full reign;
Yourself you never would restrain,
Whatever you liked, you did, posthaste.
SICK MAN: Angelic Doctor, wise and chaste,
I acknowledge your art and subtlety.
I always acted just for *me*,
Whether it was for good or ill.
But as I'm free from all that swill,
From now on I will act the sage.
From your good book I'll take a page
And follow sound advice and counsel.
O, there are many in this town still
Of rich and poor types, I divine,
Who've got diseases just like mine,
But nevertheless just cannot see
What's causing their strange pregnancy.
Yes, I'll send 'round all of these
So you can do—Foolectomies!
And gold they'll shower down on thee.
Since you haven't asked a thing of me,

For your sweet gift, I kiss your hand.
Adieu! I depart a wiser man.

He exits.

BOY *(to audience):* Now listen, if any in this convention
Desires this remedy, pay attention:
He should look for us in this place,
Here at the inn of—what's-his-face,
And to him we shall our art reveal,
And of his Fools we shall him heal.
DOCTOR: Masters, as you've now seen enacted,
So many Fools from one extracted
That grew in him full many a day,
To preserve you from the like dismay,
I leave you this nostrum at the end:
Each one, as he through life may wend,
Let Reason his sole master be
To bridle in all vanity.
And let each one be circumspect
With rich or poor, of either sex;
If any seem by Folly tainted,
With him one should be not acquainted,
But all one's thoughts, words, deeds devise
According to the counsel of the Wise.
And on my faith and troth I'll swear
That after that he'll have no care;
His belly Fools will wane, not wax.
With this, farewell, from our Hans Sachs.

Translated by Martin W. Walsh

Paul Rebhun

Susanna

A Miracle Play about the God-fearing and Chaste Lady Susanna, for Entertaining and Profitable Reading

Prologue

You, sirs, a high or low birth arrogating,
Be young or old, be rich or poor your rating,
Should anyone persistent thoughts be nagging,
For what effects my figments might be begging,
At once to him I'll offer information,
So quiet down, pay heed to my narration:
Saint Paul, a principle of faith defining,
Decrees all men their minds should be inclining
To please their neighbors with goodwill unbounded,
Which but to betterment has e'er redounded.
We therefore marshal all our volition,
To please you with this play's devout rendition.
But since of usefulness we too would leave impression,
We shall not with affairs of wanton passion
Be dealing, but sincerely here desire
To show how men and women might aspire
To come to virtue's standard gladly flocking:
It's Dame Susanna's tale of which I'm talking.
The gist of it in part you must have gotten,
How by a judgment in bad faith begotten
She was to die, yet God her shackles rended
Through wonders He to Daniel extended—
What for betterment will by and by be noted
Your faith by it will also be promoted,
You'll bear your cross, the heavy one, not whining.
How wives should honor fend from men designing,
How rulers should keep law from ever failing,
What's due to lords, just tribute, what's entailing
From women, children, maids, and grooms—start heeding,
With kindness, zeal the play its due conceding.
Lest some confusion be your mind befalling,
The characters by name this boy is calling,
The drama's plot he'll also, for good measure,
Recount in brief, for all your worships' pleasure.

The Plot or Content

Chaste Susan, most devout in town,
Of lissome bodies shapely crown,
Not knowing, wishing it, in turn
Two judges made with passion burn.
They sneaked in through the garden door,
To still their lust on her they swore.·
When from her side the maid she'd sent,
Their lust she managed to withstand,
Great fear this gave her and distress;
Enraged, they threaten her with death,
A hue and cry with all their might
They raise, the servants all affright.
To law and justice grooms her lead,
Of limbs and honor to be rid.
Spouse Jochem, children filled with fright,
Her parents, sister, maids her plight
Are crying humbled by her shame.
The judges then present their claim
What the adulteress they saw do
And sentence her without ado,
The grooms the judges' orders heed,
With stoning Susan to proceed.
From God then quickly help's obtained,
Through Daniel the boy it's gained.
The judges in her stead fall down,
Beneath a flood of stones they drown.
For widows, too, see aid divine,
Whom even a magnate will malign.
This victim they no help did lend;
Her grief to God she did lament,
The judges paid and are deceased,
Joachim's kin begin to feast,
With jubilation God address
That He has Susan saved from death.

INTERLOCUTORS OF THIS PLAY

RESATHA
ICHABOTH } *the two Judges*

SIMEON
GAMALIEL
ZACHARIAS
NAHOR } *the four elders or councilors*

DANIEL, *the prophetic boy*

SUSANNA, *the chaste wife*

JOACHIM — *husband*
HELCHIAS — *father*
ELISABETH — *mother*
REBECCA — *Susanna's* — *sister*
BENJAMIN — *small son*
JAHEL — *small daughter*
SARAH — *first maid*
DABIRA — *second maid*

BALDAM, *the rich burgher*

MALCHUS, *Baldam's groom*

OLYMPA
RUTH } *two widows*

ABDI — *first manservant*
GORGIAS — *Joachim's* — *second manservant*
SAMRI — *third manservant*

ABED
GIEZI } *the two executioners*

HELI, *who administers the final cup*

ACT I

Scene 1

Resatha, Ichaboth.

RESATHA: God bless your day with joy and pleasure!

ICHABOTH: And you with years in ample measure!

RESATHA: What is the reason I am viewing
Such sadness in your face now brewing?
Your head hangs low, your eyes you're hiding,
As if a mishap you're abiding!
If something ails you that's so dire,
Can I about your woe inquire,
Or are there other weighty matters
That have occurred, that weigh like fetters
You down with care? If you assented
To have them to me now presented,
It would, besides, be rightly acting
If they our office are affecting.
With counsel you assistance lending,
Your woe I'd be forever ending!

ICHABOTH: What ties me down in mournful fetters
Does not relate to legal matters
Which folks ask to have arbitrated.
Today myself I'm implicated
Which has me with distress tormented,
For my laments cannot be vented,
As no one round her I am viewing,
Who'd help me by something construing,
So that this grief could be averted
Which by my hands became concerted.

RESATHA: Who knows what things might yet transpire,
If into them I could inquire,
For in my heart myself I carry
A woe which I deep down did bury,

And once your sorrow you have vented,
I'll tell you what has me tormented,
And get in turn your counsel's measure;
As counsels go, I always treasure
My neighbor's more, it wiser viewing
For what in fine I should be doing.
So once we two will have consented
That what's in our hearts be vented,
As erstwhile we shall be united,
When something evil may be sighted.
And if we should start recognizing
There is no manner of advising
Each other, see no thing averted,
We'll both, with our hands concerted,
Bear what has our hearts tormented,
See pity mutually vented.

ICHABOTH: With such resolve since you're proceeding,
My main concern to know you're pleading,
Your counsel shall not be resented,
Till my unbridled woe is vented.
But ere I tell all, dearest brother,
Assure me it will go no further.

RESATHA: Don't worry that you have consented
To have your sorrow boldly vented—
And should you marriage vows be rending,
I'd keep it hidden notwithstanding.
And should it prove a nasty matter,
To please you, I will make it better.

ICHABOTH: Have thanks that you're my troth abetting,
I'm sure you won't be this regretting.
Well then, this is what has transpired:
(You must have news of this acquired)
Those times in Jochem's house to action
Of plea and case we gave direction,
When folks were for our verdict suing;
You must have been there often viewing,
Herself in precious jewels gliding,
Dame Susan in her garden biding.
My eyes her closely kept pursuing,
Intently her fine body viewing,

My heart's domain by her was captured,
By her entirely I'm enraptured.
Regardless if I stand, wake, slumber,
Eat, drink, myself with tasks encumber,
At court preside, or homeward walking,
Thoughts of Susanna keep me stalking.
To flee this passion I'm unable,
In daytime, night, in bed, at table—
She has my mind of sense divested,
Her lissome shape my thoughts infested,
My heart has melted this desire,
As if I lay inside a fire,
Such are the flames, and such my lusting,
Like vapors in my eyes they're thrusting
That, under oath this I'm conceding,
My sight and hearing it's impeding.
So that's what has me so tormented.
To no one could my woe be vented.
But with your wish to know complying,
The need, for which my heart is crying,
There's nothing I will be withholding,
All to my good old friend unfolding.
So now in your resourceful fashion
Lend help and counsel with discretion,
How I by rights and my volition
Might satisfy my lust's ambition—
So help me that this lust be sated
Which has me sorely aggravated!
I cannot quench my lust's ambition,
Except achieving my volition.
But my volition craves none other
Than I and Susan, we together,
Engage in love games' lusty pleasure—
If not, soon filled is my days' measure.

RESATHA: Though I, too, in my heart must carry
  A great distress which does me harry,
  With no small joy I'm animated
  My grief to find not isolated.
  A fellow sufferer here I'm gaining,
  Fate couldn't be things better framing!

Ideas to you I'll uncover
Which in my heart in secret hover:
When in a hospital I languished,
On torture's painful rack lay anguished,
The same distress to me you vented
My being also had tormented.
For lovely Susan also yearning,
My heart is in my body burning,
This love crowds it beyond all measure,
I feel I'll die without the pleasure
Of every day her person viewing,
Near her when I'm my walk pursuing.
When exercising jurisdiction,
My heart can foster but one fiction:
How I should gain of space some measure
Where I'd indulge with her my pleasure.

ICHABOTH: What views, dear sir, do you now vent?
Though this be so, I won't lament—
Though generally it's consented
Two dogs who'd have the same bone scented
To peace would hardly show propension,
But over it fall to contention!
Yet not to that extent let's blunder
That we should driven be asunder!
But, mostly when such things proposing,
One's weak, two easier might be closing
In on what does feed our ardor.
I hope the truth won't make things harder;
As one asks help when cart's upended,
Let's pull it out, from where it's stranded,
And bring the matter to fruition.

RESATHA: You'll see the same I do envision.
What help I can with words and action
Give you to find the right direction,
As you've this matter boldly noted—
Would that our cause were thus promoted!
You must yourself have been reviewing
This deal with Susan, how it's doing:
With fear of God alone she's burning,
Her body for no vice is yearning,

Her spouse to honor always heeding,
Would never swerve from where he's leading,
Her children in virtue but raising,
The same to servants she is praising:
In righteousness she's always basking.
I fear that when we start her asking,
Apprise her of our keen volition,
She won't accede to such ambition.

ICHABOTH: The same concern I am confiding,
What good is, brook no overriding,
This business we must start pursuing
With guile, our stratagems reviewing
To see, if force succeeds in bending
Her will to what we are intending.
What means to this are you proposing,
To danger neither one exposing?

RESATHA: We must be clever, use discretion,
And act in a most cautious fashion,
An oversight in what we're doing
Would make us rue what we're pursuing.
We must do all that's in our power
To ascertain the time and hour
When we will find her unattended.
Thus all the danger will have ended.

ICHABOTH: For this I recommend a measure—
I often pondered it at leisure:
At times, when sunshine's warmer glowing,
She'll dash to where the fountain's flowing,
Alone there in her bath she'll tarry,
Not deeming handmaids necessary.
An effort hence we should be making,
On dog days ourselves betaking
To Susan's garden, there go hiding,
In secret her arrival biding.
Would that a moment came, conceding
What our passion's lust is breeding!

RESATHA: I praise this counsel as sheer wonder,
Hence there is nothing else to ponder.
This course then we will keep pursuing,
What we've agreed on will be doing!

ICHABOTH: God grant hot days now hither lumber
  And soon my mind thus disencumber!
RESATHA: This weather we have can't be bested.
ICHABOTH: God grant our cause wins uncontested!
RESATHA: This further in her house pursuing,
  Let's go there, see how things are doing!
  Her spouse to leave is getting ready!
  Luck! for the rest your course hold steady!

Scene 2

Joachim, Abdi, Ichaboth, Resatha, Susanna, Benjamin, Jahel.

JOACHIM: Groom Abdi, with me out-of-door
  Come walk three miles and maybe four.
ABDI: Yes, sir, for travel I'm not lame,
  To get us under way I aim.
  At once, as escort I'll assume
  The duty of a loyal groom!
JOACHIM: The cloak and boots for me to wear
  Immediately you'll prepare,
  Whatever I can't do without,
  In proper order you'll lay out!
ABDI: Whatever's needed to appear
  I've packed together over here.
  Can I of more assistance be?
JOACHIM: Yes, help me dress, and speedily!
  In getting ready do your part,
  That we may get an early start!
ABDI: For being slow I won't take blame,
  To dress now quickly is my aim:
  It won't take long to count my clothes,
  This our leaving hardly slows!
ICHABOTH: Sir Joachim, my belief you strain!
  Your wife alone will here remain?
JOACHIM: Some business calls me out-of-doors,
  Sharp house surveillance, friends, enforce,
  When in and out your way you wend,
  All chance of mishap this will end,
  One can't protect this house of mine
  Too much; it would be out of line!

Could I you in some quandary aid,
No toil nor strain I'd abnegate!
RESATHA: This favor you don't seek in vain,
No dragged-in stuff will there remain!
You won't return soon to the fold?
JOACHIM: It all depends how things unfold—
Man knows when he'll go out-of-doors,
When he'll be back, though, he ignores.
SUSANNA: But sir, what can be your intent
That you on leaving here are bent,
Which means grief-stricken I'll be left,
My heart of every joy bereft,
Each day I know you are not near,
Unable you to see or hear!
JOACHIM: Ah, dearest wife, do tell me why,
You are so mortified thereby
And so distraught? Regardless where
I am, you in my heart I bear.
SUSANNA: Yes, sir, most joy will disappear,
It leaves with you, it's true, my dear!
Just God before you I adore,
And nothing in this world love more
Than you, and when you're set to go,
It causes me the sharpest woe,
And all the time I worry so
You might be also struck by woe.
So if no harm one might presume
In staying, I'd my plea resume
That from this journey you refrain,
That free from worry I remain!
JOACHIM: Dear wife, believe me what I say:
I do not like to go away;
It must be under some duress
That for this lengthy trip I press,
If matters were not pressing there,
To make this trip I wouldn't care.
To business, though, I must attend,
You, too, my plight should understand!
SUSANNA: Since there's no changing your design,
You must be off, dear husband mine!

My only plea do not disdain,
Abroad do not too long remain!

* * *

JOACHIM: In this regard, don't fret, my dear,
  I will arrange so, do not fear!
SUSANNA: Come, children, from your father part,
  He's ready through the gate to start,
  Him to a swift return incline,
  And he might bring you something fine!
BENJAMIN: Return, dear father, presently,
  And something fine bring back to me!
JAHEL: Please bring me whatever is sold
  That is exquisite, made of gold!
JOACHIM: Be always pious, children dear!
  I shall then, when I come back here,
  Bring something fine, just you to please!
  To God turn always all your pleas!
  That in good health I come back here.
BENJAMIN: We shall stay pious, never fear!
JOACHIM: May God you in good health uphold!
  I'll soon be back within our fold.
  High spirits at all times sustain,
  Abroad I will not long remain!
  May you, sirs, too, God's blessing see!
ICHABOTH: And, day and night, you, equally!
SUSANNA: The Lord help you your health retain,
  And joyfully this home regain!
RESATHA: God grant a year he'll stay away,
  So with his wife we'll have our way!

THE FIRST CHORUS

Dame Venus, what a force you wield
In Adam's lorn descendants!
To you, the young and old must yield,
All sin's enthralled dependents!
Your lovely child's sharp-cutting dart
Will quickly pierce the human heart,
In tethers it ensnaring!
Who foolishly himself will spend,

At once himself does not defend,
Will your cortege be sharing,
Will your cortege be sharing.
Though mostly young folks by your rule
Your cruel fraud seduces,
From time to time an older fool
To dancing it induces.
They have been by your tethers felled,
No honesty at bay them held,
With shame and sin they're branded.
On all of them thus shame you hurled,
Before our Lord, before the world,
Who're on your sash suspended,
Who're on your sash suspended.

ANTIPHON

But those who have, if young or old,
Your stratagems deflated,
Did thwart you, being stern and bold,
Are justly venerated.
Who with your bonds won't bind their hands,
Who will stay true to nuptial bands,
Keep to their bounds adhering,
Respect their spouse and hold spouse dear,
Those will the Lord himself revere,
And them all men are cheering,
And them all men are cheering.

What's nobler on this earth down here
Than spouses tenderhearted,
Who to each other true and dear,
Themselves not let be parted
By bad luck, love that breaches trust,
By nagging, nor an evil lust?
Their vows they're not defying.
Such love Dame Venus cannot bring,
Those who Paul's writ are following,
Them we are glorifying,
Them we are glorifying.

ACT II

Scene 1

Baldam.

BALDAM: Once again I've been reviewing
How my coming crop is doing.
I can't say I am contented,
Neighboring fields their yield augmented,
They must be as better rated,
And this has me aggravated.
Mostly it's my next-door neighbor's
Field that boasts the richest harvest
When around my gaze I'm sending,
None my pride is so offending.
I am pondering what's required
That this field might be acquired.
To no action I've resorted,
Though I've many ruses sorted,
On his death, what machination
Could procure me that location.
Now, since he has quit the living,
To myself no peace I'm giving
Till the field's in my possession,
And the widow yields by cession.
So that things go as expected,
This slick lie I have selected:
That I earlier my neighbor
Cash have loaned upon this cornfield
While he lived; no inclination
Showed he for debt's liquidation.
With a suit, that sum be granted,
Will his widow be presented!
If it's money that she's lacking,
Then this field, the loan once backing,
I'll claim as its liquidation—
This is my fond expectation!
By her countersuit contended
With a *no* the suit be ended,

I'll resort to intervention
With the judges, her contention
Making sound like she's a liar.
To achieve this will require
Gifts for them; this acquisition
Through a bribe boosts my position.
If my case the judges favor,
To my side they'll start to waver,
For delay no keenness showing,
They'll be the field on me bestowing.
Where on law they are advising,
Where their skills they're exercising,
To that place repair I'd better,
Introduce to them this matter.
Once again it may transpire
They to Joachim's house retire,
There to judging are committed.
It's nearby. I'll be admitted,
I'll observe how they are doing
As the docket they're reviewing,
See if they're involved in pleading,
With respect their pleasure heeding.
But, what's this that I am viewing:
Beadles are their task pursuing
By the doorway in position,
Whence I form the supposition
That inside, to business tending,
Are the two—I see them bending
Over pleas that they're reviewing.
Next, my bidding they'll be doing!

Scene 2

Ichaboth, Baldam, Resatha, Abdi, Olympa.

ICHABOTH: Legal briefs I'll stop reviewing,
   Check how things at home are doing.
   Clearly if things don't get better,
   Staying here won't really matter.
   But this thought is idle labor,
   Here comes Baldam, our good neighbor,

Some complaint brings to be vented.
Let's hear what has him tormented.
BALDAM: May your bliss last unrelenting!
RESATHA: Thanks! What case are you presenting?
Or another's cause you're pleading?
Sit, your words we will be heeding!
BALDAM: Gentlemen, it will be better
If I do not skirt the matter.
On this street a widow's yonder,
Whose spouse death from her did sunder;
If ten guilders she remitted,
His old debt thus would be quitted.
On that field he used as backing,
Cash which I, since he was lacking,
Gave him as accommodation,
Which has seen no liquidation.
She will—that's my intuition—
Try to weaken my position,
Penury will have submitted
As a cause the loan be quitted,
Which, though in good faith extended,
In nonpayment will have ended.
And I get for its defrayment
Neither small nor hefty payment.
Hence, dear sirs, if she is stalling,
I hereby the debt am calling
In, and so you see me pleading
With you. This petition heeding,
All your legal might unfolding,
In contempt the widow holding,
Make her, since she in cash is lacking,
Forfeit what the loan was backing,
And I'll add, as compensation,
What is good consideration.
And for you, dear sirs, from pleading
Profit, too, should be proceeding,
Lest about this you should wonder,
On a gift I'll money squander
Just for you. My case abetting,
Not a thing you'll be regretting.

RESATHA: If it's this you're advocating,
  We should be reciprocating
  What you wish we should be heeding
  And see nothing this impeding.
  Bring her now, she made a blunder,
  She lives on this street down yonder!
  Abed, you Olympa squire
  Hither, as the laws require,
  To produce an explanation!
ABDI: I'll deliver this citation!—
  Dame Olymp, to litigation
  You're commanded, this citation
  A tribunal's order being.
  What's to see there, you'll be seeing.
OLYMPA: I will go as your require,
  But to know I do desire
  Who this lawsuit has invented!
ABDI: I present what they intended!
OLYMPA: Bless you, men of wisdom, greetings!
  What's the need for these proceedings?
RESATHA: Baldam, Dame Olymp, required
  To be heard, and this transpired:
  That your husband, money lacking,
  Using that field there as backing,
  Cash on loan from him acquired,
  To be used as he desired;
  No repayment, though, conferring.
  Baldam his demand is airing
  For ten guilders' compensation,
  As the debt's full liquidation.
  This to pay you'll have consented,
  As here's duly represented.
OLYMPA: Gentlemen, such debt assigning
  To me, is excessive fining!
  In this fashion if proceeding,
  Me of lifeblood white you're bleeding!
  For such debt there's no accounting,
  Up to seven guilders mounting,
  Or to eight or nine, ten even,
  That my spouse back hadn't given.

Nor against that field there furrowed
Had he ever money borrowed.
Though we knew in life privation,
This has been his aspiration:
That I and my children never
Get in debt he would endeavor.
Therefore, sirs, my pleas be heeding,
This indebtedness impeding!

ICHABOTH: Still the same end you're pursuing?
No such thing will you be doing!
Baldam honor's code is heeding,
Never wrongfully proceeding,
Only to what's right committed!
Proof enough is here submitted—
Therefore your complaints stop venting,
To what we command, consenting!
Cede the field, if cash you're lacking,
Which the loan had once been backing—
If its price exceeds the payment,
He'll take care of its defrayment.

OLYMPA: Lord, why suffer dereliction
Of a right through this man's fiction?
God on high shall have compassion
With me, treated in this fashion!
Everything which keeps us nourished
On this fertile field has flourished.
If to take it you've concerted,
All the strain my hands exerted
Won't help with my children's feeding,
Their starvation not impeding!

RESATHA: Pleas and tears in vain you've vented!
Baldam will his claim be granted;
No more on this need we to ponder:
From her field we here her sunder
And you'll pay, as compensation,
What is good consideration.

BALDAM: Sirs, what kind and wise proceeding,
Your just verdict I'll be heeding!
Satisfied with her conviction,
What I owe upon eviction—

Now's as good a time as ever—
I'll pay, and it's mine forever!
RESATHA: Never mind, the compensation
Can await the right occasion.
BALDAM: Very well! I won't be ruing
What as proper you are viewing!
Deeply grateful you were heeding
What I wished, and to my pleading
Lent an ear, and in this matter
From delaying barred the debtor.
OLYMPA: But injustice was done to me!
Telling young and old behooves me!
Therefore, Lord, who pledged as father
In your fold you'd orphans gather,
Make provision for their feeding,
My devout entreaties heeding,
For this case your vengeance taking
Which against me they've been making!
ICHABOTH: Shut your trap and stop your ranting,
Lest your words you be repenting!

Scene 3

Malchus, Resatha, Ichaboth.

MALCHUS: Learned sirs of great renown,
My lord Baldam from our town
Sends me hither, his design
Is to give a paltry sign
Of respect. This on his part
As well as he could impart
Due to haste—to you I bear:
That no effort he will spare
To reward you as is meet.
RESATHA: To your lord you this repeat
That to keep his gift we aim,
And we thank him for the same!
Should he from our service gain,
From no effort we'll refrain!
MALCHUS: This to tell him is my aim!
                    (to the audience)

Apter saying I can't frame:
To roll well, on grease rely!
And my heart does this reply
That my master bribed the pair
Of old judges, who found fair
My lord's claim in litigation,
But wrought heinous depredation
Turning down the widow's claim,
Who her woe now does proclaim.
Well then, everyone take care
That a reckoning he can bear;
Anything goes for a mere
While, but nor forever here!
God will some day in his way
Harshly every wrong repay,
That's when crime and mischief bold
Squared are harshly hundredfold.
And gold guilders, by which ye
Dazed have been here wantonly,
For which down here you did try
Every right to twist awry,
For false judges the sole gain
Will be brimstone, pitch, and pain,
When the sentence they will hear
Passed on them. So those who here
Sit in judgment, keep your hands
Off the gift that blindness sends.—
But on this, wise men, indeed,
My advice you do not need!

Scene 4

Benjamin, Susanna, Jahel, Dabira, Sarah.

BENJAMIN: Dear mother, what a thing I heard most dire!
As I crossed now the kitchen near the fire,
No reason why I should be there repairing—
When awfully I heard the maid there swearing!
To our dear Lord she won't be presented,
For you at bedtime to us represented
That we're to honor God, with fear him heeding,

And shouldn't curse, nor our wrath keep feeding,
Can by the Lord her trespass be remitted?
SUSANNA: Dear child, she'll find it hard to be acquitted.
Make sure that from her ways your own you sunder,
Avoid on sin's and devil's paths to wander.
God all the children who are misbehaving
Will punish hard, when sin them is depraving.
Yet those who treat his will with veneration,
Eventually in heaven find salvation.
JAHEL: To heaven, mother dear, may I aspire?
SUSANNA: Be pious, child, you'll have what you desire.—
Get busy, maids, start on the cleanup working,
Throw out all dirt, the labor don't be shirking,
Make sure the master, once he's back, is praising
His staff, not thinking they're inclined to lazing!
DABIRA: Our chores, dear lady, we won't be omitting,
We'll clear up, just as soon we've finished eating.
SARAH: When will be coming back the kindly sire?
SUSANNA: He wasn't certain, when I did inquire.
Keep cleaning, since he such a cleanly type is—
He'll be returning, when the season ripe is.
Once warmer grows the sunshine, this I'll do:
Its warmth from me down in the garden shoo,
A cooling bath there for my pleasure tending,
Hence one of you I'll have me there attending.
But first let's check to see how Mother's doing,
Remember, maids, the chores you are pursuing!
SARAH *(to Dabira):* Clean up, I'll be the lady now attending,
Betimes to other maids a hand be lending!
DABIRA: Dear girl, you are a fine one thus to pother!
That work might bite you causes you some bother!
Her train to carry too would have consented,
Before I'd be by labor here tormented!
SARAH: Hold on! Where's this reproachful outburst leading?
With sweeping, once I'm back, I'll be proceeding!
DABIRA: Sure, if it could be done with oily chatter!
SUSANNA: Why wrangle so? What is with you the matter?
Dabira come, with Mother it is time to visit—
You, Sarah, I entrust to keep them busy!
DABIRA: It's only fair that you're the one at home remaining!
However high your flattery was aiming!

Scene 5

Resatha, Ichaboth, Ruth.

RESATHA: Would you hear some news of perfect timing?
ICHABOTH: If it's good for what we are designing!
  To Susanna might you be referring?
RESATHA: Yes—now start yourself from here bestirring.
  Susan gave her handmaids intimation
  That she plans this noon a visitation,
  To the garden fountain will be striding.
  Let's be off, her advent there abiding,
  This rare chance with diligence pursuing.
  God knows when another time will be ensuing,
  That, like now, he pays her no attention,
  Traveling the world's far-flung extension!
  Hence our chances, too, are now much brighter,
  Let us court, since danger, too, grows slighter.
ICHABOTH: You are right! Our fortune let's go testing,
  Furtively inside her garden nesting,
  If our cause can show a fair progression,
  And with luck and pleasure life can freshen.
RUTH: Listen, sirs, to my distress and torment . . .
ICHABOTH: Come back later; we can't lose a moment!
  We can't stay, but quickly must get going!
RUTH: To my cause no diligence you're owing?
  Else what's mine in ruins will be buried!
RESATHA: Onward, let her be, enough we've tarried!
RUTH: All I own now faces sure perdition?
  Swayed be, Lord, by my distraught condition!
  Look, my dispossession is entire.
  How to quash my right they did conspire,
  These two no defense to me have granted,
  Nor my being wronged have they prevented.

THE SECOND CHORUS

That's how the world goes round,
Who ponders it, is bound
To find that violence
As right will find defense!

With wealth, all comes out best,
While penury's oppressed.
Who hasn't land and hearth,
Will suffer sorry dearth.

All men like patronage,
Who gains its favor's pledge,
His game's won in advance,
Injustice he won't sense.

Friendship and high noblesse
Lend many righteousness,
But men whose birth is low
Injustice often know.

Widows and waifs not grown
Are always left alone;
As sin it isn't seen,
If they injustice glean.

ANTIPHON

If this may be the poor folks' fate
On earth, who take the scoffing
By those who force them, subjugate,
A change is in the offing!
On them God will his gazes bend,
If they to Him themselves commend,
For this is what He plighted:
When anyone his woes presents,
And God's eye travails apprehends,
They won't stay unrequited!

Be resolute and of good cheer,
When others should you harry,
For into joy will turn your tear,
When you the cross can carry,
By patience and staid courage trained,
By God's commands alone restrained.
He plans a happy ending,

When he appoints the proper day.
Don't falter, it's not far away;
His help he will be sending!

ACT 3

Scene 1

Susanna, Sarah, Dabira.

SUSANNA *(coming back from her mother):*
    Mother's getting old, that's clear,
    Growing weaker, precious dear.
    Wrapped in a despondent pall,
    What misgivings on her call?
DABIRA: There, Milady, comes a day
    When her life won't be so gay.
SUSANNA: Should the Lord on high ordain
    That alive she's to remain,
    With my father share each day,
    Gladly I will to His sway
    Gratefully pay proper heed,
    From all fears of trouble freed.
DABIRA: Yes, God might your prayer hear,
    Grant her much more than a year.
SUSANNA *(to Sarah):*
    In my absence, you worked hard?
SARAH: Yes, there's left a little part,
    All the rest you'll find quite neat.
    With Dabira, who's so fleet,
    Soon the cleanup will be done.
SUSANNA: Oh, this stroll has me undone!
    I feel faint, completely spent,
    As if by a burden bent.
    Such a walk did never faze
    Me, I'm sure, in younger days!
    Suddenly, with pouring sweat,
    By the day's heat I'm upset!
    I would my spouse overcame
    Travel rigors, in God's name!

DABIRA: Don't you plague yourself with care,
    If God wills it, He will spare
    Him misfortune. You are drained,
    From the sunshine growing faint.
    Do as you have said today:
    Since this is a sultry day
    And the sun does sting and seethe,
    To the fountain's soothing peace
    Let's repair, you bathe in it,
    Then your pangs, I hope, will quit.
SUSANNA: Very well! Your chores give up,
    Till we're back your cleaning stop,
    To the garden let us press,
    Clean up later all this mess!
SARAH: Dearest lady, right away
    We'll attend you on your way,
    What is it you recommend,
    We should take as we descend?
SUSANNA: Bring some soap, and also, please,
    Take this oil jar underneath
    And a cleanly laundered, sheer
    Cloth, to dry myself, my dear!
    Also bring along some lye
    So that I my hair may dye.
SARAH: All that's needed, with great care
    For your bath you see us bear!
SUSANNA *(in the garden)*:
    On this bench the oil jar set,
    Then take off, but do not chat,
    Finish in there all the chores,
    Then come for me out-of-doors,
    When you deem the time of day
    Proper that of help you may
    Be to me, then bring from here
    Hair lye that is pure and sheer,
    But take care now that you do
    Shut the door well after you,
    That no entry can be gained—
    Will alone bathe, unrestrained,
    To prevent a rude surprise,
    On the garden keep your eyes!

DABIRA: Rest assured, Milady, we
    Will be watching carefully,
    We will lock the door, and heed
    All precautions that we need!
SARAH: You want something else down there?
SUSANNA: Nothing else, just do your share!

Scene 2

Resatha, Susanna, Ichaboth.

RESATHA: Right on! Today's our lucky day,
    Good fortune has prepared the way.
    For satisfaction we are bound,
    No wonder that our hearts do pound!
SUSANNA: Good grief! My breath I here resign!
    You send cold shivers down my spine!
ICHABOTH: Dame Rich-in-Virtues, fear not, we
    Have hither come, just you to see.
    For this you must alone be blamed,
    Your figure, too, lithe, unconstrained.
    For this alone our hearts must beat,
    Consumed by an unceasing heat
    Unsnuffed, which on itself must feed—
    Unless you heed our lustful need!
    The two of us beg, since you deigned
    To bathe here and alone remained,
    That you surrender to our will,
    This lusty ardor in us still!
SUSANNA: My God, what are you asking for?
    There's nothing I would keep from more!
    You urge me to commit a deed
    Which you in others would impede?
RESATHA: One time means nothing, who will care?
    It does a lighter sentence bear!
    You did so both of us ignite,
    Our every sense has taken flight,
    You rule our craving totally,
    Dame Rich-in-Virtues, this say we:
    If love for all this is to blame,
    Let's savor it, most worthy dame!

It's not for free, you understand,
In our favor you will stand,
While you're on earth from worries freed.
Besides, you'll profit from this deed:
A noble gift to you we'll give,
The likes of which, while you will live,
You will not see, and this I stress,
If we with lust might you caress!

SUSANNA: For such a favor no one pleads!
My husband satisfies my needs,
When in his arms I lie constrained,
Nor has your boon my favor gained.
The gift you promise I don't need,
For nothing more on earth I heed
Than for my spouse, as God decreed,
Keep wedlock pure, my honor, neat.

ICHABOTH: Your reputation's honest air
This in no manner will impair,
If you do what our passion wills.
Such matters secretiveness stills,
To see or hear it, who's around?
And we won't on such thing expound
Nor will a trace of it remain
When you have done as we ordain!
But if upon our wish you frown,
Refuse for what our hearts kneel down,
Amidst mishaps you truly stand,
Which you have thought forever banned!
For, first of all, of honor we
Will dispossess you presently.
We'll spread the word from door to door
And shout that just a while before
We've witnessed both that you have lain
Right here with some young, lusty swain,
In sordid turpitude embraced,
Till our shouts away him chased,
And that you've sent away your maid,
Lest this affair be public made.
And since we here the law uphold,
Pass judgment on both young and old,

Your lot will bitter be like gall,
Doom will your flesh and blood befall.
To find you guilty we have vowed,
Let grooms the sentence carry out.
You'll fare as did that sorry band
Who really did their marriage rend!
With all your honors you'll proceed
Your life to lose with utmost speed.
To fight against this there's no need,
For we're the masters people heed!
All might's been vested in us two
To whom all men here homage do!
And only what we say here goes;
There's no one who would us oppose!—
Don't love your strong resolve's constraint
So much that you'd be sorely pained.
Hence do assent to this demand,
Yourself from such distress defend!

RESATHA: Yes, lady, think on it, be wise,
And listen to what we advise!
Your life's and honor's welfare heed,
And do the dictates of our need.
We act thus by a favor spurred,
Which ardent lust on us conferred;
As secret it will buried lie,
And no way you're impaired thereby;
To world and spouse, that's undisclosed—
If joy to bring you are disposed!

SUSANNA: Of fear I get a double share;
Much woe and worry, too, I bear.
There's absolutely no way out;
The danger is the same throughout!
Were I to do for what you press,
I would be courting certain death,
God passing sentence on me here
To everlasting pain I fear.
Refusing, though, for what you prayed,
Your hands I still will not evade,
Your verdict will my life not spare—
Such judging does injustice bear

And innocence finds no defense
In it, if rage does you incense.
Yet it appears it's better that
My life should here be forfeited,
That I should perish by your might,
Than into sin I should take flight
Before the Good Lord's gazes, where
No human works dissemble dare,
Who on all humans will some day
Pass judgment in His righteous way!
And so, by you, dear God, sustained,
My grief I suffer unrestrained.
Let by your will their hands be stayed;
Your knowledge long their vice has weighed!
Maids, squires, quickly come this way,
Come, help me chase this woe away!

ICHABOTH: Ah—as you wish, if that's your game,
    Your pay you'll right away obtain!
    While I'm this woman holding tight,
    So she would not from here take flight,
    Dear friend, you to the door will hie,
    Her servants call here by and by!

RESATHA: Maids, grooms, where are you, come in force,
    Where are you, quick, come out-of-doors!

Scene 3

Gorgias, Samri, Dabira, Resatha, Sarah, Ichaboth, Susanna, Benjamin, Jahel.

GORGIAS: Be quiet, listen, folks, it seems,
    I don't know whence, but I heard screams!

SAMRI: They're from the garden, sounding faint!

DABIRA: Let's go! At us they may be aimed!
    It seems some hardship on her weighs.

GORGIAS: What? She's there?

DABIRA: No more delays!

RESATHA: What, you believe she has remained
    Completely chaste, and free of taint?
    No longer is the cat confined:
    You search its bag, and shame you find!

GORGIAS: No, God forbid!

SARAH: What's this I hear?

DABIRA: Such things were never noticed here!

SARAH: Sweet lady, how has this come up
  That in such pitfall you should drop?

ICHABOTH: No sooner has he access gained
  Than lust the rascal has unreined!

DABIRA: Sir, not so fast . . . !

SAMRI: What's that you claim?
  You best make clear what you proclaim!

ICHABOTH: We glimpsed down here a youthful swain
  With her, and doing, what my shame
  To represent here must prevent.
  We'll have it to the council sent,
  That all of her deceit may hear,
  Which she concealed here, year by year,
  In virtue's and decorum's shine,
  Like purity's own paradigm!
  We, too, would normally not care
  Had we not ourselves been there
  And saw all, patently displayed.
  The matter, though, we'll have delayed
  Till morning, so that all can see
  What ought to be her destiny.

GORGIAS: What happened to that lusty swain
  Whom you did in this place detain?

RESATHA: The rogue was strong beyond compare,
  From our grip himself did tear,
  He leapt toward the door like light,
  A wind gust, or a stag in flight.
  But when we find him in the end,
  His wages to him we will hand.
  But you, good people, we advise,
  If you your life do highly prize,
  Make sure this woman won't run off,
  Else you'll get paid off soon enough!

SAMRI: Your beadles, then, we have been named?

ICHABOTH: Shut up! Else in the coop detained,
  Eight weeks you won't step out-of-doors,
  And suffer treatment even worse.

Those who would lend this vice support
Incur displeasure of this court.
SUSANNA: Of vice I do not bear the blame,
As witness God Himself I claim!
RESATHA: Before the council we'll proceed
To bring the case, as we agreed.
If you've not done as we contend,
How come before this court you stand?
DABIRA: The garden how could you explore
When I securely locked the door?
ICHABOTH (*as the judges are leaving*):
You ask, big mouth impertinent,
How we about this business went?
Tureen, can, dish, those are your game,
Don't meddle in this, in God's name!
SUSANNA: Lord, how can I stand being bent
By filth which they about me vent!
Have I not every day kept clear,
Why comes the rod down at me here?
Alas and woe for those big lies
Which troubles for us maximize!
I sensed it all along, deep down!
DABIRA: Stop crying so, dear lady mine,
Your honor, for which here you pine,
So rudely you should not defame!
SARAH: Now come indoors and ease the strain!
Let's hope this grief will soon retreat
We'll find a way to deal with it!
SUSANNA: I wish my husband were at hand
And to my sorrow would attend.
Now one of you do this for me,
Ask Mother to come presently
And Father also, if you please,
My Sister too, to witness this!
BENJAMIN: What has you, mother dearest, pained,
To show your face with tears all stained?
JAHEL: What makes my mamma look so faint?
SUSANNA: It's hard to tell who should be blamed.
To tell you more I've no intent,
God only will hear my lament.

DABIRA: The two old judges are to blame,
  Who knows how they have gained their aim!
  It's on her name a foul design
  That makes her cry so much and pine!
GORGIAS: The case will not on right depend,
  Because we cannot understand,
  Although they'd show us, bend our ear,
  That she was one of whom we hear. . . .
  She, who both maids and grooms each day
  Warned not from chastity to stray,
  To faith and virtue us inclined,
  How could she change to be that kind?
SARAH: I also would this thing deny,
  To understand it do not try.
  A proverb with you I will share:
  Old age will folly not forswear!
  Old men do evil, who'd deny,
  Today like young ones, on the sly.
  I therefore think those two indeed
  Against Dame Susan did proceed,
  Some villainy would have her do,
  And when their plan she'd not pursue,
  Their anger now at her is aimed,
  They'd have her outraged and defamed.
GORGIAS: Quite likely they'd have her disgraced,
  But with one thing she can't be faced:
  We dare not ask about th' event.
  When to her parents she'll lament,
  That way, we, too, will understand
  How actually the matters stand!

Scene 4

Helchias, Elisabeth, Rebecca, Susanna, Samri, Gorgias.

HELCHIAS: Dearest child!
ELISABETH: Let peacefulness here reign!
REBECCA: You, dear sister, may the Lord sustain!
ELISABETH: May the Lord Eternal show, I pray,
  How it is that my dear daughter may

Be beset by overwhelming pain,
Which the maid to me could not explain!
Shall you, who to virtues' peak proceed,
Now be seen as one of those indeed,
You, who since your youth have led a life
As behooves a pious, faithful wife?
That such violence should make so bold!
God will soon your innocence unfold!

SUSANNA: Even if my honor God restores,
Shortened will be my life's normal course,
With a threat of death to me they came,
Since I wouldn't play their shameful game.

HELCHIAS: Dearest daughter, stop now your lament,
Your distress to God we will present,
Who'll be surely our supreme resource,
Irrespective how the truth they force!
But, pray tell us now, by summing up,
How into their pitfall you did drop?

SUSANNA: Since the sun shone with a warmer glow,
To the garden I went down below,
For the fountain, as I'm wont, did start.
Hurriedly my maid I made depart,
To make sure the garden's locked secure,
While I would enjoy its peaceful lure.
Suddenly, these two, with ill design,
Sneaked in, gave a start this heart of mine.
Me for their trespass they wished to blame,
With harassing claims at me they came,
And they also promised much more still,
Were I to surrender to their will.
Since by goodness I was not subdued,
With injustice they their suit pursued,
With their might then threatened me the two,
Told me all that to me they would do,
How of life and honor they'd bereave
Me, unless myself to them I'd give
For their lust; when then I didn't heed
What the two of them for me decreed,
Suddenly they both became incensed,

Summoning the help with yells commenced.
As a such and such by them designed,
Saw my honor dastardly maligned.
SAMRI: This whole matter haven't I judged right?
As two rogues these judges did indict?
GORGIAS: Who'd have dared to think what lurked within
These two rascals in so ancient skin?
That we're fooled, besides, the two made sure—
God curse vice so wantonly impure!
HELCHIAS: May, dear daughter, God your aid remain!
He will surely show you bear no stain!
SUSANNA: If you only were here, husband mine,
If you could this heavy blow divine!
ELISABETH: Hush! It seems he is back just in time!
REBECCA: Here he comes, God help us, sister mine!

THIRD CHORUS

David, prince of seeing minds,
Reminds,
The Holy Ghost's rule learning:
That only who in God abides,
Confides,
Is safe from overturning.
Like Zion, motionless he stands,
And never bends
To winds' wild lashing,
Which have the devil, flesh, and world,
Against him hurled,
No sin's him bashing,
Which he has sent down crashing.
His house upon a cliff stands sure,
Secure,
It has a mighty grounding.
Water, wind to move it strain,
And rain.
It's whole, sends them rebounding.
The fear of God is its redoubt,
By devil's clout
It can't be shattered.
The Word that comes from our Lord—

His arm and sword.
He won't be battered,
By sin nor relapse fettered.
But those who our Lord vilify,
Won't try,
His word and ways obeying,
Reedlike, they will in a breeze,
With ease,
Upon the pond go swaying.
Their house, because it's built on sand,
Has no endurance, will go under.
When just a venial sin them brings
What barely stings,
They break asunder,
Let evil rule and plunder.

ACT IV

Scene 1

Resatha, Ichaboth, Simeon, Gamaliel, Zacharias, Nahor, Abed.

RESATHA: Since your wish, dear, wise, old scholars, you're
    unfolding,
  Court this day to be together with us holding
  On which customarily it's not required
  That you sit, we'll not conceal what has transpired:
  Yesterday we saw an outrage much resented,
  Dared not suffer justice circumvented.
  Presently to hear it all you'll have occasion,
  When Sir Ichaboth will make his presentation:
ICHABOTH: Gentlemen, it's clear, and anything but hidden,
  What through Moses erstwhile our good Lord had bidden:
  That adultresses should for their dereliction
  Be condemned to death and all face stern conviction,
  Irrespective of their class, the judge not heeding
  If they're young, old, rich, from noble stock proceeding.
  Not by person, rank, or might the case construing,
  Judges pass this sentence on them, nothing ruing—

Else the Lord withdraws His favor, and sweet life's donation.
That we not succumb to such a sin's temptation,
And that men forever keep us righteous judges calling,
We believe about such matters we cannot be stalling,
When adultery before our eyes is stewing.
Yes, if we were only through the person viewing,
Or pretended not to see, the law not heeding,
To the call of friendship, rank, or honor ceding,
We would not reveal just how it did transpire.
But our hair did feel the tug of Moses' ire,
On our necks the Lord's law heavily is weighing.
Therefore rank and power we shall be dismaying,
And the one that trespassed by the right name calling,
With your help before this court we shall be hauling.
You all sensed it, and gave recognition,
To her prominent and righteous life's condition.
Susan, Helchis's daughter, Jochim's wife discerning,
Had us think no vice was in her body burning.
Yet we in adultery have the selfsame wife detected—
Where and how what we observed had been effected,
You'll find out when we her case will be reviewing.
Now you'll let the bailiffs, their sworn duty doing,
Fetch her, if you do agree with this proceeding.
First of all, though, I'm for your opinion pleading!

SIMEON: What you say brings sorrow, and my faith, it's shaking,
Hearing that Dame Susan was her troth forsaking,
I would not believe it, but, the case when weighing,
I saw you two never from the true path straying.
Since you've everything, as you relate, been viewing,
I cannot deny the claim for which you're suing.
Hence do bring her hither, whence you have her hidden,
Make her face the verdict, as the Lord had bidden.

GAMALIEL: Who'd believe Susanna's crafty and designing!
Or see her as "one of those" to vice inclining?
How could be so suddenly such bent begotten?

RESATHA: Sir, your grief should be, but not your word, forgotten!
We were ourselves struck too by consternation,
Like the others pondering upon her aberration!
Had we with our eyes not seen what did transpire,
Do you think we would to hide the truth conspire,

Or feel well when ruling in our jurisdiction
On a guiltless man, who merits no conviction?
That we Jochem, whom as friend we always treated,
See, while he's abroad, with such disaster greeted?
For his sake, we might have left it undiscovered,
Hadn't Moses, frightening law above us hovered!

GAMALIEL: Dearest gentlemen, your word I'm not assailing!
Fine! Before this court we should be Susan hailing!
Let her be, as you're demanding, here arraigned,
Duly her of her trespass attaint!

ZACHARIAS: As the word goes, female wiles are customary;
That's why this one I don't think would vary,
Of her pureness like fresh fallen snow conceited,
And have never dreamt with lust to be repleted
If she saw the slightest chance to get things brewing.
On that score, and since you saw what she was doing,
Fetch her, as the law prescribes, and time don't squander,
As your claim would have it, from her house down yonder!

NAHOR: Granted, gentlemen, your train of thought pursuing,
That you may have seen Susanna mischief doing,
There's no man who's righteous to the point he'd never
Fall, like all of us, alas, all life forever.
But, would you have bailiffs Susan hither dragging—
Don't you think that to our fame this might cause sagging?
From a woman, whose good name was never lagging,
Whose illustrious lineage never has gone begging,
If too quickly we've repute and honor taken,
That will in some stalwart burghers anger waken.

RESATHA: Rest assured about this we have also wondered,
Everything like you beforehand weighed and pondered.
But, since earlier we told you of the dire
Consequences which did Moses' laws require,
Not by rank or person each event reviewing,
So you should approve as right what we are doing.
How for public view her virtue was alluring
As so many mock fights, soon you'll all be viewing,
Once the facts are one and all shown for conviction.

NAHOR: Very well, proceed, I lift all interdiction!
Now the path is clear for legal intercession,
Bring her, let us hear the details in progression.

RESATHA: Listen, grooms, as guards to her you'll be repairing,
  Lady Susan's mischief here we shall be airing.
  If she balks, use force to slap her in detention.
  Don't let anyone cause hindrance or prevention—
  Otherwise yourselves your laxness will be ruing,
  If this task you're not with care and haste pursuing!
ABED: Learned sirs, we will as grooms complete this mission,
  Properly and justly enacting your volition.

Scene 2

Abed, Giezi, Joachim, Abdi.

ABED: A cause there's for complaining
  That we should be restraining
  Dame Susan, send her walking
  To trial, oh, how galling!
  What crime has she committed
  So harshly to be treated?
GIEZI: It's surely no small matter,
  Why else should we her fetter
  In bonds' and ropes' retention,
  By shameful intervention
  Make public her perdition?
  Who'd have an intuition
  So shamefully she'd blunder?
  What made her change, I wonder!
ABED: All this we shall be viewing,
  When her at court they're suing,
  And charges are presented.
  To no one this be vented!
GIEZI: But if she won't submit then
  To words, our task's not quit, men!
  To force shall we submit her,
  As those two wish to treat her?
  This could be averted
  If folks, by force concerted,
  Her from our hands retire.
ABED: Go quickly, henchmen hire,
  Three, four will be sufficient.
  They'll get their due commission

To help see she's committed,
To where the court is seated,
Our fears of mishap dampen,
In view of what might happen
Should Jochem's men come racing,
Once he hears what she's facing.
We could be overtaken,
Our hold on her be shaken.
If angered they grow bolder,
He'll easily withold her.

GIEZI: Quite true. Our task dividing,
Help I'll soon be providing.
Guard weak points from invasion,
Stay clear of accusation.

JOACHIM (*speaking while returning home*):
Untoward things are brewing—
I don't know just what's stewing.
Dark feelings my heart's breeding
Which are its beat impeding;
By millstones weighed, it panted
For days. I sense implanted
A portent that's deep-seated.
God will have it deleted,
As soon as I'm confirming
No pain her body's burning,
Nor grief her life does mire!

ABDI: His aid God won't deny her,
To what is best her leading,
Your cares will start receding!

JOACHIM: There's real danger nearing.
Things rather grim I'm fearing,
Whatever plight we're meeting.

ABDI: I wish I knew what's fitting!

JOACHIM: Whom are the beadles dragging
Away? The law's gone begging.
Why is my house invested,
By pikes and ropes infested?
These noisy beadles striding,
And grooms their orders biding,
With fetters them attending,

Whom are they apprehending?
What was here perpetrated?
Who's been investigated,
With shame goes to detention?
ABDI: It's past my comprehension.
Might those two judges molding
A trial here be holding,
A custom oft repeated?
JOACHIM: They never have mistreated
Me thus, with bluster thundered,
Though oft they've hither wandered;
No verdict they've begotten
That might have been called rotten.
They've sent now grooms detested;
Before the door they're nested.
Such violence unfolding,
As if their court there holding,
To shackle they're intending.
ABDI: We'll know soon what's impending.

Scene 3

Abed, Elisabeth, Joachim, Susanna, Helchias, Giezi, Benjamin, Jahel, Rebecca.

ABED: Hail!
ELISABETH: Praise the Lord, you're home again!
JOACHIM: Why have you started raising Cain?
SUSANNA: Oh, dearest spouse! . . .
ELISABETH: Dear son, which way
Are we to turn in our dismay?
It's good you're back now in our fold.
In check this fury help us hold!
JOACHIM: The grooms? Quick, call those grooms of mine,
I'll quickly a defense design!
What's this, that you with fury bold
My people here as hostage hold?
Who is it that you should indoors
Tie up and drag out with main force?
ABED: The judges here to come us bade,
To have your wife by force conveyed

To court, where we will now repair.
Of what she's done I'm not aware.
JOACHIM: There's not a chance that through these doors
I'd let you take my wife by force.
For what misdeed is she to blame?
HELCHIAS: Her conduct never brought her shame!
She's charged by judges from this town
With things on which she'd always frown!
JOACHIM: Then what's her crime, in heaven's name!
SUSANNA: Dear sir, in this I'm free from blame!
HELCHIAS: They faked it out of spite, those two:
That as adulteress she did woo!
JOACHIM: My wife! Oh, what a foul design,
Her honor basely to malign!
GIEZI: Enough delays, it's getting late,
At court she soon will learn her fate.
The judges sternly warned about
Us staying for too long without,
Lest someone loosen up our hold.
By force we'll take her where we're told!
JOACHIM: At court her case I would present,
And try this error to prevent!
ABED: You're free to go there, by and by—
But what our task here does imply,
And what we've come to do up here,
You plainly word for word will hear:
Your wife to trial must repair
Right now, or else we'll badly fare
And pay the piper for the feast
On which for us they will insist.
So come with us, yourself apprise
Of all events that did arise.
Our task has been enough delayed,
You've heard now what our masters bade
Us do, and sternly they'll exact
That we upon their orders act!
JOACHIM: Alas, whence comes this vile charade?
SUSANNA: To you, dear Lord, all bare is laid,
I'm guiltless, know not what they deal,
If it's ordained, though, do your will!

HELCHIAS: Hush, do not let your heart grow faint,
  God's aid and grace you'll soon obtain!
ELISABETH: That I should live to see the day,
  My child with woe watch waste away,
  And for such sorrow bitter cry!
ABED: Hush! God his succor won't deny!
BENJAMIN: Why, Mother, under so much strain?
SUSANNA: Oh, dearest child, it's mortal pain! . . .
JAHEL: My mamma, please, let her remain!
GIEZI: No, child, you're begging us in vain!
  You'll have her back, just like before!
JAHEL: No, no! You have bad things in store!
SUSANNA: Resign yourself, child, don't complain,
  What's fated, fated will remain!
REBECCA: May God with you commiserate,
  Dear sister, your woe mitigate!

Scene 4

Abed, Resatha, Joachim, Ichaboth, Helchias, Simeon, Gamaliel,
Zacharias, Nabor, Giezi.

ABED: Learned Judges, fettered and arrested,
  We bring Susan, as you have requested!
RESATHA: Bring her here within the range of vision.
  Make her stand up straight that with precision
  All can view her at this courtroom visit,
  Her, who with chaste worship herself busied!
JOACHIM: Learned Judges, why have you berated
  Her who vice has never tolerated?
  Why are you such shame to her imputing,
  Why are you her innocence disputing,
  Which to keep was her life's avocation,
  And for which she earned such admiration?
  For which debt am I to be accounting,
  I, who've always been as honor counting,
  I, who in my house your court permitted,
  See now here against my wife committed
  Gross abuse, who nothing could be doing
  To your harm. What end were you pursuing
  While I was abroad? Why are you trying

To arrest my wife, with ropes her tying?
Should my station not respect inspire?
Or is this how you your debts retire?
ICHABOTH: Dear friend Jochem, rest assured that our
Debt to you we'd pay this very hour.
But this path we now can't be pursuing,
Since God's law such favor bars from doing.
It forbids to ask: If of high station?
Men or women are, or high vocation,
If they're mighty, rich, of noble breeding,
Or if they've the righteous way been heeding—
Only should they off the right track wander
And the Law of God thus break asunder,
Therefore should to punishment be driven.
Else we judges could not be forgiven.
Yet your wife as guiltless represented
You won't find, once this case is presented;
We shall tell how everything transpired,
Of which firsthand knowledge we acquired!
Resatha, to you I am appealing,
Publicly start everything revealing!
RESATHA: Let's proceed with legal application,
And depose a detailed attestation.
Now to hear it all, sirs, you're invited:
Yesterday at noon a tort we righted,
Which at Jochem's house we had been hearing,
To conclusion then the matter steering,
After all our work, to chase vexation,
In the garden we sought relaxation.
Stretched out, there we sought the shade's protection,
Which was in the garden's backward section,
Unforeseen Dame Susan then came walking,
To the garden, with two maids her stalking,
To the fountain bathing she was going,
Orders to depart on them bestowing,
To secure the door of them required,
Her misdeed to hide she thus desired.
But, alas! we were exposed to viewing
What she thought in secret to be doing.
From the garden, as the maids were leaving,

Came a youthful swain toward her weaving,
To embrace her rushed, his time not biding,
As if often they've done this in hiding.
From his arms herself she didn't sever,
But allowed him all with keen endeavor,
Sinking down, caresses on him lavished
As we watched; from sight they never vanished.
Quickly she did yield to his volition,
Played the love game's prurient rendition,
As in sprawling shame their lust they vented.
We ran out, their flight would have prevented,
But, old age with weakness us enfolding,
Sapped the strength we needed for his holding.
Nimbly he our groping hands averted,
Through the door sprang, little disconcerted.
But we grabbed Dame Susan in quick action
And we placed her under stern exaction
To reveal who was this friend fine-feathered,
Who her ample charms here so well gathered.
But to give his name she has been stalling.
This we state, as fits our public calling,
What with our own eyes we have been viewing.
From all this the lesson we're construing
That her baited virtue fished for praises,
So that she might hoodwink our gazes,
While her vice evaded recognition,
Letting no one know her true condition,
Till this hour came wherein were captured
All her wiles, and her deceit was ruptured.
That's why everyone now must be viewing
This fine lady as a lie pursuing,
Though her fame has us so often blinded,
Till God's grace our moral clock rewinded.
JOACHIM: Learned sirs, I'm stunned, my mind is reeling,
For more time to you I am appealing,
That I might, unflaggingly now striving,
My wife's forfeit honor start reviving!
While I was abroad, these claims' weird texture
Wouldn't even warrant a conjecture,
For by confidence I have been driven

That to pious modesty my wife was given.
All this time I surely would have noted,
If she any mischief had promoted.
Therefore, please, don't be so quick in judging.
For a query time to me not grudging,
A few hours, ere she is indicted,
To examine, what here could be righted!

ICHABOTH: Jochem, what is further to inquire?
We to skimp on truth have no desire.
As you heard the details by us vented,
All this happened just as here's presented.
That we're of such hostile mind do not conjecture;
Not a jot we'd plan from you to capture
Of what's yours, much less in such a matter—
But the law we follow to the letter.
We don't gloat about her dereliction,
And ourselves would hold it for a fiction,
If on hearsay the report depended.
In the act, though, we her apprehended!
That God had not willed us to discover,
What she chose to practice under cover!
But since God sent us her sham to shatter,
How are we to alter now this matter?
Can postponement be indeed required,
When we saw so plainly what transpired?
Would we not of wisdom prove most needy,
If in sentencing we were not speedy?

HELCHIAS: Sirs, there's something that needs to be vented:
Proof that my child's guiltless be presented!
Of the case she tells a different story . . .

ICHABOTH: She'll tell lies, of that you shouldn't worry
Since to such an outrage she consented,
As by us has been here represented.
We have caught her in lust's lewd diversion.
Let no ear lend credence to her version,
Which she did concoct as purest fiction.
Now by law she's in our jurisdiction,
We shall sentence her and duly punish,
On this earth whom sinful ways thus tarnish!
To our case that's now here been presented,

Sirs, we hope you all will have consented,
Since her black offense is so appalling,
For the pain of death this crime is calling!
SIMEON: If so heinous then was Susan's blunder,
Which you here report for us to ponder,
I decree, the course of law pursuing,
Judge adultery, as we're used to doing!
GAMALIEL: Since her execution you pronounced thus,
And her crime in public have denounced thus,
On the strength of evidence presented
She must perish, as the law intended
Which commands: the breach of troth atoning,
Put adulteresses to death by stoning!
ZACHARIAS: Of my views I make here presentation,
What she's done calls for her life's privation,
As it stands long in our Lord's code written,
Till she's dead, with rocks she's to be smitten!
NABOR: Your indictment does not bear assailing,
What's both just and lawful is prevailing.
Stone her dead, as bids the ancient fashion,
Following the law without compassion.
ICHABOTH: Since what's right by law you are recalling,
Down on her old Moses' ordinance yet calling,
Since with verdict you've the case concluded,
Never mind on whom grief has obtruded.
As is meet, the staff above her breaking,
Her adultery we'll be thus unmaking.
Haul her off, grooms, and pay close attention,
Keep her shackled while she's in detention,
Stone her, as the law her fate decided.
Stay unruffled, if for this you're chided,
Lest on you pour mighty torrents spewing
In a bath of grief you, too, imbuing.
Any meddler this pursuit impeding,
On him too heap stones, these orders heeding!
GIEZI: Gentlemen, concerning this conviction,
You will hear from us no contradiction!
Since to punish her you us are hailing,
So we'll do with zeal and without failing,
Though we'd rather, this we are admitting,

Not act, but as might the court find fitting,
Lest unjustly blood we should be spilling.
To forgive our errors, Lord, be willing!

THE FOURTH CHORUS

Of all the world judge, mighty Lord,
Down here you did accord
All sovereignty and powers:
You won't let order pass away,
You will yourself survey
How we do spend our hours.
Full well you understand,
When you your hand
Withdraw, how things are doing!
No vice, however low,
Men will forgo—
Not justice they're pursuing
As we right here are viewing.

And on this earth, poor innocence.
That, wretched, rates defense
Is trampled in each instance.
From pharaoh's heart that never yields,
Who here much power wields,
It can't expect assistance.
Just you, Lord God, you heed
Our every need,
Your flock's ordeal you're sharing,
And all the devil plots
Your wonder blots,
Toward what's best us bearing.
High praise deserves your caring.

Your custom it is in no sense,
As in the Writ it stands
(A point worth our believing)
That you will choose our human way,
With zeal, hard work, good thoughts display
In all that you're achieving.

Whom you intend to elevate,
You first let wait,
With deep woe him undoing,
And when we think there's no way out,
We've lost the bout,
Your help you start revealing,
To know it, we're appealing!

ACT V

Scene 1

Susanna, Joachim, Giezi, Helchias, Elisabeth, Rebecca, Abed.

SUSANNA: Eternal Lord, you see what people bury
  In secrecy, things great or ordinary.
  Aware of everything ere it's ensuing,
  Your gaze, what's hidden also, can be viewing.
  You recognize that by false accusation
  Of perjurers, from life to condemnation
  To death I'm led in this unlawful matter—
  Oh, God, send succor to me you had better,
  My innocence grant juster jurisdiction.
  I'm free of vice and don't deserve conviction
  Which was imposed when they to lies resorted.
  I'm sentenced, to my death I'm here escorted.
  Since I'm to render my own soul as payment,
  Receive it in your hands as debt's defrayment;
  My pleas, oh, Lord, you wouldn't have me squander,
  But will a vengeance for my sorrow ponder!
JOACHIM: That innocence in silence should be ending!
  That, prostrate, laws before their might be bending!
  How long will you permit truth's lamp to darken,
  And to our fervent prayers will not harken?
  Why must we suffer now this greatest evil ever
  From which, oh, Lord, your hand won't us deliver?
GIEZI: Dear Lady, in God's name, grant exculpation
  That our hands should cause you aggravation!
  For this dread business we see scant expedience,

But to the elders' law we owe obedience.
Surrender to your life's harsh immolation,
Hold out your hands in patient resignation!
SUSANNA: Their tying, could it be a while averted,
That I might hug my own ere they're deserted?
God bless you, spouse, our love bond is now ending—
Don't let my death forever be your dear heart's rending;
Some day for this will God revenge have taken,
My innocence their lie asunder will have shaken!
Accept my children as a fervent commendation,
They'll help you to uplift yourself from your prostration.
Keep steadfast fear of God in them unfolding,
As friends in your old age your faith they'll be upholding—
On earth no greater treasure can be cherished,
Than when in children godliness is nourished!
JOACHIM: Then, best of wives, to God's embrace go soaring,
Upon your face no longer I'll be poring.
God's hand His care for you will have asserted,
Your sorrow will then be to joy converted!
SUSANNA: To you, dear parents, also goes my blessing,
May you receive a wage that's less distressing
For virtue and devoutness in me breeding.
Great comfort these in me were always feeding.
Since I die innocent, no guilt me hounding,
The strength you lend me should prove quite abounding,
The Lord will have my plight to good converted,
And when you die, your bliss, too, is asserted.
The Lord will keep you all from going under,
Which you have had the chance till now to ponder!
HELCHIAS: O, daughter dear, this grimmest disappointment,
Forever will deprive us of enjoyment.
We too, crushed by this grief for what we cherish,
Are going quickly from this earth to perish!
And yet, since naught can remedy our sorrow,
Depart and we shall follow on the morrow.
ELISABETH: Oh, daughter mine, you whom I once did carry
Beneath my heart, no pains did me then harry
Like these which now for you my heart encumber.
Hence I'll, too, rush toward eternal slumber.
I wish to God, beneath these sorrows bending,

In this departure you I were attending,
But since the will of God can't be forfended,
Your life I'll see to my deep sorrow ended.
Dear God, in yonder world as compensation,
Life grant us both unceasing in duration.

SUSANNA: Stretch out your hands, dears, soon to be deserted,
Before to ashes I shall be converted!
The Lord is bound to show you his compassion,
Extend his hug's protective intercession,
Because no longer he will be conceding
That I should lead you and should keep you feeding.
On you, dear sister, God bestow his blessing,
Prevent that grief your life should be oppressing!
To parents, chosen by the Lord of all creation,
Like me, for their entire life's duration,
A child's obedience you will accord unblinking,
From serving them your efforts never shrinking.

REBECCA: Dear sister, since you now await such dire
Demise, may God you through his grace acquire!

SUSANNA: It's time to start the children elsewhere shooing,
My dreadful death prevent them thus from viewing.
Their health this likely would be aggravating!
You also, parents, cannot go on waiting,
What's bound to come do not insist on viewing,
My death you would be only deeper ruing!

ELISABETH: How can be, daughter, our eyes averted,
God grant this world by us, too, were deserted!

ABED: It's time to shackling you that we attended!

SUSANNA: All chance for mercy for me has then ended?
I'm bowing to your force with resignation.
Surrender life to God as my oblation!
A moment grant me! In this favor basking,
From Him protection for my soul I'm asking!

Scene 2

Susanna, Resatha, Giezi, Daniel, Simeon, Gamaliel, Zacharias, Nahor, Ichaboth, Abed, Heli.

SUSANNA: Oh, God, Lord over all unbounded,
Your own you can, whom woes surrounded,

Redeem, by your dread might unfolding,
Redeem who're to your message holding.
They won't taste death, though close it hovered,
Though by his gruesome pall they're covered:
Do turn to me, my terror heeding,
For proof of troth from you I'm pleading,
That everyone your name start calling,
Themselves inside your host installing!

RESATHA: How long will you drag out this matter?
You'd better quickly end this chatter!
In vain your tears are and lamenting,
Your folks you're only more tormenting!

GIEZI: Your soul to save if you desire—
Of waiting we begin to tire,

HELI: Hold on! A parting cup her pouring,
Will ward off faint, her strength restoring,
From losing heart she'll be prevented,
Before to death she is tormented.
Drink, lady, first, stop your lamenting,
Fresh courage to your plight presenting!

DANIEL: To share in bloodshed not intending,
Beneath its burden I'm not bending!

SIMEON: Hush, listen!

GAMALIEL: Eh?

ZACHARIAS: Whence this hellfire?

NAHOR: A boy's voice, since its pitch is higher!

SIMEON: Stop, stop, you grooms, your zeal do slow down,
Lest we should rue this hurried showdown!

RESATHA: Your screaming mouth you'll be regretting,
When black-and-blue it will be getting!

GAMALIEL: It's gone too far, sir, hold your fire!
Who knows what might herefrom transpire!
Let's hear what has in him ignited
Such tumult, and these screams incited!

NAHOR: Dear son, what message finds expression
In such a brash, vociferous fashion?

DANIEL: Oh, folk of Israel, with folly lavish,
Your foreheads donkey's ears embellish!
You have no grasp of what you're doing,
Truth nowhere capable of viewing,

Your folly's daze is so amazing
The best among you you've been raising
Must here now suffer condemnation?
So, back to court, the litigation
Reopen! These two have reported
False evidence, to fraud resorted,
And ruled as rogues complete, entire,
And learning this will fan your ire!

ICHABOTH: Such lies why does your gullet spatter?
You'd call us bunglers in this matter?
The headsman have her—Nothing doing!
Do you pretend the truth you're viewing?
That you're possessed aren't you admitting?
Your wits transgress against what's fitting!
So, hold your tongue, unless you'd rather,
Like her, feel rocks your body smother!

NAHOR: No way! not so! Your pace start slowing,
Don't rush the boy to where he's going!
Till now what's right he didn't slander,
God knows the path on which he'll wander!
Prevent rash action from occurring;
Let's not important facts be slurring!

SIMEON: Dear son, if you have dispensation
From God that by your presentation
Be shown what tricked us in this matter,
Whereby we might His justice shatter,
We are hereby now recommending
This case as chairman you'll be tending,
Though proper to our jurisdiction,
We couldn't judge not risking friction!
But if with men you this concerted,
About the chance be well alerted:
The threat of death for you looms dire,
And sentenced with her you'll expire!

DANIEL: The Lord himself the verdict's breaking,
Injustice nearly done unmaking,
He sent me here this fact asserting,
The sentence just in time averting!
Arrest these two, your duty doing,
Their might without compunction viewing!

ICHABOTH: This rowdy kid gets jurisdiction?
  We're calling for an interdiction!
  If, sirs, to felony you're given,
  Would see us to injustice driven,
  Unpunished will not go your doing—
  Great harm for you will be ensuing!
RESATHA: Instead of us the boy you're calling
  As judge? To exercise our calling,
  Who God knows whence came hither straying,
  To gloat, for shame on us is preying?
  When did indeed such thing transpire
  An underaged boy should inquire
  Into our verdict, start assailing
  What right procedure is entailing?
DANIEL: Your new resolve for fear don't damage,
  Their meanness can no longer ravage!
  Arrest them both! To jail them taking,
  Much tamer both you will be making,
  Of haughtiness they'll be there quitted!
  Against them God himself is pitted!
  To no avail will be their railing.
  Their custody on grooms entailing,
  In turn start Susan's fetters rending.
  Of guiltlessness proof God is sending!
GAMALIEL: The lady's bonds, grooms, quickly sunder,
  With ropes tie up those judges yonder,
  Stop being of their power leery.
  It was short-lived and made us weary.
  You count to two, and what transpires
  Are only lies, made up by liars,
  The charges that they were presenting
  Against her turned to angry ranting!
  How blind we were to all their doing.
  They cocked a snook, their goal pursuing!
  A youngster has to us presented
  What long since should have been prevented!
ABED: You heard the truth, now start it heeding!
  The process you can't be impeding!
  Give up, at your arrest stop balking,
  Else, with main force your movements blocking,

We'll force you, clinch the arrestation!
Submit with quiet resignation!
ICHABOTH: Good Lord, how come that in this matter
A boy act as mistake's abettor,
With shamefulness our name oppressing?
I bet he's for traducement pressing!
DANIEL: Don't let their threats change your position—
The huddling twosome next partition,
Thereafter I will broach the matter,
Their evildoings' veil I'll shatter!
To one the court's attention turning,
The other somewhere else interning,
As soon as one's interrogated,
The other'll be evaluated!
SIMEON: Quick! What he says have implemented,
Do it, and no more questions vented!
Let them their anger be transporting,
With ease its brunt you'll be supporting!

Scene 3

Abed, Ichaboth, Giezi, Resatha, Joachim, Helchias, Susanna.

ABED: Stand by, and pay now close attention,
Bind Ichaboth, and to detention
Dispatch him hence as they intended,
Until to this one they'll have tended!
Securely him you should be gripping,
Lest from your grip he manage slipping!
ICHABOTH: For force to seize me you are asking,
With bonds and guard my person tasking?
Grooms, has your recent occupation
Not been to act on our dictation?
GIEZI: To know, who better is empowered,
About the tricks you on us showered,
And what might further be occurring,
Since down on you we thus come bearing!
ICHABOTH: That's how behaves a finger licker,
A snotty brat, and fawning slicker!
To shame the people here consented
A boy more trust and faith they've granted

Than wise old men who'd never tire
Of being judges in your hire.
Have then all honors been forgotten?
For years from us you've justice gotten!
To prostrate now do you endeavor
Those who before so high did hover?

ABED: Luck can be to and fro diverted,
  Who's honored now, soon is deserted!

JOACHIM: Here, dearest, luck its gifts will lavish,
  The Lord will make your hardships vanish,
  And for the best have all converted.
  The boys He's not in vain alerted!

HELCHIAS: Avenged must be their vile aspersion.
  God's help remains a firm assertion,
  He'll salvage those from going under
  Who from true faith themselves won't sunder!

SUSANNA: Your justice, how sublime, unflagging,
  O, Lord. Let insight be not lagging!
  How oddly you design all matters,
  My innocence to rid of fetters!
  What man would ever have conjectured
  That Your compassion I'd have captured?

Scene 4

Daniel, Resatha, Ichaboth, Simeon, Gamaliel, Zacharias, Nahor, Abed.

DANIEL: One of the oldsters now bring hither,
  To question him I will not dither!

RESATHA: What for, dear sirs, serves this proceeding,
  Which with your mouths unlocked you're heeding—
  You execute this youngster's bidding
  As if we two were vices breeding?

DANIEL: Enough, old boy, you've questions vented,
  At once the answer here's presented:
  You think, when you're injustice molding,
  The Lord will keep your cause upholding?
  To evil in your youth addicted,
  By virtue you were not restricted,
  Beneath false pretense vice you'd bury,

As pure and pious yourself carry,
To pretense lend a truthful flavor,
Till you've gained everybody's favor.
Into the saddle once you'd gotten,
The Lord completely was forgotten,
The law of justice you divested,
The guiltless to their knees your wrested,
The crooked, who to you presented
Rich gifts, went free and ne'er repented,
But who proved to your wish resistant
The piper paid, that very instant!
And in your crooked deals and pandering
Without the fear of God meandering,
Your thought the Lord's commands ignore,
Which Moses taught us to adore:
The guiltless, filled with pious rapture,
For execution you shan't capture!
All this you've never even pondered,
Nor in your heart have ever wondered
That God might tear your foul play's texture.
Nor did you bother to conjecture
That nothing here has such fine weave
That someone's eye it won't deceive!
But long enough your fraud's abided;
God's justice has your fate decided!
Precisely in this put-up matter,
Since pious wife's good name you'd shatter,
For this foul lie on you we'll lavish
Disgrace before the world you cherish!
So, tell us, justice never-wronger
—Nay, better still, you fictionmonger—:
Tell us, while in the garden biding,
Which tree you saw their lewdness hiding,
As you have been your yarn pursuing,
Pray tell, those two, where were you viewing?
RESATHA: Beneath an ash tree there they rutted!
DANIEL: By God's decree may you be blotted!
What pack of lies you are confecting!
Your villainy they are reflecting!
Behold, the sword is God's donation

With which the angel's fulmination
Your life will slice, not giving quarter,
Will pay you for your sin by slaughter!—
Remove this one, the one remaining
Bring here, to question him I'm aiming!—
Come here, bad seed, forlornly sired,
From Canaan's land in vices mired,
And not from Judah's proper lineage,
Struck by God's anger-cloud's fierce visage,
Since you a case made past detesting,
Of her unfaithfulness protesting.
Your heart a wanton lust was breeding,
On lewd desire often feeding,
For Israel's fair daughters craving,
Whom to your will you were enslaving
And used for sensual satiation.
They couldn't voice their protestation,
Lest they would be your anger courting,
Which they were fearful of supporting.
Because this lady crossed your yearning,
Her soul and body from you turning,
Her charms refused which you would plunder,
She had no way out and fell under
Your anger's brunt. Her extirpation
You planned, and forged this fabrication,
And with your friend you did conspire
That by your verdict she expire!
Once you alleged that you'd been viewing
Dame Susan her lewd act pursuing:
So let it be by you presented,
Beneath which tree their lust they vented!
ICHABOTH: Beneath a linden they lay lazing!
DANIEL: God strike you with his vengeance blazing!
Foul lies to us you have presented,
Against her evidence invented!
Behold, God's angel is now broaching
Your punishment. The time's approaching
And growing short. To strike, alerted,
Is poised his sword. By both deserted
Will be this world. Your lives now end.

And freed will be the innocent!
Be off! To questions I presented
You offered lies, by you invented!—
Here, gentlemen, you're plainly viewing
That only lies was all their doing.
Now, being men in your position,
Do justice, as behooves your mission!
You are the angel, awesome fighter,
Whose sword has never glittered brighter,
The villainous to be assailing.
Hence peace for pious people hailing,
Make sure truth by it is asserted,
To evil ends not be diverted.
Its blade turn 'gainst all ill intention!
Its blunt back pay devout attention!
That means, as bearer them attending,
Upon your backs welfare's depending.
This precept do especially treasure:
That never here, to soothe his pleasure,
A magnate see a claim be sounded
To his advantage, though unfounded,
Ere, closely you the case review,
And know exactly what to do.
A lord, by wrath or envy baited,
Will have some wretch oft aggravated.
When such a ploy's to no avail,
He'll try by lies still to prevail,
Upon his fame and office playing,
Who would suspect what traps he's laying.
His word, not brooking confrontation,
At once gets certain approbation—
The way the judges tried to do!
Thus carefully henceforth pursue
What's lawful, never shake or cower,
Should flashing teeth bare naked power;
So fast don't bite those misbegotten,
By God the righteous aren't forgotten!
SIMEON: To God eternal thanks we're sending
    That he's to us in time attending
    Impeding such a harsh accounting,

And guiltless sacrifice surmounting.
You, chosen boy, did save the day;
Through you to Him we'll honor pay.
Now we will be by nought affrighted,
Because the Lord in you delighted.
To difficulties never ceding,
Your lesson we'll be always heeding.
What verdict, elders, have you reached
Regarding these two men impeached?

GAMALIEL: God offers a determination
Against which there's no protestation.
No lengthy pleas be here presented.
Be death their penalty, intended
For her, to which they were committed,
As bitter wrath their spirit heated.
They made a false denunciation;
They're sentenced to life's deprivation.
The verdict's rigor unabated
Declares for stoning they are fated!

ZACHARIAS: I find this view the justest ever!

NAHOR: I hail it too with sincere fervor!

SIMEON: Let then in God's name be concluded,
Their blood is here to be exuded.
Grooms, take away each fictionmonger
For judges they aren't any longer,
According to deserts them bleeding,
With stones begin their limbs impeding.
And as a favor, don't give quarter,
Or else, your life will be cut shorter!

ABED: Right proper with them we'll be dealing,
Make sure their wages they are feeling,
If thoughts of flight these dogs should favor,
Then let them learn life's weighty labor.

Scene 5

Giezi, Resatha, Abed, Olympa, Ichaboth, Ruth, Heli, Baldam, Malchus.

GIEZI: Well, gentlemen, be on your way.
It will you both cause great dismay!

But whether pained or cheered thereby,
What lies ahead you can descry!
RESATHA: Of these reports we've heard our fill!
ABED: You were the ones that made this deal!
OLYMPA: You, sirs, have you a thought retained
Of that injustice by you framed?
My field I lost, all thanks to you,
But God on high your crime did view.
The debt is paid off now at last,
Which He allowed so long to last!
I trust those who the law uphold,
Will snare the fox that made so bold,
And through his guile and might undue
My field had stolen thanks to you.
To gauge by what's correct and just,
It's time that snake should bite the dust.
RUTH: You, sirs, have you not time to spare,
My case before the court to air?
For what you yesterday did pine,
Has now become a heavy fine!
ICHABOTH: Woe! fickle luck, how you've declined!
Just now with honors wined and dined,
But now the world would us berate,
In dire straits steers our fate.
On earth is nothing safe indeed!
Who'd ever think we would proceed
Toward an end so ill-designed!
Oh, luck, how sadly you've declined!
HELI: You, sirs, this wine cup first you'll drain,
A parting draft you shall obtain,
Fine malmsey here for you we pour.
But you'd drink water, if therefore
You could go home, and there remain,
And thus relieved were of the pain
Which follows, once you quenched your thirst.
Since from this wine the stone has burst,
Which will your loins not only bash,
But back and head will also smash.
How sweet the cup, though, that you drained,
With fresh resolve you'll be sustained,

The stone you won't resent in fine,
Though crushing you be its design!—
So, cheer up, don't be bashful, drink!
You've pushed too far toward the brink,
It's far too late to make it good,
The evil hour has ensued.
Since your designs on her depart,
The tankard's fill will give you heart!

ABED: From other people's pots who nabbed,
Will by his head be also grabbed!

HELI: Who is with others' kitchens free,
By stone enlightened he will be!

RESATHA: To our grief we bear rebuff,
The wage for all that sinful stuff.
If young or old, from troth who stray,
Behold what dish is on its way.
It's venison of stones they bear,
Lest you break teeth they've taken care,
When snapping, in a frantic craze!
We, too, were caught in such a daze,
And now we're choking on the same,
Because we rushed to chew the game,
This uncooked meat, and not well-done,
Which our stomachs were to shun!

GIEZI: Take heed! It cuts your life's duration!
Your spirit faces expiration!

RESATHA: My head, oh, woe!

ICHABOTH: Oh, woe—my back!

GIEZI: Don't look around! Throw on, don't slack!

RESATHA: Oh, Lord, stand by me in my plight!
My soul through lips is taking flight!

ICHABOTH: Oh, Lord, don't view my sinful shame
Which since my youth I couldn't tame!
With my distress commiserate,
Eternal death don't make my fate!

ABED: Enough, they're full, and lying down,
Their limbs the rightful place now crown!
Now women neither one maligns,
Nor on their honor has designs.

GIEZI: Oh, yes, we offered them therefore

A cure, it lies there past the door.
Saint Steven's bread the name it gained,
For such an illness it's ordained,
One penny the prescription filled!
ABED: Not I, to buy it I've not willed,
This physic, for my limbs to burn.
Nor for a woman do I yearn,
Her name and honor to malign—
So for this salve I do not pine.
GIEZI: And everyone massage would I
With flint lard, thickly it apply,
Who for shame neighbors will upbraid,
Though of it found in them no shade!
Their tongues I'd rub with it and twist,
Three days from moving they'd desist.
And unto those I'd too attain,
Who after their own meal would fain
Of others go the tidbits sharing,
While their own cake inside still bearing!
They only bend the law, they swear!
Who thinks so, in his mind must bear
To stop, ere bending is a break,
Revenge for which the Lord will take!
ABED: Yourself all further effort save,
Entomb these two inside a grave.
To let them lie here there's no need,
This idle calk would only breed!
GIEZI: Blast! This one's fat like suety kine!
We'll sweat when making him recline!
ABED: The cakes upon which he had dined,
With heaviness his belly lined.
Hey you, pitch in, you are not lame,
You'll earn a tip, if you are game!
BALDAM: Alas, I see it all too well:
I will be surely cast to hell!
I robbed the widow with my claim,
For cheating many I'm to blame;
The judges bribes and gifts I gave,
Their law with falsehood made my slave!
And now they're gone! My turn to drop!

All my affairs a dismal flop!
Vile gold, by you I set such store—
You drove me to hell's gaping door,
You stay on earth, just like before,
What use you offer any more?
As deity you I used to rate—
You leave me death as only fate!
Run, boy, and those who're friends of mine,
Bring quickly! My life's in decline!
The filthy wealth I did pursue,
Brought anguish that I never knew!

MALCHUS *(runs to get friends, returns):*
I found no friends, so back I came—
Bring help! He's dead, what crying shame!
A stroke has caused his quick demise,
For cheating her with wrongful lies!
How awfully, Lord, you punish here
Those who your wrath did never fear!—
The body I won't destitute,
I'll bury it with promptitude!
The law his wealth to friends will deed,
When into dust his limbs recede!

Scene 6

Susanna, Benjamin, Jahel, Joachim, Helchias, Elisabeth.

SUSANNA: God, Whom alone I just presume,
You brought me vengeance in their doom,
And saved me from a deadly fate.
In all distress you only rate
As helper, for you never let
Down those who by you store have set.
What you have promised, is ordained.
Who'd dare accuse you of a feint?
Your children you assured to aim
At building on you as their claim,
To you their vengeance they should leave,
Through you they will revenge receive—
You showed by me this to be true,
Your pledge was carried out by you!

Your praises thus I can't conceal,
Life stirring in me I can feel,
Henceforth, I'd like to, as before,
Beseech you, that I, on this score,
In all distress could, soon or late,
To you as faithful God relate.
Dear, pious parents, how you pained,
Dear spouse, as patient as a saint,
To praise from our own hearts proceed
Almighty God, and Lord indeed,
Who from on high leaned, none too soon,
And sent to us this friendly boon!
In you, dear children, be ingrained
This model that we have obtained,
Of fear of God to tend the seed,
His love and His respect to heed,
Because you here directly faced
How God the Lord my cause embraced,
How He did lead me through my grief,
And brought me safely home to live.

BENJAMIN: Dear mother, much from this we've gained,
   Our piety will not grow faint!

JAHEL: I will obey, my faith won't faint!

SUSANNA: Yes, daughter, do as is ordained!

JOACHIM: Susanna, dearest spouse regained,
   A stony heart would have disdained
   To thank the Lord for granting grace,
   Which has today here taken place,
   As to deliver you he deigned,
   And had your pain of death restrained!
   Your loss I did already grieve,
   When you returned with us to live.
   New heights your worthiness attained,
   Since you have pure throughout remained.
   Your innocence God public made,
   Because your shame to fix he bade
   On your accusers' wily ploy,
   As he against them roused the boy.

HELCHIAS: For me your merit also gained
   That you intact throughout remained,

And honors must to you concede
Who God and worldly masters heed.
Forever, too, in mind I'll bear
That God your innocence did bare.
ELISABETH: Of course I can't this boon divine
Requite with anything that's mine,
Which He down here to us has paid,
When He the boy sent to our aid,
Your innocence to vindicate!
No longer therefore shall we wait,
But praise the Lord, forever that
He our wishes kindly met!

Scene 7

Abed, Simeon, Susanna, Daniel, Joachim, Nahor, Abdi.

ABED: Learned gentlemen, we've done what's been concerted,
Life's last breath the evildoers has deserted,
And they've been entombed, according to tradition.
Hopefully you'll find we've done well by our mission!
SIMEON: Praise the Lord! He did her innocence betoken,
And the nasty judges' power has been broken.
Into the abyss of sin we started gazing,
When God sent the youngster by His grace amazing,
Who the lady's innocence to us detected,
And the wrongful bloodbath caused to be rejected!
Lady Susan, lest by us you be forgotten,
Don't consider, please, our plan as misbegotten
That against you for a verdict we've been suing,
Which to you a great injustice would be doing.
This is what we think: the Lord this case converted
That the judges' knavery could be by you averted.
All the clever men will be your virtue viewing—
To both parties thus just merit is accruing.
Proper wages now the judges are betiding,
For the mischief they till now have both been hiding,
But your virtue will be widely represented,
To more folks than ever it will be presented!
As to people's ears your story is proceeding,
More respect and awe for you this will be breeding.

You will serve for decent wives as inspiration,
To a chaste and spotless life an invitation.
Just because you stood, with shame above you hovering,
Briefly here, to our eyes your grief uncovering,
Seven times more honor on you we'll be squandering—
How much you the boy and God owe pondering,
Whom God graciously to us had sent as witness,
Demonstrating to the world that you are guiltless!

SUSANNA: Dearest gentlemen, the verdict you've presented
Will not be in coming days at all resented,
But the will of God this verdict they'll be calling,
Gratefully as wonder all of it recalling,
When He, at His wretched handmaid kindly winking,
Let his gaze to me so fatherly come sinking,
You too, dearest child, I'll always honor, wondering,
How the Lord such bounties on you has been squandering,
You through me from their defiant tricks redeeming,
And, while I'm alive, most highly you esteeming,
As God's envoy you within my heart installing.
After Him, my life's redeemer you I'm calling.

DANIEL: Dame Susanna, for such honor I'm not pining,
Since I haven't come here by my own designing.
But the Lord your innocence had so admired,
Knowing how your trusting heart to Him aspired.
That's why He to your entreaties paid attention,
Making me the agent of your death's prevention!
Hence you should to God all merit be assigning,
Thus you'd all have done whereto my heart's inclining!

JOACHIM: As appropriate, dear elders, this I'm holding,
Nothing should be our praise of God withholding!
Hence to sing His praises let us all here gather,
Our gratitude to demonstrate together.
All his bounties never will be here forgotten,
But the people who together here have gotten,
With them in a friendly fashion I am pleading,
That without objections, my example heeding,
Should assist this day to have as feast asserted,
Since for me the Lord my woe to joy converted.
Hence our thanks and praise through song let's give expression,
Let us dance, make merry, leap with frenzied passion—

Thus to praise and honor our dear Lord proceeding,
Having no regrets, expenditure not heeding!
As upon death's ferry this day she's been pining,
"Widower" as name myself I was assigning—
Since the Lord, though, gave her life renewed duration,
And my matrimony granted renovation,
Like a wedding, let a feast here start unfolding.
To a promise once more, elders, you I'm holding;
Don't deny my wish: I'm for your presence pleading,
For God's praise, my pleasure, my wife's honor heeding!
NAHOR: For our sake to answer him, your wish we'll treasure,
  We won't argue, but do likewise, with great pleasure!
SIMEON: Dear Joachim, we're aware of your intention,
  Rest assured that on that score there's no contention!
  We are yours and will intone your spouse's praises.
  Joy, whatever may befall, our spirit raises!
JOACHIM: Heartfelt thanks upon you, gentlemen I'm heaping,
  How to be of service will in mind be keeping!
ABDI *(to the audience)*:
  To assist my master you who have consented,
  And your pity for Dame Susan here have vented,
  Joyfully you ought at once again here gather,
  God the benefactor let us praise together!

CONCLUSION

Most gracious friends and gentlemen,
And the entire gathered clan,
Who time to see the play have found,
Pay heed to what we here expound:
The play was written with great care,
And was designed to bring to bear
True awe of God, make it burn bright,
That all should glean some use and light
Who saw it here. So pay now heed
For what from you we here now plead:
That each some lesson from it store,
And take it to his dwelling's door,
To better thus his human state,
Regardless how his name might rate!

The judges teach us how to frown
On vice. The old in shame must drown
When wayward they to dally vow,
Who'd ardent youth this disallow.
And what a thing it is debased,
If anyone can be disgraced
Without recourse, at someone's will
For whom no crime's lost its appeal!
Likewise of government who hold
The sway, with violence make bold,
The personage of magnates heed,
But aggravate the paupers' need,
Whom only greed and favor sway,
From justice they will turn away.
That this will not go unassailed,
That God's own vengeance hasn't failed,
Here recognize—and each one heed:
When men disgrace dispense through greed,
False witness bear employing lies,
Foul shame will also be their prize!
The councilmen have shown today
For fear we shouldn't turn away
From truth, but law and right should groom.
Although some drawback we assume,
We should not let injustice gain,
As yes-men evil help sustain.—
And, too, no lord need it repent
Should him a word of praise be lent
From someone of a lowlier line,
According to the boy's design.
For Daniel to all men proves
How much of children God approves,
How often in them He'll ingrain
His spirit, ere they reason gain,
How God through children's mouths can act,
His constant praise thus does effect!

Dame Susan may us best outline
The Christian doctrine's fair design:

It's, first, a mirror crystal-clear,
In which should view themselves the dear
And pious women, who do heed
The path, on which to walk they need,
For virtue and for honor pine—
She'll teach them how to toe the line,
To follow men's unquestioned lead,
As masters their commands to heed,
Men's wishes with their acts approve,
And more than anything will prove
Their solid love's undying flame,
Set at no other man their aim!
And much and oft she's to appeal
To child and staff to do God's will.
All times, besides, on guard she'll be
Lest servants stray from God's decree,
Ward off the wild seduction game—
Ere life and limb be lost to shame!
And she in us can trust infuse
That God our rescue won't refuse
When we're about to suffocate,
So long as Him we advocate,
And bear our cross without lament
Imposed on us by God's intent.
Ere God will aid to us disclaim,
His miracle the threat will tame.
This was to you made clear and plain
As Daniel did just explain.

The widows to expound succeed
That those who to God vengeance cede,
The best revenge to get are bound—
Much harsher than themselves could mount.
A model Jochem's for our life,
That men do right, who for their wife
With love and honor do abound,
Who care that no one should confound
Her in a cruel, wrongful way,
Nor will without cause stay away.

And judging by her parents' life,
We see respect and joy are rife
At last in one's declining days,
If children we do rightly raise.
On grooms and maids, too, one can view
What can good supervision do.
Good teachings them to good incline,
Which wife and lord for them define,
They loyally will do their chores,
With which they're charged behind closed doors!

So, too, the children, this is plain,
Should children teach, in minding train,
So that with love, and not with clout
They should pursue the righteous route,
Their games with teachings implement,
Which parents to them represent.

What other thoughts this play of mine
Holds that to virtue might incline,
To count them all is not my aim,
But profit everyone that came
Should draw from them, as best he deign—
God, too, his prize from it should gain.
Grant to the poet, and us all,
That our loftiest wish befall.

But, dearest gentlemen, do heed
For what we furthermore here plead,
Since principally for you all,
Your benefit and joys galore,
To take such pains we hither came,
We learned the play, began the same.
This service as our gift now claim,
With thanks and pleasure it acclaim!
And where we not as well did fare
As would seem fit, our views to air,
Put up with us, till, by your leave,
We've practiced more, give us reprieve,
Till time and tide make us more wise,

Take wish for finished enterprise.
The goal at which we all did aim,
In best intentions we did frame:
To praise the Lord, our sole design,
That youth to fear of God incline,
That honesty be helped to grow,
That godliness and virtue glow.
Make sure this spreads throughout the town,
The honored council honor crown,
Which we at this occasion ask
That it should glory in the task
Of now accepting with acclaim
The service which to give we came!
And this we'll do in every case,
So as to earn it with good grace!

Translated by M. John Hanak

Andreas Gryphius

Leo Armenius
A Tragedy

Content of the Tragedy

Michael Balbus, Emperor Leo Armenius's supreme commander, after having been charged on several occasions for his disloyalty and libel, takes an oath against the Emperor, who often warned him through Exabolius, his privy counselor, to desist from his irresponsibility. However, because Michael persists with his intention, he is unexpectedly taken prisoner and condemned to death by fire at the court in which the Emperor serves as plaintiff and judge. However, as Michael is being led to the stake, the Emperor postpones his punishment until after the Christmas celebration due to the fervent insistence of his wife, Theodosia. Meanwhile, Michael seeks every possible means to save himself. Because the Emperor is upset by fear and (Michael's) audacity, he personally visits the prison at night and finds Michael asleep, dressed in purple. Michael, in utter despair after being informed of this by a guard who had recognized the Emperor because of his embroidered shoes, threatens the conspirators that he will expose them if he is not aided immediately. The conspirators, however, successfully enter the palace by means of a special ruse and they mercilessly murder the Emperor before the altar.

This takes place in the year 820 after the birth of our Lord, in the seventh year and fifth month of his rule, as the ghost of Tarasius had prophesied in a vision shortly before the event. Cedrenus and Zonarus relate the history in greater detail in their *Leo Armenius and Michael Balbus*. The tragedy begins at noon before Christmas; it continues through the night and ends before sunrise. The setting is Constantinople, primarily in the Imperial Palace.

ACT I

Scene 1

Michael Balbus, the Crambonite, the Conspirators

MICHAEL: The blood that you ventured in vain for throne and
crown,
The wounds, which you bear openly on your every limb,
The unrewarded service, the care-filled life,
Which day after day you must yield to plundering;
The cruel intent of the prince, the discord in the state,
The controversy in the church and dishonesty in the council,
The unrest in the palace: oh, most flourishing of all heroes,
These matters struggle in my soul and force me to proclaim
What cannot be kept silent! Who are we? Are we the ones
Before whom barbarians have so often dropped to their knees;
Before whom Saracen and Persian and even he, who injures
more
When he flees than when he stands firm, are terrified?
Who are we? Are we the ones, who often in dust and despair
Yet filled with blood, with courage and spirit, defied cruel
death?
Who covered the broad land with the enemies' hide
And overturned Sidas and set ablaze
Whatever showed us weapons? And do we now fall asleep,
Now that everyone wants to be tyrant over us?
But ye heroes, wake up! Can your fighting hands allow
That realm and land and state will thus go to ruin
While Leo cleanses himself in his subjects' blood
And always quenches his thirst for wealth with your goods?
What is the court anymore but a den of murderers?
But a place of betrayers? A dwelling of bad boys.
He who skillfully flatters and lies as much as he can,
He is presented to princes: a straightforward man
Who has often forced a well-equipped army to flight
Remains unheralded and withers! What does this weak
lamenting accomplish?
Nothing! if a woman's heart beats in your breast!
But much, if a hero's courage, which no fear terrorizes!

Whoever is hesitant, has heard too little from me:
A hero has heard more than enough. And yet a woman destroyed
The imperial power not long ago, as you know.
The mother had her child taken from throne to prison
Where it had to end its life in greatest torture
As both its eyes were cruelly torn out.
A weak arm accomplished this. How can we boast of ourselves?
Irene is worthy of praise.

THE CRAMBONITE: Let him boast who wants to follow!
Look, hero! Here is a sword, and this fist can stab
And cut, if necessary, and can smash the heads of princes.
What is a prince? A human being! And I'm as good as he!
Indeed, better! If it weren't for me, if it weren't for my sword,
Where would his crown be? The dazzling diamonds,
The purple-golden garb, the multitudes of servants,
The scepter's brilliance, are all but an empty splendor.
It is an unwavering arm that makes the prince
And, when necessary, displaces him.

FIRST CONSPIRATOR: Oh, Judge of all things!
Must your revenge at last awaken from its dreams?
So it is! It summons us, when we least expect it.
Who is there who knows not what vexes my soul
And eats away at my heart and liver! That honest spirit,
The more than pious prince, the image of gentle goodness,
The trusted Michael,* was forced to lay down his staff and crown
When the Lion became enraged and charged him
With cruel treachery and mad power. He relinquished the royal purple
And put on a hair shirt with the intent of dedicating
The rest of his brief time at altars to his god.
But no! Leo, who was impassioned by nothing but murder and ridicule,
Broke his loneliness and banned him from church and the realms,
Forcing him to shrink before him from throne to dust.
Exiled to the isle of Prote, he who once held this great land

*Emperor Michael I. Rhangabe preceded Leo Armenius as emperor from 811–13.

Encompassed in his command, is now encompassed by a narrow
   grave in sand
Which each moment is washed by the desolate sea!
His son Theophilactus! What has he not felt?
When his male parts were torn from his loins
And his brother's penis was rubbed in his face!
Break forth, oh long awaited day, which so many thousand tears
Demand! Oh break forth! My life may pass away
If only my foot can first trample on your head,
You bloodhound! You tyrant! If I can avenge the atrocity,
Then let a quick spear stab me to death on the spot.
SECOND CONSPIRATOR: Let him suffer what he committed! Indeed
   that day is breaking forth.
Insofar as the human spirit can divine the future—
Insofar as the wise soul can escape from the prison
Into which the flesh and dire necessity and time and labor force
   it,
And, feathered by reason, can soar through the air
And observe the obscure: so must the tyrant land
Fall, even sooner than anyone thinks, as booty to the sword.
Already I think I hear the trumpets of revenge resound!
MICHAEL: What does this speech imply?
SECOND CONSPIRATOR: The splendid chamber
Up at the castle which is decorated from floor to ceiling
With alabaster, precious metals, and marble
Is not so much embellished by the splendor of gold and riches
As by writings with higher meanings. Many an old parchment
Presents to us the heroes who knew Persia and Scythia,
Who sacrificed their lives for their fatherland
And dampened their proud swords with enemies' blood.
What can the pen not accomplish, which gives life to him
Upon whom death and time have executed their power!
The course of the suns, the fleeting essence of the stars,
The characteristics of plants, all can be read on a thousand
   pages.
The art of the Greeks, the ways of distant lands,
And what a human mind conceives is preserved on paper.
And what is more, how one can know that which is hidden
And how and when a person's life will end.
Often before, and to be sure not fruitlessly, I have

Searched through an unknown work filled with drawings
In which, as is thought, everything that every prince
Who has occupied this throne has done is chronicled in
    symbols.
How long this realm will stand in full blossom:
How in the future each prince will rise and fall:
One learns from this book the anxiety, the burden that
    oppresses us
And the means to untangle the distress in which we're bound.
The lion of a former time corroborates what is believed;
The years point out the one who strangles and robs everything,
Who with inflamed spirit and claws seems to threaten:
He tosses his front paw into the air as if enraged;
His hair flies about his head: yes, the portrait shouts
Of his cruel manner; his bright eyes burn,
Inflamed with mad rage; his jowl can scarcely be discerned
Due to the foam and fresh blood that flows on the ground
As he begins bite upon bite and murder upon murder.
What could be more clear? His strong back is covered
By a purplish red cross, through which a hunter thrusts
With a more than rapid hand a sharply whetted sword
That penetrates through skin, flesh, and bone into the heart.
You know the wild beast: the cross is Christ's symbol,
Before whose birthday passes, this lion will pale and die.
MICHAEL: I want to be the hunter. Whoever stands with me
    For honor and country and life; whoever sets his spirit
    As security for fame and freedom; whoever has the courage to
        dare;
    Whoever desires revenge and reward; whoever can trample death
        and eternity
    With his feet—let him contribute at this time
    With counsel and action, and help seek out the means
    To carry out the attack without delay and suspicion.
THE CRAMBONITE: We'll go wherever you command.
MICHAEL: I swear to venture
    Body and blood for the commonwealth and the realm.
    Do what you consider necessary.
THE CRAMBONITE: Hand over your sword. We swear
    To transform the cruel power of the prince into powdery dust.

Scene 2

Leo Armenius, Exabolius, Nicander.

LEO: So he no longer heeds either advice or warning?
EXABOLIUS: That's right. Warnings, requests, and threats are
 scorned.
 He races like a horse that has snapped the reins;
 Like a powerful creek, when the streams pour out
 And sweep houses, trees, and cattle into the sea.
 His courage grows more and more, and if I understand
  correctly,
 He has undertaken with others a greater project
 Than has ever before reached our ears.
LEO: Faithless fool! More than cursed man!
 Ingrate, more depraved than depravity itself!
 Bedeviled spirit! Cursed senses,
 Which no honesty or charity can gain!
 Didn't I bring you, mad dog, from the gutter to the court?
 And here on my very own lap make you famous and great?
 Has the cold snake, which now strikes, cheated us?
 Was this basilisk raised at our breast?
 Why weren't you strangled when you committed this insolent
  deed,
 Before the treason was revealed to the great council?
 Have noble courage and reason befooled us?
 Did I strengthen the arm that now rises against us?
 But what is a prince, beyond a crowned knave,
 Injured every moment by that which is splendid and which is
  common
 Through word and deed; always embattled from both sides
 By envy, faithless suspicion, hate, pain, anxiety, and fear.
 To whom does he entrust his body, when he spends the long
  night
 In ceaseless worry and remains alert for the nations
 Who observe his trappings more than his raw distress
 And (because he is no longer free) scorn that which deserves
  fame?
 Whom does he bring to the court? The one who risks his life

First for him, and then against him, and chases him from the
court
When the game changes. One must honor his mortal enemy,
See with blind eyes, hear with deaf ears.
No matter how his heart burns with anger and zeal,
One must be courteous in words, and elevate to honorable
offices
Him who tramples regiment and crown with his feet.
How often this crime has been forgiven of the perpetrator!
How often! What do we lament? No lamenting will help here,
But only quick counsel.

NICANDER: Stop it, before he himself stops it.

LEO: If he should die, who would not grieve for him without
judgment?

NICANDER: A prince must not question weightless words so much!

LEO: A weightless word often sets off not-weightless uproar.
The populace, officials, steed, and knave look only to this man.

EXABOLIUS: Let him be bound and arraigned at the palace.

LEO: How? What if, as before, he reduces the complaints to
nothing?

EXABOLIUS: The charge is too clear!

LEO: So was the last one, yet he got away.

NICANDER: That's why he breathes revenge and murder.

LEO: His following is too great.

EXABOLIUS: If his head is cut off, then no other limb can cause
damage.

LEO: I would burden myself with the hatred and malice of many.

EXABOLIUS: One heeds no hatred if it's a matter of crown and
scepter.

LEO: He has filled South, East, and West with his fame.

EXABOLIUS: Now South, East, and West will curse his crime.

LEO: If only East and West don't avenge his punishment.

EXABOLIUS: A bird flees the tree, upon which thunder strikes.

LEO: The great wild forest is moved by the strike.

EXABOLIUS: Moved and also shocked. One learns to avoid the
cliffs
On which a foreign mast has had to suffer shipwreck.

LEO: He has the hilt of the sword; we have, unfortunately, only the
sheath.

EXABOLIUS: Hold firm before he stabs; we must strike or suffer.
LEO: Who will be able to clap his audacious fist in irons?
EXABOLIUS: When strength is useless, one must resort to cunning.
NICANDER: Let him be seized unexpectedly as soon as he comes
    this way.
LEO: With regret we support what can't be changed.
  We feel our soul compromised by his guilt;
  We hear his long service plead for his crime.
  The overgenerous favor which we have often granted to him,
  His marble-hard frame of mind, which no warning can bend,
  Inflame our wrath. We regret his strength.
  Yet our spirit becomes enraged if we even superficially
  View his deeds! It will have to thunder,
  Since no lightning frightens him. Tell him once again
  He is to appear upon our summons in the palace.
  If he can be changed, if (as we hardly suspect)
  He confesses his guilt and honors the one whom he injured
  In pious humility, no sword will be sharpened here.
  Insofar as he (as is customary) wants to sing the same old song,
  Nicander, tie him up. Let the proud head roll
  That cannot bow.

Scene 3

Nicander, Exabolius.

NICANDER: Conclusion not unhoped for!
  Yet much-too-late concern. Pardon me, but I must
  Make known what oppresses me. The Emperor is too mild
  And jokes with his well-being: whoever wants to watch the
    flames
  When the raw winds set up camp around the embers
  Until his own roof and house are consumed
  Unfortunately cries but in vain. The archtraitors wake;
  We fall asleep, assured. They seek our death;
  We worry about their fortune, and now that dire necessity
  Already begins to embattle us with a bare sword,
  We think of lulling them into a dream with words.
  But why, Exabolius, does one speak to the deaf?
  The snake plugs its ear. The sword alone will bring peace

To the Emperor, to you, and to me. I'm supposed to tie up the
    murderer!
Why not penetrate his breast with this dagger?
That's how to end his defiance. This is Nicander's advice!
A great performance is lauded only when the deed is done!
EXABOLIUS: I'll gladly confirm that his damaged conscience
    Can atone for all his atrocities with nothing except blood and
    death.
    Yet if punishment is meted out to a man without a hearing
    He is always revered as righteous, no matter how tainted he may
    be.
NICANDER: Do you intend to contain the rampant pestilence
    which spreads daily
    With an extended trial? Do you mean to fight using the law
    When he's grasping the pike? He errs, who tolerates
    But for a day the one whose neck he might soon break.
EXABOLIUS: A long time won't be lost with lawsuits here!
NICANDER: I can execute a quick sentence with this sword.
EXABOLIUS: The Emperor's reputation doesn't allow such harsh
    judges.
NICANDER: The Emperor's welfare commands and condones what
    I do.
EXABOLIUS: Why would you want to give envy opportunity to
    calumniate?
NICANDER: Why should this head of the revolt live on?
EXABOLIUS: His demise is certain if he doesn't reverse his ways at
    once.
NICANDER: If his sword doesn't pass through our hearts first.
EXABOLIUS: Your zeal is indeed good, Nicander, but too heated.
NICANDER: Exabolius, don't make the accusation all too pointed
    Or he will stab us yet, himself.
EXABOLIUS: Do what the Emperor bids;
    Station a guard in the hall and court; in the event the cocky soul
    Won't keep within his limits, then let him be seized straightaway.
NICANDER: The strongest contingent must be brought to the
    adjoining chamber!
EXABOLIUS: Stay behind the tapestry with the footmen.
NICANDER: Right you are! In this way I'll hear how the game will
    end.

Scene 4

Exabolius, Michael Balbus.

MICHAEL: Where might I be able to find the Emperor, Exabolius?
EXABOLIUS: I believe he'll be granting you an audience right away.
MICHAEL: Why this "I believe"? What does he do without you?
EXABOLIUS: He himself does whatever occurs to him. The
    Emperor rules by himself.
MICHAEL: Why so crestfallen? So still? So lonely? So dismayed?
  What is that sigh about? Has he, whom you loved,
  Has Leo, who now spares no friends at all,
  Rewarded your long service with disfavor, as is his custom?
  He's silent! He turns away! I've found what it's about!
  Does one thus have no more to hope for than such gratitude?
  One who plunges himself into burning danger and deep distress
  Even as the Prince passes time with a thousand pleasures.
  He swims in a sea of bliss beyond desire
  While we stand in armor and suffer dust and sun
  And campaign against enemy and air and land.
  We risk our life, but if they flee, he who sits
  In the garden is lauded. The symbols of victory
  Are engraved with his titles when we pale in the grass;
  For our fame and strength and courage and estate
  And deeds and service are covered with a handful of sand.
  If one brings his tired body, his wounded limbs,
  His half-mangled head and chest, back to court again
  Then he beholds us as those on loan to him
  And wherever there's a wretched job that no one can do,
  Wherever there's a desperate place which no one knows how to
    keep,
  Wherever there's a dangerous office—that's what we're bid to
    manage.
  And he staffs us with traitors to keep himself informed—
  So that if peace reigns, we're more frightened than if war reigns,
  Until we make a mistake or the Prince takes a certain notion,
  And then we're robbed of honor and goods together with our
    head.
EXABOLIUS: My friend! Your loose mouth will bring you to
  greatest distress.

If anyone should hear you, you're a living corpse.

MICHAEL: I protest that it's no longer permitted to say aloud
What unfortunately is more than true. A careless word
Is treated like a crime worthy of sword and pillar.
Where has freedom fled? Freedom, whose place
Has been taken by a honey-sweet mouth, a flatterer
Who by wheedling has arrived at this place
Which my fist earned. I myself spit upon me
For being able to watch this crooked game so long.
The man who pushed himself onto the throne by trickery
(As earth and sun well know); who put down no enemy
Except with a foreign sword; who hears no proposal
That is a little unpleasant; who honors gossips
And suppresses virtue and suspects honesty
And bothers himself with strange fear and false suspicion:
Who never laid waste a foreign nation with steel and fire
And constantly dyes his claws in the blood of Byzantines;
Who lets himself be ruled by every knave and lad
And scandalously lets himself be led around the light, as if by
   the nose.
He is the one, whom you and I must behold with trembling!
He is the one, to whom we entrust our realm, our goods, our
   lives.
   How long will fear, illusion, and terror still blind us?
   Insofar as you want what I do, then in these hands exists
   The end of tyranny.
EXABOLIUS: The beginning of new pain.
   I request what I may.
MICHAEL: Withhold all requests
   And do what suits your honor and bravery.
EXABOLIUS: I do what friendship bids; whoever shows to one who
   is misled
   The proper way, whoever restrains a man
   Who is dashing towards the chasm, and whoever subordinates
   himself
   To this one who now falls, does more than just wishing.
   You seek what is hardly found by blood, by strangling and
   laying waste
   And flame and death: let alone the proud calm
   Of the safe countries! Can you believe without doubt

That all rob not for themselves, but just to benefit you?
And another thing! Who will join us? Four hands can't do it.
Many hands could, if one mouth doesn't break the oath of all.
Granted, too, that we already were pressing with a thousand
    armies
Into the imperial palace and were occupying the court and city:
Would Leo most likely be standing alone without sword and
    shield?
Certainly not! Those who now walk at his side,
Those who supported his power, and who only live through
    him,
They must give their hearts and necks for his crown.
Why? His fall would be their ruin.
Also, the one for whom he's doing something bitterly joins in
    reply:
Whoever always pleads for a new age and new masters,
Whoever lauds what is hoped for and curses what is at hand,
Whoever boasts of nothing except his strength and of rusty red
    spikes
And what the hard Persian lost in such and such a battle
He is bold enough to kill the tyrant and prince.
When the reveling with filled glasses at midnight banquets
Melts away in heated fear, when the trumpet sounds,
When swords are grasped and the armor rattles,
Many wish only to curb the power of the prince,
Not to do away with him entirely. Many can put up with
    strangers;
More can stand only their own blood! The uncertain power
Of weapons is not steady. Whoever intends through coercion of
    battle
To force his way onto the throne can disappear by battle;
This which he may aspire to and whatever he actually holds in
    his hands
Will find fear and woe and pain-filled despair,
And after experienced torture will find the port of lamentation:
    death.
Heaven itself watches over crowned heads
And supports the scepter. They struggle towards their bier
And reach, unexpectedly, a quick and horrible end
Who are bedazzled by the jeweled gold of a heavy crown.

Consider also what it's like to always move as a captive
Of so many thousand worries. When the confounded morning
Exposes the world's anxiety, to hear what
The Persians' sword suppresses, towards where the Scythian
  horse
Sets its swift foot into action, what Susa has undertaken,
How far the Barbarian might be, how far the Goth has come,
That now the Huns' wrath already penetrates the Danube,
That Cyprus is estranged, that Asia is offended,
That Colchos conceives new intrigues and Pontus invents new
  cunning,
That soon the proud Frank will gain in Greece,
That Taurus is no longer loyal: now the great city,
The queen of the world, dictates what can be hoped for;
Now Illiris, soon Sparta, send us emissaries;
Soon Egypt demands aid, and our allies
Make known what oppresses them. Soon the army calls for pay,
The nations withhold grain, the cities lack gold.
Now the foamy waves want to roll right up to the walls;
Now the envy of heaven doesn't want to water the fields;
The severe Titan singes away the dry sheaves
With glowing-hot light: the earth itself breaks
And can no longer stand when the peak of Mt. Hemus trembles;
When the great burden of the heavy towers collapses
And temple and altar and castle and court and house
Are covered in a moment with dust and rubble.
Now the foul breeze hastens to sweep in diseases
And infects the nations; soon the borders are surrounded by
  those
Who are nourished only by robbing; soon an unknown
  doctrine,
Aroused by superstition and dark illusion,
Is brought into action (oh, sickness of these times!),
Which holds the power of leading the whole realm and its
  people astray
So that the base of the pillars which bear the crown and royal
  symbols
And support cross and scepter, trembles and moves.
This doesn't affect everyone, yet everyone must suffer
His own part for himself. The prince can avoid nothing;

He feels the entire burden. When someone commits a crime
Who works in his service, the rabble doesn't fear
Ascribing the guilt, however great it was, to the Prince:
Can anything he does remain unrebuked?
He is afraid of his sword; when he goes to dine,
Is the mixed wine, which has been poured into crystal,
Transformed to gall and poison? As soon as the day fades,
That blackened band, the army of anxiety, comes creeping
And keeps watch in his bed. In ivory,
In purple and scarlet, he can never be as peaceful
As those who trust their body to the hard ground.
If brief repose be granted to him,
Then Morpheus attacks him and the night paints for him,
Through oppressive fantasy, what he thought by day
And frightens him first with blood, then with a toppled throne,
With conflagration, with sorrow and death and a snatched-away
   crown.
Do you want to exchange your peace for this burden?
Why? The stream of highest goods rushes toward you!
Do you also yearn for fame? You have climbed so high
That you see the entire empire lying at your feet.
The immense power of war rests in your hands.
Whoever is sent to the Emperor's palace by princes
Has himself presented to you and then by you to the court.
The Prince can command others: you can command the Prince.
Tolerate something above you! He whom vanity chases,
Who ventures into the wide expanse of light breezes
With wings which illusion and pride have bound to him,
Is, before he's found himself in the throne of the burning suns,
Drowned in the sea. Indeed Phaeton grabbed
The reins, but as the strong chariot coursed
And singed the Niger, Euphrates, and Nile in bright flames,
Even as the thunderbolt exploded on his head,
He cursed, although too late, the greatly desired power.
MICHAEL: Tell this to children! A heroic spirit laughs
   At this feeble scare. If a man may live crowned but only a day
   He will place himself in the greatest danger.
   This which seems impossible becomes possible if one ventures.
   The scepter is considered to be oppressive, yet the one who
      complains

Doesn't lay it down freely. Indeed, can a social class be found
That doesn't have to encircle its own pain with worry?
Fear hovers as well around straw and sackcloth as scarlet.
If Phocas, if Irene sanctioned your counsel
They never would have seized the crown.
If Leo himself delved so deeply into each matter,
If feeble fear intimidated him so effeminately,
Would Michael likely now be garbed in armor?

EXABOLIUS: If Phocas, if Irene had been more cautious
Would he have been killed, would she have entered the cloister?
If Leontios would have paid more frequent attention to this
He would not have had to give up the ghost in the public square,
Surrounded with disdain and scorn and martyrdom and fear!

MICHAEL: If only Justinian would ever have trampled on him with
his feet!
If he had moved the Bulgarians to his aid
When he laid his tender hand gently in his lap.

EXABOLIUS: He aspired to his empire, from which he had been
exiled.

MICHAEL: Whoever followed your advice would have remained in
misery.

EXABOLIUS: He was driven out by false cunning and unrest.

MICHAEL: Is it believed that Michael doesn't complain about
unrest?

EXABOLIUS: He willingly gave up this which opposed him too
much.

MICHAEL: Yes, when Leo totally confined him to the palace.

EXABOLIUS: He could resist no enemy, armed.

MICHAEL: Thus he learned to go from the court into the desolate
cloister.

EXABOLIUS: Then a hero had to support an empire that was
already exploding.

MICHAEL: Why not right now, since the supports will be of no use?

EXABOLIUS: What is it that can justly and truthfully be rebuked?

MICHAEL: This: that the emperor never did anything that was
praiseworthy.

EXABOLIUS: The vast empire is seen blooming in tranquil peace.

MICHAEL: Because I, not Leo, must wage armed campaigns.

EXABOLIUS: Provisions enter the country with the sail-billowing
wind—

MICHAEL: Because the Ister and Hellespont are secured by me.
EXABOLIUS: The Persian gives us gold.
MICHAEL: That I have forced from him.
Exabolius: The primitive Shiite is peaceful.
MICHAEL: He is subdued by me.
  What all is attributed to others, that I have brought into being?
  His life, his crown, exist under my power.
EXABOLIUS: Please don't exaggerate!
MICHAEL: Yet more! Should I keep silent?
  Before me, the Franks and Thracians must bow their proud
      heads;
  The Hellespont fears me. The world which ever-present frost
  Holds imprisoned in ice recoils in fear before me.
  The white-toothed Moor is terrified of the deeds
  Which my hand committed. Those who roast in Cyrene
  Tell of my deeds and my palm of honor.
  What would you have (if it weren't for me)? No more Emperor.
  I raised him to the throne, when Michael was defeated:
  I forced him, so that he had to enter the fray
  And am I no longer the one who I was before all of this?
  My life is his salvation, my threat his funeral bier.
  His scepter, crown, and blood rest upon this sword
  Which has the power to lay his corpse in a cold grave;
  Which, now that he's become a tyrant and is filled with dark
      suspicion,
  Shall penetrate the cruel fountain of his veins.

Scene 5

Michael, Nicander, the Footmen, Exabolius.

NICANDER: Surrender!
MICHAEL: What are you doing?
NICANDER: Upon command of the Emperor!
MICHAEL: Traitors!
NICANDER: Accuse us of what you have so often committed.
MICHAEL: How?
NICANDER: Take his sword away!
MICHAEL: From me?
NICANDER: Right now!

MICHAEL: My sword,
  Which protects your body?
NICANDER: And desires our death.
MICHAEL: Heaven help us! What is this?
NICANDER: What you had planned to do
  Has now, doubt not, fallen on your own head.
  Bring chains!
MICHAEL: Chains? For me?
NICANDER: For you, murderer.
MICHAEL: Chains? No!
  I want to be unfettered, even if I should die.
NICANDER: The Emperor wants something more.
MICHAEL: Ha! Servants of the tyrant.
  Go, executioners.
FOOTMAN: Murderer, come.
MICHAEL: Do you want to put in shackles
  The one who guarded your blood and freedom?
FOOTMAN: You may go to sleep now.
MICHAEL: Alas! Is the man scorned
  Before whom the earth trembles? Do you know whom you
    scorn?
FOOTMAN: The one whom perjury has not crowned in Byzantium.
MICHAEL: What incites you against me?
FOOTMAN: Your unjust splendor!
  Your regicide.
MICHAEL: Cursed is he who makes himself a slave
  When he can rule. You lead me into bondage,
  Thoroughly embittered soul. Abyss of the most evil shame!
  Court hypocrite! Ambiguity! Assassin! Smithy of lies!
  What prevents me from tearing you limb from limb in a rage,
  You basilisk, and from rushing to stamp in the dust
  Your sly viper's head? What prevents me?
FOOTMAN: The chains.
EXABOLIUS: I showed you the snares.
MICHAEL: You thrust me into death.
EXABOLIUS: I warned you, yet in vain. I threatened you with
    danger,
  Yet my rescue attempt wasn't effective.
MICHAEL: Therefore your chicanery must take effect.

EXABOLIUS: When one is free of vices, one can rebuke virtue itself.
    Innocence acquits me.
MICHAEL: Ha! Be silent, tyrant's knave.
    Where am I? Heaven help! Where is great justice sleeping?
    Imprisoned, not accused! Condemned, yet not tried!
    Betrayed by my friend. Him, whom the barbarian honors,
    The prince of his own race strangles.
FOOTMAN: Away! Away!
OTHER FOOTMAN: He will escape.
FOOTMAN: To the imperial throne!
MICHAEL: One should sooner draw and quarter me
    Than lead me if I'm unwilling.
FOOTMAN: Stab him.
MICHAEL: Yes, stab the dagger,
    Stab, hangman, through my heart, as long as my limbs are
      moving
    Michael is still free. Drag along! strangle! stab and shove!
    Beat! bind! I am free. Suppress! martyr! wrench and tear!
    Even if I were standing in glowing sulfur, I will proclaim this:
    That this is the reward of virtue. That this is the gratitude given
      heroes.

ACT I

CHORUS OF COURTIERS

STROPHE

The miracle of nature, the wise and then some creature,
Has nothing comparable to his tongue.
A wild beast makes known with mute signs
The meaning of its inner heart: we rule with words!
The burden of towers and all that weighs upon the land;
The building of ships and all that crosses the sea;
The majestic power of the stars,
Whatever creates air and flame,
Whatever Clovis displays in her gardens,
Whatever established law requires of all nations;

Whatever God revealed of himself to the world;
Whatever now bursts forth in blossom,
Whatever has perished through time,
Will be discovered by this device alone:
Friendship, which abhors death and finality,
The power that has forced wild tribes to civilized ways,
A person's life itself depends upon his tongue.

ANTISTROPHE

And yet there's nothing quite as sharp as a tongue!
Nothing which can cast us poor ones so low.
Oh, would heaven but grant becoming dumb
To him, who is much too free with words!
The rubble of cities, the corpse-strewn field,
The burning of ships, the sea discolored by blood,
Black magic,
The vapor of vain doctrine,
The power to thwart the fates by poison,
Bitter hatred among nations, that monster war,
The quarrel which engages church and souls,
The decline of virtue, the victory of raging depravity:
All are born by the power of the tongue,
Through which love and loyalty are lost.
How many the tongue has forced into the grave!
A person's death depends upon each person's tongue.

EPODE

Learn, you living, to keep a tight rein on your lips,
In which salvation and doom reside,
And that which condemns and rewards.
He who seeks advantage in words should ponder each word.
The tongue is this sword
Which protects and wounds;
The flame which so consumes,
And yet so well delights;
A hammer, which builds and breaks;
A rose branch, which perfumes and pricks;
A stream, which refreshes and drowns;
The medicine, which restores and destroys;

The course on which failure and success often occur:
Your life, my comrade, and your death, always depend upon
   your tongue.

ACT II

CHORUS OF COURTIERS

1. Oh, thou changing of all things,
     Ever-enduring vanity!
     Does nothing course through the spheres of time
     Except inconstancy?

2. Has nothing merit but falling and standing,
     Nothing but crown and hangman's rope?
     Between the depths and the pinnacles
     Is there barely one sunset?

3. Eternally fluctuating fortune!
     Do you respect no scepter?
     Is there nothing in the world
     That can escape your whim?

4. Mortals! What is this life
     But a totally mixed-up dream?
     This, which honor and hard work give us,
     Vanishes like the foam on the waves!

5. Princes! Gods of this earth,
     Behold what falls at your feet!
     Think how suddenly you could be
     Suppressed beneath foreign power!

6. Even just a moment upsets
     Yours and the enemy's throne:
     And it's a brief instant that adorns
     The one you hate with your crown!

7. You, who with collected honors
     Make yourselves beholden to a prince,
     How soon it can be heard of you,
     That you've been bound in chains!

8. Poor ones! Seek yet to climb high!
   Before renown rightly glimpses you,
   Your flowering will have to fade
   And death will have ensnared you.

9. Boast, you who convulse the world,
   Boast about the power of your weapons!
   When something melancholy scents the air
   The weak fist is scorned.

10. The one to whom precious metals flow,
    The one to whom the Tagus offers up treasure,
    Often begs before the day is done,
    For just a piece of mouldy bread.

11. Beauties! Those snow white cheeks,
    Which entice souls after them;
    The noble splendor of the face,
    A high fever bids to flee.

12. While we count the years
    And anticipate one hundred harvests,
    We must be wanting at the hour
    When Clotho calls: "It is over."

13. Frame up castles! Build palaces!
    Sculpt yourselves from hardest stone!
    Alas! Nothing is too firm for time!
    What I build, another will destroy.

14. Nothing! There's nothing that yet today
    Couldn't go to ruin in a hurry!
    And we! Alas! We blind people
    Hope to remain forever and ever.

ACT III

Chorus of the Pages

Strophe

Do we agree with the opinion
That fate frightens us before our destiny?

That a ghost, a dream, a sign often reveal
<blockquote>What can be expected?</blockquote>
Or is it mere fantasy that troubles the tired spirit
Which, as long as it's in the body, loves its own misery?

ANTISTROPHE

<blockquote>Is the soul itself also supposed to envision,</blockquote>
As soon as sweet slumber has overcome the body,
(In which, as is taught, it dwells as if imprisoned)
<blockquote>What's to be hoped, and what has taken place?</blockquote>
Those consumed by contagious epidemic, those whom near-death
embraced,
Have indeed often prophesied what took place after their death.

EPODE

We who've endeavored to know everything
From the beginning of time
Can still not fathom
What we daily find before us.
Those whom heaven warns through omens
Can barely, indeed, they cannot escape.
Many, too, even as they take pains to evade death,
Are seen advancing toward death.

ACT IV

CHORUS OF PRIESTS AND VIRGINS

FIRST STROPHE

VIRGINS:
The joyous night
In which the true light autonomously appeared to us,
In which He, Whom earth and sea and sky serve,
<blockquote>Before Whom hell fails,</blockquote>
Through Whom all that draws breath must live,
Entered into the vale of tears;
In which God came from the canopy of heaven;
The precious night refreshes the great world.

FIRST ANTISTROPHE

PRIESTS:
The ever-shining brightness
Which darkness shrouds, which obscurity has hidden,
Now rends the cover asunder. The sun, which before morning,
    Before the starry galaxy
Adorns heaven's vast firmament,
Before eternity itself is glimpsed
Beaming forth in gleaming bright splendor,
Suddenly rises in black midnight.

FIRST EPODE

VIRGINS AND PRIESTS:
Let earth stand firm, the sky breaks,
Yet not split by hot thunderbolts;
Behold the host of angels hastening toward us
Because the creator speaks to us.
Yet no longer encircled with mighty storms, with wrathful
    passion:
Ah! His gentle whimpering is heard,
While his lofty host sings.

SECOND STROPHE

PRIESTS:
We erred without light,
Exiled in black night by God's solemn curse:
Therefore the blessed Savior will seek us in the darkness.
        Don't you hear His calling?
You, who have lost the image of the Highest,
Behold the image born unto you.
Ask not, "Why does it enter in a stable?"
It seeks us, who are more bestial than a beast.

SECOND ANTISTROPHE

VIRGINS:
The shadow comes to an end,
The ancient prophecy is fulfilled by this child;

By His tears the fire of hell is extinguished:
    He offers us mouth and hands.
If you couldn't recognize our members
We now may call God Brother!
He is no more a fire that consumes;
The Lord has transfigured Himself into a servant.

SECOND EPODE

PRIESTS AND VIRGINS:
    Glory be to God on high,
    Who honors our flesh beyond merit,
    Who has extended His grace without end.
    May His ever-firm peace remain
    Longer than the sun shines upon us:
    May this child grant us all
    To will His will, so that we shall always well please Him.

ACT V

Scene 1

Theodosia, Phronesis, the Highest Priest, a messenger.

THEODOSIA: Alas! night of horrors! Ha! Terrorizing time!
    Dismal darkness! Must the fierce pain
    Of worry deny even the repose of weary sleep?
    Does nothing surround thrones but harsh bitterness?
PHRONESIS: Does Her Majesty lament? What is it that bothers her?
THEODOSIA: A bitter dream prevented our brief rest.
    My cold breast freezes, yet all my limbs sweat
    And my whole body shakes: we sat down,
    Dressed as if we were at a celebration: as my soul remembered
    And contemplated that year, a slumber overcame us.
    The earth, as it seemed to us, began to split in two;
    We saw our mother come forth from her grave:
    Not blithe, as she was when she lived,
    Not as father adorned her with luxurious gold.
    The purple was asunder, her gown lay torn to shreds,

Her breast and arms were bare, she stood on bare feet,
No diamonds, no ruby adorned her lovely hair,
Which sadly was all tousled and wet with tears.
We kissed her face, and called, "Oh, welcome!
Welcome, worthy lady. Now nothing has been taken from us,
Since the Lord of Lords, whom you loved so devoutly,
Snatches you from your grave and gives you to your child.
Lay aside your mourning garb, and sing praises to Him who
Smiles in the manger. The desolate cliffs listen
To the angels rejoicing! The narrow lake resounds
While joy-filled Byzantium offers thanksgiving upon
      thanksgiving."
"Alas!" she spoke, "alas, my child!" and turned her pale hands.
"It is not time to rejoice! Your rule is coming to an end.
Arise, if it is not too late (if one can still rescue
Once death has already grasped) and save your son and
      husband.
The holy night shrouds the greatest atrocities;
The safe church, murder! Alas! You cannot be helped—"
She wanted to say something more, when a stream of tears
Flowed down both cheeks and her voice broke.
A bloody sweat appeared on each of her limbs,
The drops clung like corals to her hair.
When (before we suspected) she vanished in a gentle breeze,
Our purple gown was transformed into a sack.
We wandered, lost, all alone in unfamiliar deserts,
In which ferocious bears and fierce tigers dwell,
Until an enraged beast flung his claws at us
And tore off both our breasts and ripped our heart out.
Then anxiety rubbed the sleep from our tear-stained cheeks.
What can the omniscient Being have ordained for us?
Omnipresent Eternity! Let the power of your lightning,
The glow of your grave thunder, and what the solemn night
Threatens your poor maid, vanish in profound favor.
And yet, if we ask in vain, then let this head feel
What your judgment declares. Accept us as a sacrifice
For him, without whom this country cannot live in peace.
PHRONESIS: Where there are worries, there are dreams.
      A troubled conscience is terrified even at that which we need not
      fear.

THEODOSIA: Where there is a scepter, there is fear!
PHRONESIS: Fear is but a game and a joke
 Where there is nothing to fear.
THEODOSIA: Oh, would, would but God!
 Where is the Prince?
PHRONESIS: Ahead in the temple.
THEODOSIA: We tarry
 Really too long here! Come, virgins, let us hasten.
HIGHEST PRIEST: Murder! Murder!
THEODOSIA: God, help!
 What is it?
PRIEST: Murder, murder.
PHRONESIS: Where?
PRIEST: At the altar!
THEODOSIA: Oh, Heaven. Our dream is sadly only too true.
PHRONESIS: Princess! She's dying! Behold her lips and cheeks pale,
 The gleam in her eye petrifies, as in deceased corpses:
 Bring balsam, ointment, and wine. Princess! She's fading.
 Princess?
THEODOSIA: Alas! Were we elevated to this fall?
 From where does this misfortune come?
PRIEST: I cannot know the reason.
THEODOSIA: Where is the Prince?
PRIEST: He was still there when I ran away.
THEODOSIA: He stayed, of course he stayed, the one who can't
 escape.
PHRONESIS: Has someone been attacked?
PRIEST: Look at my wounds.
THEODOSIA: Tell us how this tragedy began:
PRIEST: The third part of darkness had passed
 When the chorus of priests entered God's church;
 The songs began, the sound of the sweet chords
 Resounded more pleasant in the stillness:
 Each person was reminded to honor the great night
 In which the One who is like God in power and being
 Came from His glory, the realm of the highest Father,
 Into flesh. Devotion could be felt
 With holy fervent passion, and it ignited heart and soul
 With chaste flames. Sighs pressed forth
 And rose high above before the vapors of incense.

The Prince himself began to sing of Christ's multitude,
Which neither tyrant, nor death, nor henchman can force.
Meanwhile an unknown mob emerged,
Unseen, from every corner, and tore up the barriers
Which separate the priests from the congregation, choir, and
    temple.
In a flash swords were drawn from sheaths,
From candles, canes, and robes. The gleaming weaponry
Shone more frightening by light, and flashed
Its quick reflection back and forth; everyone was numb with fear
    and timorous
And knew not what he did, and asked the one who asked him
Like when bright lightning strikes the tall fir trees
And turns branches, trunk, and stump into a glowing fire;
A tired wanderer, in such a swift cracking,
Thinks nothing else except that he's already in the jaws of death.
The wrath finally breaks out; the daggers strike at me;
Before I realized the danger, I received this wound.
I cried: "Ye heroes, spare, spare my venerable hair,
Think of the holy time: you're strangling by the altar
The one who never harmed you." They backed off when I
    hollered,
And attacked others. This one wept, that one ran,
The next fell—I escaped from the storm, I know not how.
THEODOSIA: Doubt not: body and realm have been taken from the
    Prince.
    The storm lashes out at him! What do I say? Alas, he lies fallen!
    The treachery of our crazed enemies has conquered us.
    Did our being tolerant kindle the hot flame,
    In which everything we had, envisioned, or wished for, perished?
PHRONESIS: It's still unclear.
THEODOSIA: What? Can anything be much clearer?
PHRONESIS: Princess! Alas, she collapses prematurely in pain!
THEODOSIA: Princess without a Prince! Princess without a crown!
    Princess without a country! Whom this blow strikes from the
        golden throne
    Into the abyss.
MESSENGER: Cursed cruelty!
    Unheard-of wrath, never anticipated sorrow,
    Has the Christians' enemy, the Bulgarian, ever perpetrated this?

Has the heated Persian? Or the one who loves only deathblows,
The depraved Scythian, ever tried such a deed?

THEODOSIA: We know what he bemoans,
His pains affect us! Ask! No, don't ask! Yes, ask!
Let him tell what he knows! Bid him not to euphemize;
We imagine even more than he will tell us.

MESSENGER: The church is desecrated. At the altar the Prince is
Stabbed to death; your crown and life are in danger.

THEODOSIA: Can the one who no longer rules hope for anything
   but the bier?
Reveal which sword will pierce through this heart;
She pleads, she commands. Just show us the hand
Which will release our soul.

MESSENGER: What the bond of blood,
What friendship, long favor, what ambition and promise
Bind to Michael, has, to end his distress, snatched up
The bare sword; and into the holy place
It has ventured, unrecognized. Much has tainted the Prince's
   fame
With crazed envy. Many who hope to make themselves great
When change occurs and the demise of others takes place
Support this gang of murderers! The raging was aflame,
And someone yelled: "Attack! Attack!" And the armed hand
Struck out for the priest's head, in error, not in revenge.
Then our Prince, filled with courage in such a confused event,
Ripped the sword from both fists of someone, I know not
   whom;
And he smote the breast and skull of the one who struck at him
Until the sword splintered like ice on the enemy's steel blade.
He saw himself surrounded! His guards were pushed back afar,
His friends without counsel; yet he stood undaunted
Like a riled-up lion, who, when the close chase
Cuts off all escapes from him, with wide-open jaws
Scares the hound, then the hunter, and tries to free himself.
In vain; since he was pressed upon from all sides
He whose warm blood now flowed from limbs and veins.
He felt that his strength was gradually leaving him
When he gripped the cross, on which He had hung,
Who dying, saved us; the tree on which the world
Was freed from fear: so that death was felled,

Before whom hell recoils in fear. "Think," he called, "of the life
Which gave itself for your soul on this burden.
Don't contaminate the blood of the Lord, which stains this bole,
With sinner's blood. If I've deserved so much punishment
Then for fear of Him who carried this staff
Refrain from banging your angry fist on the altar of Jesus the
     Son."
They stopped still at these words, like in an avalanche
When the frustrated creek stops its proud course
And the flood then rises upwards, the foaming waves rage
Until the ninth stroke surges with an enormous roaring
Over the barrier and rips everything along with it,
And hurls the mossy stone into the deep valleys.
The hardened Crambonite began only then to really rage;
He shrieked: "Now, tyrant! Now is not the time to plead!"
And thrust his murderous sword up, which came down on the
     Prince
And in one stroke amputated both his arm and the cross.
As he fell, they stabbed him twice through his breast.
I myself saw how he kissed the cross
Onto which his body sank, and departed with that kiss:
As his corpse was mutilated, as the dull dagger
Was forced through his every limb, as Jesus' last gifts,
His precious flesh and blood, which soothe weary souls,
Which refresh a languishing heart in its final anxiety,
Were mixed, oh horror! with imperial blood.
THEODOSIA: Thou sulfurous glowing ardor of thunder-hard
     flames.
Strike out! Ravage them! Ravage us together!
Break, abyss, break asunder, and if you can,
Thou cleft of eternity, devour us and the murderers!
We err, no, not they! only us, only us alone,
They, too! Yet far from us, let weep whoever wants to weep.
The eye's spring congeals; what's happening? Is our heart
Transformed into hard steel? Does the bitter pain disengage
Feeling from our breast? Is our body becoming a corpse?
Come where the stroke of lightning will not reach your head:
Where, distant, the earth is deaf: come, thou desired death!
Thou end of dark anxiety! Thou port of wild distress!
We call in vain to Him, who avoids the melancholy

And only touches the spirit who suffers no oppression.
Come! Come, assassins! And cool the burning courage,
The hell-inflamed revenge, in the blood of these veins.
The Prince is not yet gone. While our limbs still move
He lives in this breast. Approach, and thrust the dagger
Through this, which beats in me. A quick demise
Is a certain comfort, when one can no longer stand.

HIGH PRIEST: Princess! The One who created you has predestined this death.

THEODOSIA: And He predestined that we long for our grave.

HIGH PRIEST: He bids us to deal patiently with whatever oppresses us.

THEODOSIA: Then why didn't He send patience with the cross?

HIGH PRIEST: Can there be such an evil, that no solace can reach it?

THEODOSIA: Can there be such an evil, that it can be compared to ours?

PRIEST: God doesn't burden us with more than we can bear:

THEODOSIA: He takes on one day throne, crown, realm, and husband.

PRIEST: He takes, Princess, that which He previously has given.

THEODOSIA: One thing alone He doesn't take, that which isn't wanted: life.

PRIEST: He proves in fire of anguish as gold those whom He loves.

THEODOSIA: Those, whom He hates, go free while He afflicts us.

PRIEST: He who strikes your wounds can heal all wounds.

THEODOSIA: The stroke is noxious that can sever hearts.

PRIEST: What isn't severed by time? Death ends everything.

THEODOSIA: The Prince must enter his troubled grave before his time.

PRIEST: He doesn't die before his time, who ends his own epoch.

THEODOSIA: With blood, which was spilled in the church on God's table.

PRIEST: One doesn't die as one would wish, but only as the Highest wills!

THEODOSIA: Then does the Highest will murder and such tragedy?

PRIEST: Can he, who is mortal, comprehend His judgment?

THEODOSIA: Speak thus! and teach the masses to topple princes from their thrones!
Restrain your comforting! The pains are too severe,

The wounds are too fresh, the clanging weapon
Trembles before the door: arise, spirit, the murderers come!
Well! Let us, comforted, follow after him whom they took from
us.
Arise, my spirit. She pays little heed to the enemy,
She, who lives imperially and wants to die royally.
Farewell! Don't weep for me! Open up! Bolting is useless here—
Open up! One must greet death when he arrives.

Scene 2

The First Band of Conspirators, Theodosia.

FIRST CONSPIRATOR: The hard-as-diamond yoke of dreadful
    tyranny,
The heavy-as-stone burden of harsh torturing,
The scepter of metal, the throne established on blood,
The all-consuming anxiety which lays waste to cities and fields,
And whatever else a ferocious prince puts into action,
Is finally, albeit late, abolished by us.
Your reign is now over. The unbridled raging,
The arm striking everything is atomized into the air:
Learn now to obey those whom you ruled; and understand,
That there's often only one night between falling and the
    pinnacle.
SECOND CONSPIRATOR:
The heavily oppressed country that is relieved of its weighty
    burden
Now inhales fresh air, and rejoices that your glory
Deteriorates in such disdain: yet everyone laments
That tyrants can't be punished according to what they deserve.
He offers but one corpse for thousands of misdeeds;
When a commoner offends, no pardon spares him.
A simple offense receives wheel, pillory, noose, and sword,
Oil, seething lead and pitch, a horse of glowing iron;
A tyrant becomes great through evil, and blossoms when those
    fade
Who stand with heart and hand for honesty.
FIRST CONSPIRATOR:
What can a person ultimately do? Whoever grasps what is going
    on:

He charges him with so much until the increased burden
Crushes his neck and spine. If one should refuse
To carry more than is indeed possible (however great his
     courage!),
Him he besmears with rebellion! He has incited the populace,
Impugned the prince, insulted majesty.
He clears him out of the way. Did anyone have more to risk
Than he? For he who doesn't strike down tyrants is stricken
     down!

THEODOSIA: So have you, as you boast, murdered tyrants?

FIRST CONSPIRATOR: Who doubts?

THEODOSIA: Listen to us! Who places you in power?
Who entrusts you with this sword? Who so endowed you,
That you, who were nothing before, now have more than
     everything:
Who? The one whom you now inveigh against. When he, with
     most sublime splendor,
Elevated you next to himself and turned you virtually into gods,
Who was he? A tyrant? You sang with different tongues.
Now, since you've succeeded with your prank, your murder,
His name is: I know not what. As long as a prince gives to
And loves as well-deserved those who are unworthy
And seeks to satisfy their greed with gold and honors,
His praise must fill the realm, his fame the world.
As soon as he no longer gives, indeed no longer can give,
As soon as he punishes insurrection, disloyalty infects you.
As soon as this pestilence strikes you and rogues unite,
The desire for new power and political might is easily kindled;
Then he becomes a tyrant: the one who lies dead is slandered.
Thus is a dead lion often attacked by a mouse.

SECOND CONSPIRATOR:
The lion, whose life was cut off by this sword!

THEODOSIA:
Oh, fame-worthy deed! You have felled in death
Whom? One person! So many of you! You have, in the black of
     night,
Betrayers, murdered more through deceit than wounds,
The one, to whom previously you often swore oaths:
What weapons did you not employ against him,
Who went unarmed? May this atrocity

Be compared to anything? You've desecrated the glorious
    moment
In which God gave Himself to us with regicide:
And in the holy place, which releases sinners,
You've spilled innocent blood: who can henceforth doubt
Whether you're still Christian: behold in the temple
The mutilated corpse which lies on the cross
Upon which Jesus conquered hell:
The true flesh of the Lord, which you splattered with blood,
His blood, which you have mixed with the Emperor's blood.

SECOND CONSPIRATOR:
    It's not a matter of how, when, or where evil ones are eradicated.

THEODOSIA: A human differentiates, not you, you monsters!

FIRST CONSPIRATOR: Guilt is punished with justice.

THEODOSIA: Who gives to you this power?
    A prince serves Him alone, who keeps watch in the clouds:
    He who places us on the throne can ban us from the throne.

SECOND CONSPIRATOR: The most lowly of the populace is master
    of the tyrant.

FIRST CONSPIRATOR: The Highest executes His justice with the
    arms of men.

SECOND CONSPIRATOR: And with men He topples tyrants and
    their house.

THEODOSIA: Thus can one without effort disguise a dastardly
    deed.

FIRST CONSPIRATOR: Does one call what a thousand souls are
    praising a dastardly deed?

THEODOSIA: And ten times one thousand disdain?

SECOND CONSPIRATOR: Do you know to whom you say this?

THEODOSIA: To you, who stand charged with this murder before
    the court of God.

FIRST CONSPIRATOR: Your life, blood, and death rest in these
    hands.

THEODOSIA: Therefore hasten to end the tragedy with our death.

SECOND CONSPIRATOR: Courage which is mighty strong before
    one senses reality
Diminishes when distress enters in.

THEODOSIA: Strike! My breast is bare!
    Do you think Leo is dead? He lives in this heart
    And calls revenge out of us. Through his pain,
    Through his wounds, we are dead. It is his spirit that moves us,

That draws breath in us, that moves this hand,
That beats in these veins: come, open the door for him,
Open the prison, this flesh, so that he might lead us with him.
Yet use the same sword that went through his heart,
When his hacked-up arm embraced cruel death.
There's nothing more beautiful, than when two so firmly bound
    souls
Withdraw from the caves of the body at one time and place.
FIRST CONSPIRATOR: After the heroic hand has executed the lion
    Before whom the world trembled, no attention is paid to the
        dogs.
    Nor can the blood of a woman stain the glorious steel
    Which the holy night found thrust into the tyrant's breast.
SECOND CONSPIRATOR: Let someone else kill you; it's more than
    enough for us
    That your fallen spirit doesn't want to see the light of day.
    It's more than enough for us, that we can kill you
    And yet spare your life, which you yourself don't spare.
THEODOSIA: Compassionate cruelty! Disguised tyranny!
    Poison disguised with gold! Gentle barbarism!
FIRST CONSPIRATOR: Follow us.
THEODOSIA: Where are we going? What misery is at hand?
    What is intended for us? Shall this body
    Waste away in bondage without solace? Will the raging mob
    Of the riffraff be given this neck for a sacrifice?
    Come, fear, however great you are, and hasten to abort
    The misery-filled remnant of life.
    Farewell, ruled realm! Farewell, possessed throne!
    Farewell, lost court! Farewell, stolen crown!
    Farewell, thou splendor of the world! Farewell, confused life!
    The sugar-coated poison, encircled with a pearl-studded cross,
    Palaces full of anxiety, thou scepter, heavy with woe,
    Thou purple, red from blood: we pass away, farewell.

Scene 3

Michael, the second and first group of conspirators, Theodosia, the corpse of Leo.

MICHAEL: You now give to me light, freedom, soul, and life!
    You give to me myself: what will I give in return,
    I, who saved from death and tomb and ignited conflagration,

And what is even more terrifying, from the tyrant's hand,
Through your loyalty, now mount the great throne:
And I show the shaken world with my example,
That friendship goes beyond crown, and love beyond scepter,
That a hated prince stands on shifting sand.
There he lies, who lowered me. I rule in these chains
In which I plan to mount the throne
From which the lion was toppled. How will I reward this
    courage
Which risked intrepid blood for me
In greatest peril? Will I ever find anything
That has the power to bind you and me more powerfully
    together?
Yet if my arm is too weak; believe that the world at large
Which you took out of dark anxiety to golden freedom;
Believe, that the wide realm which you, in a few hours,
Yet not with little courage, bound to yourselves for eternity;
Believe, that whoever here and there, up until the noble night,
Languished in prison, in chains, in dungeons;
Believe, that whoever shall be born into light after us,
Will praise you heroes. Yes, when the earth's orbit
Vanishes in flames, your excellence,
Crowned in perpetual honor, will deride death and time.

THEODOSIA: Alas, wellspring of our anguish!

MICHAEL: Ha! Widow of the tyrant!
Your binding, your power, your burning and banishing
Now banishes itself!

THEODOSIA: This is still unheard of,
That one, who is so exalted and honored,
That one, for whom so often such enormous guilt has been
    forgiven,
Whom we kept alive, thus causing our own death,
Should call us cruel! And yet we've proven
So much, who alone it is that may rightly call us cruel;
In that we gave you such full rein
And tore you from the flame, which you deserved!
Did our enraged fist whet the sharp sword
Which your bloodthirsty arm holds at our throat?
He is the most cruel on earth, it's true,
  Who must, like us, be his own executioner.

MICHAEL: Thus he who
Digs trenches for others falls in himself.
THEODOSIA: Thus one gets
Mockery for gratitude, and pain for long-standing charity.
MICHAEL: You get what you deserve: grievous anguish for grievous
sins.
THEODOSIA: Fine! Thus in time revenge will find you, too.
MICHAEL: Whoever commits no crime is not afraid of revenge.
THEODOSIA: Is it just that the oath and princes' necks are broken?
MICHAEL: If princes first break their oath themselves.
THEODOSIA: When did the Emperor ever break his solemn
promise?
MICHAEL: His life and his terrible end demonstrate that.
THEODOSIA: A vice is judged before the law, not by the manner of
death.
MICHAEL: Justice is for the populace: on princes swords are
sharpened.
THEODOSIA: They will, in the end, also pass sentence on you.
With this wish mount the oft-sought throne;
Take the crown, which you won through treachery, blood, and
murder,
We know the court and the injustice of palaces:
The jealousy, false fidelity, and those cursed guests
Of princes, trouble and fear. Elevate yourself, as you will;
Strike, rage, kill, and stab, while your hour is at hand,
Elevate those beside you, stained with our blood,
Who inherit greater honor and fortune through our fall.
Elevate what has loved perjury more than integrity,
What has trained itself so masterfully in regicide,
What has power to destroy church and court and prison.
And sharpen a sword, which yet will pierce your breast.
MICHAEL: You know that the future holds, yet not your own
peril.
THEODOSIA: Which prophesies your misery.
MICHAEL: You grasp toward your death,
Which is imminent.
THEODOSIA: We ask for the life
Which you owe to us: bid sword, bid dagger to be given
And end our torture: insure your power,
Prove what you can: grant that the night

Might cover my eternal sorrow with constant darkness:
Grant that they be placed in one grave,
Whom one love, one marriage, one throne, one realm, one
    station,
One heart, one spirit, one fall, one demise, united.
MICHAEL: Your dying does not benefit me, your living cannot
    harm me;
Your living can bestow fame, your death, hate, upon me.
Therefore I am not the one who plans to judge her,
Who, as she boasts, gave me my life.
THEODOSIA: This evil is now impossible to endure;
That after so much anxiety, death will be denied to us.
What in the world can she hope, she who cannot have this
Which is given to enemies. You people behold us:
You spirits, listen to us: she, who when daylight paled,
Who before midnight had crept upon the earth,
Was accustomed to ruling the great world like a goddess;
She finds herself, before time lets the sun greet
The now approaching day, disdained, scorned, reproached,
Discarded, deposed, crowned with woe and anxiety.
She learns how close together the heights and falling stand;
How little time passes between throne and prison.
She who ruled everyone, she asks but in vain
For the end, not of the burden, only of her toppled life.
Whom does the grim mob drag along? Oh, agony! It is the one
Who rules this realm. What precipice, what sea
Of pain swallows us up? What can we recognize
That isn't battered? Can a single limb be named
Which the sword hasn't mangled? Where is his lovely hair,
That was just encircled with bejeweled gold?
Where is the strong hand, which bore sword and scepter?
The breast, which shining steel, as well as royal purple,
    embellished?
Woe unto us! Where is he himself? Behold! His innocent blood,
Aroused by our anxiety, surges and spurts anew
From all his wounds! His blood calls eagerly for revenge,
Even if his lips are silent. His blood exposes the injustice
Of your cause, bloodthirsty ones!
MICHAEL: Take the tyrant away!
THEODOSIA: Take us with him! Death will bring you and us gain:

Strike with pike and sword! Use flames and cruel weapons!
We wish (leave us here) we wish to fall asleep
On his paled mouth, on his beloved breast.
MICHAEL: Take the body away from her.
THEODOSIA: Where are we? What kind of pleasure
   Do we now experience? The Prince has not faded away:
   Oh, joy! He lives! He lives! Now this sorrow is vanquished.
   He wipes away our tears himself, with a gentle hand.
   Here he stands! He angers and brandishes sword and fire
   Upon the betrayers' heads.
FIRST CONSPIRATOR: The pain has cracked her!
   She rages in dire distress.
THEODOSIA: My light! They are overcome!
   The murderers are strangled! He offers us his kiss:
   Oh, unexpected bliss! Oh, soul-refreshing greeting!
   Welcome, worthy Prince! Ruler of our senses!
   Comrades, mourn no longer: he lives!
MICHAEL: Take her away!
   We'll hasten to the church: announce to the whole state
   The fall of tyranny: call the great council.
   I want the patriarch to crown me now, here
   In the presence of my sons and in your presence.
   You, keep watch on the castle! You others tell the troops
   What's needed. Bear witness to that which enemies have to gain.
   I am the one who will suppress those who are hostile to us and
      elevate our friends:
   Be firmly assured of this.
THE CONSPIRATORS: Long rule and live the Emperor!

Translated by Janifer G. Stackhouse

Daniel Casper von Lohenstein

Sᴏᴘʜᴏɴɪsʙᴀ, ᴀ Tʀᴀɢᴇᴅʏ

CHARACTERS

SOPHONISBA, *Queen in Cyrtha*
MASINISSA, *a Numidian prince*
SYPHAX, *Sophonisba's husband and King*
SCIPIO, *Roman general and proconsul*
VERMINA, *Sophonisba's stepson*
LAELIUS, *Scipio's adjutant*

ADHERBAL ⎫
HIERBA ⎬ *Sophonisba's sons*

HAMILCAR ⎫
HIEMPSAL ⎪
MICIPSA ⎪
HIMILCO ⎬ *officers of Cyrtha*
JUBA   ⎪
BOMILCAR ⎭

MANASTABAL ⎫
DISCALCES ⎬ *Masinissa's advisers*

BOGUDES ⎫
MAMERCUS ⎬ *priests*
TYCHAEUS ⎭

TORQUATUS ⎫
FLAMINIUS ⎬ *two captured Romans*

ORYNTHIA ⎫
HIPPOLITE ⎪
MENALIPPE ⎪
ELENISSE ⎬ *ladies in waiting*
ELGADA   ⎪
AGATHE   ⎭

ELAGABEL, *a priestess*
The ghost of DIDO
A CROWD OF ROMAN MILITARY OFFICERS AND SOLDIERS

ROYAL LADIES IN WAITING
A PARTY OF NUMIDIAN PRINCES AND CAPTAINS
A CROWD OF MASINISSA'S SOLDIERS
TWELVE CUPIDS
CHORUS OF DISCORD, HATE, JOY, TERROR, DESIRE, ENVY, FEAR, SOPHONISBA'S SOUL
CHORUS OF LOVE AND HEAVEN. WITH PASSION TO RULE IN THE PERSON OF *JUPITER;* THE ABYSS; CRUELTY IN THE PERSON OF *PLUTO;* EARTH; VIRTUE IN THE PERSON OF *HERCULES;* WATER; HONOR IN THE PERSON OF *JASON*
CHORUS OF JEALOUSY, REASON, ENVY, FOLLY, DESPAIR, TOGETHER WITH BEAUTY AND CONCEIT WHICH APPEAR AS MUTES IN SYMBOLIC ATTIRE.
CHORUS OF *HERCULES,* OF VOLUPTUOUSNESS AND VIRTUE, OF EMPEROR LEOPOLD'S SPIRIT
CHORUS OF FATE AND THE FOUR MONARCHIES

ACT I

The action presents King Masinissa's tent.

Masinissa. Bomilcar. Hiempsal. Himilco. Micipsa. Syphax. A throng of Roman soldiers.

MASINISSA: Guilt swarms round ruin as round light will swarm the
  moth.
He springs the trap himself who treaties breaks and troth.
So Sophonisba falls and Syphax's hope is shivered,
Since she the breach of peace conceived, and he delivered.
Now you can figure on the fingers of one hand:
If you deserve of us that we assistance lend,
That we your crackling house to save from flames endeavor,
Your town in dire straits from gore and gutting sever.
The stinger of the bee is too its honey duct.
Who feels offense will have from vengeance far more sucked
Than sugar in his heart, for sweet is without rival
What fervor cools. No dew so sparks the snail's revival
As to insulted men the blood of foes lends zest.
With this reviving balm the heavens have me blest.
Now Europe from herself has Moorish shackles shaken.

Down has gone Sicily, Hispania's been taken,
And Hannibal himself, entangled and beset,
Observes here on our fist dead Hanno's blood still wet;
The fleet turned brimstone, was into the air sent flying,
The camp of Hasdrubal and Syphax's host defying,
The burning reeds consumed. What left was of the foe
By sword and flame, just now my arm has here laid low.
The sparks already flew round Carthaginian towers.
Yet if your hardheadedness your counsel overpowers,
By harm and time made wise, then mercy should forgo
Revenge and harshness: this, once open to us though
Stand castle, palace, town. But if spite's not abolished,
Until your walls we have dismantled and demolished,
Within his mother's womb no child there will be spared.

HIEMPSAL: None but the timid beasts by threatening words are
    scared,
The raucous hunting horn frights chamois, but no lions,
A wave alarms no cliff; hot threats we bid defiance.
The Prince himself may judge if such a city might,
Which thirty-thousand men can muster for a fight
Who in their bosom feel a heart intensely beating,
Fall to the foe, itself with perjury defeating?
The realm's head to protect, till blood's last drop is shed,
By every limb is pledged.

MASINISSA: Heroic dare instead,
Your pluck at last gone limp, behind weak walls chose stalling
Itself, so tightly squeezed? Your skin should now be crawling
Limbs growing rigid, as the Rubricat you view,
Its stream with corpses swelled, these corpses being you,
As with your blood the Moors' white sea it is now making
Into a sea that's red. How long resisted taking
The capital unconquered, that wonder Syracuse?
New Carthage fell as soon as Scipio did choose
To set foot on its ground. How often was unsettled
By us your Utica? Yes, Carthage now is rattled,
What strange conceit is this that Cyrtha spites and scorns,
Those whom with palms and laurels destiny adorns?
What hoped relief can help you from your plight unwind?

HIMILCO: Your grace has even means gods' helping hands to bind?

MASINISSA: They're not without their means, the gods that by us
    stand.

MICIPSA: Trust me: a cobweb is a bulwark's iron band
    If gods wish to assist, a stout shield heaven forms.
    They, not your arms, set off the rains and thunderous storms;
    From Hannibal's power, that like fivefold lightning flared,
    Though rattling Rome and realm, the Capitol was spared.
    And yet our Hannibal on Italy's core keeps chewing,
    Sucks on the Roman breast.

MASINISSA: And from afar he's viewing
    As in a glass and mirrored in you his Carthage burn,
    When Capua, Tarent he lost on one card's turn.
    His brother's gory head he laves with tears, distracted,
    In Italy's nook he's stuck, entangled and impacted.
    On him you pin your hopes?

HIMILCO: God has our trust and he.

MASINISSA: Like you an ostrich thinks the hunter he can flee
    When out of fear inside a hole his head is hidden.

HIEMPSAL: The Punic flag of luck has often higher ridden:
    When Hannibal both Alps and nature overran,
    At Trebia, Ticinus, and at Transimen
    The eagles downed, then, Rome at Cannae overthrowing,
    Sent through Tarpeia's rock a shattering tremor flowing.

MASINISSA: The tables are now turned.

MICIPSA: And they again can turn.

MASINISSA: When, crackling in the flames, your Carthage we'll see
    burn?

HIMILCO: When one more Regulus his head thereon will smash!

MASINISSA: When will an ant hill, roused, against the lions dash?

HIEMPSAL: When Syphax all of Africa's lands brings with him.

MASINISSA: Who, Syphax?

MICIPSA: Syphax, yes!

MASINISSA: Who barely can a limb
    In our fetters move?

MICIPSA: Sweet dreams these bonds remain.

MASINISSA: Such stiff-necked scornfulness I bid you to restrain!
    In bonds and irons, quick, bring Syphax here to us!

HIMILCO: **Ah,**
  Who would this believe? The mishap's sea will thus
  And Rome the whole world drown, rise over it high cresting,
  This Rome whose triumphs wit nor force succeeds arresting,
  Although sun, dust, and wind in our aid emerge,
  With dragons, elephants to raze the Roman scourge.

MASINISSA: Shall this man Cyrtha's fort and Byrsa's palace save?

HIEMPSAL, HIMILCO, MICIPSA: Once weighted down by
    crowns,—gods, can it be we rave?—

MASINISSA: Does now our king wear bonds?

BOMILCAR: Whose fraud and trickery
  From Masinissa stole them.

HIEMPSAL: It's true then? It is he?
  The king and our Prince thus slavish bonds oppress?

HIMILCO: On Syphax's knee, foot, bonds we kisses wish to press.

BOMILCAR: At Masinissa's feet, the victor's, bend your knee,
  He who is prostrate should obeisance never see.

SYPHAX: This is Dame Fortune's game: last night I shone,
    resplendent,
  Still more than you. For might and fall a twin are pendant.
  As Croesus I for you play the example's role:
  That no one ere his grave his fortune should extol.
  Let this as lesson then, and Solon's charge prevail:
  That victors princely should the vanquished prince regale.

MASINISSA: That Cyrtha yield forthwith, you issue the command!

SYPHAX: No fallen prince complies, if he does love his land.

MASINISSA: Unless he with himself his nation wishes tumbled.

SYPHAX: By slavish fear we will not ever have them humbled.

MASINISSA: Your head upon a stake we flourishing will see.

SYPHAX: My honor's relic, but on yours a stain 'twill be.

MASINISSA: Quick, let the hangman's ax the haughty man's neck
    sever!

SYPHAX: Tonight we're braving death more steadfastly than ever.

MASINISSA: Stand by!

MICIPSA: Ah! mighty prince, ah! to consider deign:
  That prince and column, though in ruin, still remain
  The image of the gods. The action is uncommon.

MASINISSA: That villains should be struck who spiteful worms
    would summon?

HIEMPSAL: That on account of pluck a princely head must roll.

MASINISSA: Which gave the throne and realm of princeliness small
  dole.
HIMILCO: The utmost for the King's welfare we'll have to manage.
SYPHAX: Would you the ancient fame with breach of faith
    disparage?
  The hangman let despair into your spirit sow?
  Should Cyrtha fall, would then the killer milder grow?
  For can't you be like me by him decapitated?
  Bear this last blow with joy and courage unabated.
  It brings more honor here to die, than live as slave.
  Sagunt and Estapa a good example gave:
  That virtue rather jumps in flames and conflagration,
  Than falls in Roman hands and hostile degradation.
MICIPSA: To save our liege's life, can there be found no way?
MASINISSA: Until he's ceased to rave, this nitwit take away.
  To you and town delay and mercy are now granted,
  Till Syphax's attitude to her is represented.
  Bomilcar then and you will to the Queen convey
  What was concluded here. But Hiempsal must stay
  As hostage in our camp. From now within three hours,
  If town and citadel we still may not call ours,
  The spitted head you see of Syphax on a stake.

Masinissa, Hiempsal

MASINISSA: On what cold bottom will Hiempsal his stand make?
  Hiempsal whom I'm worthy of better fortune deeming,
  And of a truer liege, because to Syphax's scheming
  He's not a party. You must to the times adjust,
  The city and you too must our staunchness trust;
  As Masinissa's eye Hiempsal henceforth act,
  His virtue, too, with more exalted worth connect.
HIEMPSAL: The King would not impute to me such treachery!
MASINISSA: Not wicked is the man who would his country free
  From ruin and bring peace, nor he who, lest he drown,
  A foreign board will grasp, and when the ship goes down,
  Swims to the enemy's shore.
HIEMPSAL: The lords our fealty need
  Until the grave's abyss.

MASINISSA: A vassal loose is, freed,
  Once ruined is his liege, reduced to slavish station.
HIEMPSAL: The traitors are on earth a dread abomination,
  To those that nurse them, too, a thorn stuck in the eye.
MASINISSA: To think of us as quite ungrateful do not try.
  Alas, you do not know of Syphax's ghastly actions,
  How many princes snared his treasons and deceptions,
  How he the pact with Rome, himself forswearing, broke,
  How treacherously he my realm stole with one stroke.
  In brief his villainies to you will be imparted.
  My father Gala from this world had scarcely parted,
  By Syphax's poisonous arts my older brother, named
  Desalces, died. His gentle son Capusa claimed
  The throne. King Syphax then Mezetelus incited
  To fiery riot, who most shamefully delighted
  In washing in his King's spilled blood both soul and hands;
  Upon Desalces' wife his wanton lust he spends,
  And steals her for his bed; the kingdom's peers dispatches,
  A plot against Prince Lucumacen hatches
  To snare himself the throne. But when at last our fist,
  Outraged by slaughter, shame, which would repel a beast,
  Upon ancestral soil, was backed by Bokhar's faction,
  The robber did assail and with successful action
  At Tapsus won the day, then Syphax at me throws
  A mighty martial force. Thereon the thieving foes,
  Dispersed by me, start from the country running;
  King Syphax Asdrubal to form new bands is dunning,
  And for one more attack is quick to mobilize
  The forces of the realm; hence I must organize
  Retreat to Balbus's cliffs; by robbing we survive,
  Yet soon in full retreat to save our lives we strive;
  I barely got away at Clupea from five
  Who pushed me in the stream; though I swam off alive,
  King Bokhar I made think I was in billows buried,
  Till I my weakened hulk, which fifteen wounds now carried,
  Inside a cave with herbs to health could nurture back.
  There, too, my scattered host, what's left of it, I track,
  A troop of forty horse, a new host reuniting:
  I drive like winds of war with grim flames all igniting,
  To Syphax's castle gate, and Hippo's rock is stormed.

Yet like a deadly foe, my plans the heavens scorned,
Both Syphax and his son Vermina now descend
Upon me with two troops, my luck in battle end.
Vermina's host forced me to flee with utter speed,
And, unconsoled, disguised, to Garamant proceed,
Till Syphax so succeeds in Hasdrubal bewitching
By his own daughter's hand, that he does venture breaching
The pact with Rome; I summon counsel, dare
With Scipio the Great my blood and heart to share,
Who for me benefits arranged to be provided,
When as his enemy I still with Carthage sided,
And he my sister's son Massiva had sent home
No ransom claiming. Once I chose to stand by Rome,
To trip me Syphax proves uncommonly inventive,
His daughter and my realm he offers as incentive,
And when my feet the snare avoids of his design,
He bribes a servant to put poison in my wine.
Hiempsal, be the judge: if Syphax is deserving
With love's true service, or if there's more profit serving
The Romans, gaining thus more honor and more fame,
By whose support you see me prospering with gain.
HIEMPSAL: I own it, Syphax's wiles inspire but disgust.
  And yet . . .
MASINISSA: A wise man must to fate himself entrust,
  Allow yourself be led, like me, by your foe's own hand,
  To mount your forebears throne.
HIEMPSAL: A problematic stand,
  Where faith and luck and fear do in one soul wage battle!
MASINISSA: The sun of reason must these murky vapors settle.
  Decide with firm resolve on fame and welfare's lures.
HIEMPSAL: So be it. Cyrtha will this very day be yours.

The scene is set in a temple.
Sophonisba. Hamilcar. Vermina. Juba. The Queen's Ladies-in-waiting.

SOPHONISBA: Oh, Africa's mainstays, gods lightweight as a feather,
  Strikes our Numidia a fresh misfortune's weather?
  Does Beelsam now concede, what Adad simply waives:
  That Rome make our Punic chief, and all of us, its slaves?

My Syphax one more time is totally defeated,
And Cyrtha is attacked. Are our wails completed?
The mourning clouds are not of lightning bolts yet freed;
From every corner now new brewing storms proceed.
You, gods, before whose feet we ourselves do throw,
By our sighs be moved, your tears let freely flow.
And if your fiery wrath is not to pass us by,
Then let our free-willed body, sword, stake, and flame defy.
Then let by thunderbolts both breast and heart be sundered,
Then let our limbs' oil be, on red grills sizzling, squandered,
Then let her craving thirst pitch, steel, and brimstone slake,
As long as Sophonisba the Romans slave don't make!

VERMINA: May to you, most serene, kind heavens lend their
    hearing!

SOPHONISBA: The heaven's help, my son?

VERMINA: With honor you endearing,
Forever at your feet he lays his bloodstained sword.

SOPHONISBA: My child whom heaven did to our wish accord,
Which gives you back to us, come, our kisses seek!
But, what is this, does blood all of your members streak?

VERMINA: In part the foe on us, in part, our own we've spilled.

SOPHONISBA: But where remains the king?

VERMINA: The fray in such heat milled.
The squadrons blended so that I no heed could pay
To where the stalwart Prince did in the battle stray!
The left-wing captaining, which Father gave to me,
A third horse riding, I stand firm, until I see
Our troops in full retreat. I flee, hard-pressed, belated.

SOPHONISBA: Oh, gods. I'm done for! Has the whole host
    dissipated,
The King still gone, so that, alas, he cannot be
Unharmed in battle?

HAMILCAR: Though grave is the grief I see,
Still, in calamities, one for the best keeps hoping.

SOPHONISBA: To her no hope remains, who with such bolts is
    coping.
Alas! we're ruined, all!

VERMINA: Most of the refugees
Toward the mountains fled.

HAMILCAR: There, too, if god it please,
  The prince found refuge.
SOPHONISBA: No! My heart so wildly pounds
  Which tells a harsher truth.
HAMILCAR: Keep grief in proper bounds.
  Just wormwood never serve the gods to us, unless
  A bit of sugar strews on it high-mindedness!

Sophonisba. Himilco. Micipsa. Vermina. Hamilcar.

SOPHONISBA: Come you two worthies news from Masinissa
    bearing?
HIMILCO: So come we, but, alas!
VERMINA: You quake, you men of daring?
MICIPSA: From fear, and yet rejoice to see Vermina here.
SOPHONISBA: Where could be Hiempsal? I for his safety fear.
HIMILCO: Oh, no, to utter it, the harsh ill luck would censure.
HAMILCAR: Speak up! And fearlessly some words you must here
    venture.
MICIPSA: Prince Syphax.
SOPHONISBA: I'm done for!
MICIPSA: Is in the enemy's hand.
SOPHONISBA: Dead?
HIMILCO: No. He is alive.
SOPHONISBA: How sad indeed things stand.
  My sea of woes' true scope, on what can it be grounded?
HAMILCAR: You know of certain grounds? The enemy oft sounded
  A false alarm, so as to gain the city's keys,
  For which his arm's too weak.
MICIPSA: The foe, alas, did please
  To show us our King in bonds and irons fettered.
VERMINA: The rabid dog on him such slavish insult spattered?
  Let's, while a drop of blood through our veins still flows,
  For town and castle fight: who do agree, all those
  Who rather in the air with brimstone would be driven,
  Than Masinissa's fist one hair by us be given.
HIMILCO: I prize resolve and pluck; your comrade I will be.
  One more misfortune though has knocked us to our knee.
HAMILCAR: Apprise us of the worst.

HIMILCO: The foe has clearly stated:
  If in three hours' time they haven't celebrated
  Cyrtha's capitulation, they'll stake the Prince's head
  For all of us to see.
SOPHONISBA: What dragon, tiger that
  Resembles Masinissa? Clouds, burst; flash, lightning; parting,
  Break forth, abyss! The dog, so raving, hotly smarting,
  Is bent upon our soul. Oh, helpless Queen, just think,
  Into what desperation will Sophonisba sink!
  Why should we see a stake by our head's head garnished?
  Should eye and heart by such dread spectacle be tarnished?
  What other ghoulish sight the heart more penetrates?
  No, Sophonisba's eye as Thyestes' hardly rates!
  No! Let the dagger be through heart and bosom driven!
VERMINA: To ranting at ourselves, dear mother, more you're given
  Than at the enemy. Let's sharpen sword and wit:
  So that his very soul a lightning bolt will split!
SOPHONISBA: My head goes round, confused, my sight quite
    obfuscated.
  The Queen concedes: what if her spouse is for the saber fated?
  The Queen concedes: what if as slave she is enthralled?
  That you, and Cyrtha too, beneath Rome's yoke are hauled?
  No! bloodhound, go on, rave, his skin from Syphax strip,
  Your cruelty and threats with fear the town can't grip;
  Yet, no! Micipsa, hasten, open town and gate,
  Go, tell the foe I'll be his slave, I'll abdicate;
  I gladly join in Rome the victor's grand procession,
  If granted is my spouse his neck's and head's possession.
HAMILCAR: To what insane conceit her sorrow makes her dart?
  Has Sophonisba lost her Hasdrubalian heart?
  Into the death-foe's maw with her she'd have us sink?
  Cannot for him the dog his spirit cause to shrink?
  More harshly play with it, when lost has been the game!
  No resolution's safe which wavering has for aim.
SOPHONISBA: Should for my spouse's neck the ax with spite be
    whetted?
HAMILCAR: Why should through fear the ax be for our necks
    abetted?
SOPHONISBA: Humility pulls swords of tyrants from their fist.
VERMINA: Your dread of Masinissa, how has it been dismissed?

SOPHONISBA: My heart dissolves from love, from him craves
    expiation.
HAMILCAR: The foes oft threaten more than reaches
    consummation.
HIMILCO: We saw on Syphax's neck the ax already set.
VERMINA: Still, not a hair upon his head was damaged yet.
MICIPSA: The stroke has been postponed, the rage is unrelenting.
HAMILCAR: Delay makes lukewarm what with rage is madly
    ranting.
SOPHONISBA: But not when in delay old foes advantage sense.
VERMINA: Highmindedness breeds fame, fear is the hare's defense.
SOPHONISBA: Alas! you do not feel remorse's anguished twinges.
HAMILCAR: Suppose the foe won't budge: thereon the King's life
    hinges.
  What's there to lose besides what from us has been torn?
  The lords who're destined to the purple to be born,
  Without their scepter sick they are, and more than dead, when
    fettered.
  To our hero-prince, would life have so much mattered?
  To our King do not faintheartedness impute:
  His neck for children, realm, would him as payment suit.
HIMILCO: It's true: what we now are considering in this instance:
  Damns Syphax, and it calls for unswerving persistence
  To seek our welfare, and be sure that his demise
  Ends our loss, because with him, his misery dies.
  Yes, when the foe found out no threat could faze his daring,
  Since he his neck, unfazed, has to the ax been baring,
  Then tyranny itself pulled back its peaky horns.
HAMILCAR: Our virtue stings the foe like penetrating thorns.
HIMILCO: Bomilcar though insists that Cyrtha should surrender.
SOPHONISBA: Good. Now that you this verdict did on Syphax
    render,
  No storm of floundering doubt my breast does now annoy
  And Sophonisba draws from sorrow even joy.
  While by our breath the breast, by blood veins are expanded,
  The dagger we will bear, were Syphax twelve times ended.
  Now take Bomilcar home, Micipsa, quickly go!
  He's not worth listening to. The foe's loose honey flow
  Instills but antimony; he should be rather trusted
  When threatening, than when ash on glowing coals he's dusted.

Rise! That the loyal town as models serve we may.
Strap on the breastplate. Pass the helmet! Cut away
This useless hair to use for bowstrings; do not waver,
Shear brow and crown! Which maid who does us favor,
Which woman unafraid, unless she hates our land,
Shall do as I now do? We shall fell warfare's brand
In our undaunted fist with you, you heroes, carry;
The town's defenders be, the foes with sallies harry.
Put quickly on, dear girls, cuirass and casque, like me
And heaven this may grant: that Sophonisba be
Tomyris to the foe, and you, the Amazons transcend,
The foe that thirsts for blood, who make his own blood spend.
Instead of Hiempsal, Himilco tell the town
Praise to them our resolve. Now bring our children down
Before this altar. My own blood be demonstration
With what a milk of love I feed the realm and nation.

The Queen's Ladies-in-waiting, Orynthia, Hippolite, Menalippe.
Hamilcar. Sophonisba. Vermina. Adherbal. Hierba. Syphax. The
Priest Bogudes. Torquatus and Flaminius, Two Captured Romans.

HAMILCAR: Unconquerable branch of mighty Hasdrubal,
Stouthearted Queen, whose star refuses to grow dull
By blows of destiny, though thousand tempests break,
You awe the world, divine your Carthage you will make;
As Africa's Penthésiléa Romans at her fume.
The realm's protectress, Cyrtha's own Paladium!
I draw now breath and nerve; such stern determination
Must flow from destiny, from gods' own approbation.
Take heart! The Queen for us a Xanthippus will be,
By her restrained, this Regulus in bonds you'll see.
And teach: when Carthage seems in dust defeated throbbing,
Her dragon from Rome's eagles their fame and triumph's
    robbing.
SOPHONISBA: The gods confirm they grant my wishes their accord.
Come, strap around my waist what was my prince's sword.
Vermina, you, too, wear this womanly attire;
Devotion dictates: our silk the hero cannot mire,
Nor be it deemed disguise. My robe, too, now put on.
To offer to the moon, a hero's dress I'll don.
This holy likeness, dressed like woman, start revering;

The goddess otherwise to pleas refuses hearing.
Do save us Kabar, you, our city's patron star!
Hear me, Baaltis, you, for whom we always mar
The noblest human blood, child flesh cede to your power,
So that your glowing image can scorch it and devour.
Look, Goddess, two of my own children face you now,
And should their scorching trunks your flame with glow endow,
Your maw start opening, the well-known beams releasing.
Yes, yes! I see the heat's intensive glow increasing.
Flames crown your head. Come, Children, and by lot decide
Which one of you is on this glowing grill to bide,
To save the fatherland, as victim here ascending.
Come, for it seems she is her arms toward you bending.
By just such sacrifice dear Anobreta has
Averted for the Punic throne crushing war's distress,
When she for gods to roast her only child surrendered.
Busir, Osirius, the Druids Teutat tendered,
Thus did Crete Saturn by such blood propitiate.
And Amon Moloch's image with this glow inundate,
And Sparta, too, a human heart on Mars's altar offered.
ADHERBAL: Blest he who for his country's good the pain of death
has suffered.
My mother, I will have in drawing lots no part,
For primogeniture, the fact that my own heart
Breaks for the commonweal, are high repute's assurance
That I the victim be.
HIERBA: You think beyond endurance
I find her charge? I have the same nerve as you do,
To offer heart and blood to save the realm; like you,
This steel against myself, or our enemy to whet.
Here stands the urn with lots. Let's draw, don't further fret.
VERMINA: From sorrow wed to joy my blood and heart now roil!
Their spiritedness does my bosom's coldness foil.
Gods have these starry twins, into two suns transmuted!
HIERBA: Rejoice! Priority is Hierba's undisputed!
Dear mother, please, remove these earthly clothes from me.
SOPHONISBA: Am I, good heavens, his blood-priestess now to be?
HIERBA: Vermina, from my hips the belt now starts untying.
VERMINA: Thus gold and virtue find flame's ardor purifying.
HIERBA: The victim's band around me Hamilcar will tie.

HAMILCAR: Our welfare's Phoenix will then from your ashes fly.

VERMINA: Numidia will crown you with laurels twice as many,
When we more altars build, than did the two Phileni
Whom Carthage hallowed, when in hot Cyrena's sand
They let themselves be buried: thereby the fatherland
Had in their noble vault a lasting landmark, gaining
More potent influence. Let Decius Mus, attaining
Self-sacrifice, his host keep whole; but here, this feat
Of children is so grand, no Roman could compete.

HIERBA: To laurel, cypress crowns Adherbal is attending.

ADHERBAL: Posterity and I will tend your cult unending.

HIERBA: Let mother lay me down into Baal's red glow.

SOPHONISBA: Here, one last kiss! How awful is this heartrending
blow!
Get on with it. State interest outweighs an infant.
Gods change you to a star, us fighters make triumphant!

VERMINA: God help us! What dread flames the image spews our
way!
What bolt the altar strikes, the gods' house making sway,
And causes earth to quake, the ground about to sunder?

SYPHAX: You fools, what's your intent that gods themselves send
thunder
Down on your mad conceit? What's this? Should Hierba's gore
A paltry offering be? Release him. He'll restore
With pluck in time Numidia's free and rightful station.
In dire straits with different blood one makes libation
To flame-wreathed effigies. Could no one else be found?
Are for their altar's flame both sun and moon then bound
Their victims from first fruits of captives to be claiming?
Quick, bring two different ones. These sweeter gifts obtaining,
The gods should be quite pleased.

SOPHONISBA: What flighty gods you are!
Should fury or kind fate my grand intention mar?

VERMINA: Oh, reason, you're so blind! With mole's eyes you're
pretending
To lynx-sharp sight. Poor fools, you're worthless, standing
Before the high court of beclouded destiny!

SOPHONISBA: Ye gods! is this a dream? am I alive, round me
Closed the abyss? Is Syphax this, a shade devoid of matter?
The king, whom foes restrained with bonds and iron fetter?

SYPHAX: I gladly, dearest Queen your Syphax aim to be.

SOPHONISBA: Come, guardian God, with soul and arms embrace
now me.

ADHERBAL: On hand, knee, feet, dear father, allow me to plant
kisses!

SYPHAX: Dear child, your sweet embrace your father sorely misses.

HIERBA: My god reveals himself to whom I'll give my heart.

SYPHAX: Doubt, sorrow, fear, and joy now through my spirit dart.

VERMINA: Dear father, for my joy is there a fitting payment?

SYPHAX: Is this my son? Vermina? and dressed in women's
raiment?

VERMINA: For you, my King, I pray to gods in women's dress.

SYPHAX: I will die happy, if round you my arms I press,
The pillar of my throne, about whose spurious dying
The enemies rejoice, yet honor flags they're dyeing
Dipped in your wounds, because the enemy and vice
May virtue not revile.

SOPHONISBA: Tell, dear, by what device
So luckily from chains you have yourself extracted!

SYPHAX: Where is the lock for which has gold as key not acted?
With it I bought the troth the Moorish guards had sworn.

SOPHONISBA: Within my bosom are breath, spirit, heart reborn,
And give thanks to the gods.

HAMILCAR: If Carthage knew the measure
Of Syphax's happiness, and of our joy and pleasure!

VERMINA: The priest brings presently two prisoners to us.
Right. God and piety it's best to honor thus.
The first's meant for the moon, and for the sun, the other.

BOGUDES: Through victims from the gods one's favors sure to
gather.
Undress the prisoners, but let them keep their shirt.

TORQUATUS: Damned be this house and service which fiendish
rites pervert.

BOGUDES: Upon your breast and limbs let molten metal rain,
This holy place with curses should you dare profane.
Another word, and in hellfire you will drown.
With May dew seven times we'll have you sprinkled down.
This wine will cleanse eyes, mouth, and forehead with its
splashes,
Then strew upon their heads a bit of dead man's ashes.

Behind their backs their feet and arms you will then tie.
The captives' dart and incense let in the fire fly.
With Nabathea's sap the glow more lively races.
Next, on the victims' board the two will take their places.
Toward Astarte's image you then will turn each face.
The sharp incision through both breasts that I now trace
Shows how great Baal the foes' control will slice asunder.
This heart burns for the sun, and for the moon, that yonder.
Accept, oh, guardian God, what piety is due,
The flesh be by the heat, the foe consumed by you.
Here, Derceto, you have their brains as an oblation,
Be dread to our foes, for us, kind constellation.
And as this heated ax has through their gullets bored,
May Rome fall thus and foe, struck by a Moorish sword.
The dead men's heads then have exposed upon a tower.
That, more than Gorgon's shield, they make the enemy cower.

SOPHONISBA: The offering is done; one thing is left to do:
My children, picked by fate for vengeance, it is you
By whom should Hannibal's oath once more be here repeated:
That Carthage by you thrive, Rome be by you deleted.

ADHERBAL: Should in our veins there run one drop of Roman
blood,
Together with my heart, quell it, oh, brimstone flood!

BOGUDES: You'll touch the altar, on the sword your fingers
placing.

HIERBA: I feel inside my breast revenge and passion racing.

BOGUDES, ADHERBAL, HIERBA: We, our tribe, and realm forever
shall be cursed,
If we don't die Rome's foes, won't foremost seek and first,
King Masinissa's end, and Rome's annihilation.
We're placing in gods' hands this solemn declaration.

CHORUS TO ACT I

*(In a mythologically allusive presentation of the complex soul of
Sophonisba, discord, hate, joy, terror, desire, envy, and fear contend for primacy.)*

ACT II

Scene takes place in front of the inner square of the royal palace.
Sophonisba. Syphax. Vermina. Juba. Himilco. Micipsa. Orynthia.
Elenisse. Menalippe. A number of Numidian Princes and Mag-
nates.

SOPHONISBA: Then, God forbid! the town belongs now to the foe?
HIMILCO: Alas, we're done for, yes.
SYPHAX: How fickle you are, woe!
  Inconstant fate, with us like water bubbles playing.
SOPHONISBA: What rage against our Cyrtha and us they'll be
    displaying!
VERMINA: Pray tell, how come the town was lost so rapidly?
HIMILCO: By our sword we fall and by foul treachery.
  By opening the fort Hiempsal troth has broken,
  Of heaps of gold to us, the simpletons, he's spoken,
  To city and us, fools, he solemnly alleged:
  That Masinissa had peace to our nation pledged.
SOPHONISBA: The fiendish cur! Should one this mothlike fawning
    bother,
  From worn mesh spun and purple, finally not smother?
HIMILCO: And as the joyful crowd from outposts starts to tramp,
  Some on a whim go even to see the enemy's camp
  Which quakes with shouts of joy, with fires brightly glowing,
  Where every banner is with olive branches flowing,
  The foe takes by surprise with just a minor force
  Which Hiempsal commands, the gate; this calls, of course,
  For countermeasures which with friends I'm quickly taking;
  Yet soon we have the foes' main body for us making,
  And when Mandrestal falls, Hiarba, too, is slain,
  And I receive these wounds, all flee; hard-pressed, I gain
  The safety of the fort.
SYPHAX.   Numidia is fated
  To see her obsequies and mine soon celebrated!
  And even Hannibal knows Carthage cannot hold.
JUBA: Woe, Prince, the fortress now the enemy's flames enfold,
  The garrison the gate, the walls, their arms surrenders,
  They jump to join the foe; those left of the defenders
  Count barely hundred still devoted to the King.

VERMINA: Let's notwithstanding boldly into action spring.

SOPHONISBA: We will campaign with you till death undoes our
    being.

SYPHAX: Too late! Would that Vermina could save himself by
    fleeing!
  For Carthage he's last hope, the welfare of the land,
  My solace, when the rest is forfeit and condemned.

VERMINA: What? I'm to seek alone in flight and fear salvation?

SYPHAX: Put on a Roman dress, a mercenary's station
  Pretend, and with them blend. The foe will, once I am
  Made prisoner, not worry much about you then;
  You, too, my friends, take off, your own escape route choosing,
  Since I'll blow up the ship, I authorize you using
  A board, to swim away from death and hurtful woe.

VERMINA: A kiss, dear father, for the one who now must go,
  And for a kinder lot to gods for you I'm calling.

HIMILCO: We'll bear whatever you, serenest, is befalling!

MICIPSA: Prince Masinissa and his force begin to spill
  Right through the gate.

SOPHONISBA: Let heaven do its will
  What fate will send we'll heed, heart steadfast and devoted,
  For even wormwood pills has patience sugarcoated.

Masinissa. Syphax. Sophonisba. Bomilcar. Juba. Himilco. Micipsa.
Hierba. Adherbal. Manastabal. The Queen's ladies-in-waiting.
A crowd of Masinissa's Soldiers.

MASINISSA: Look how this crowd of runaways itself betakes
  Out of this cage which is astir with poisonous snakes?
  Be quick! In irons clap the ones that did surrender.

SYPHAX: My gloominess is a reflection of your splendor.

MASINISSA: Your perjury's your fall. He who gods' oath will break,
  The mortals' grace and pity forever must forsake.
  Around his arms and legs have fetters tightly twisted.

SYPHAX: From having my hands tied your rage could have desisted!
  Just heavens! Oh!

MASINISSA: Quite so. Oh, yes, they're just indeed;
  Your case has shown that he's perdition's slave, the seed
  Who bears of evil.

SYPHAX: You the gods' own retribution
  Will suffer soon enough. You, dragon of collusion,

You'd swallow Africa; you under Roman yoke
Would chain your liberty, a she-wolf make your cloak
Next to your bosom which will soon you too devour.
BOMILCAR: On victors prisoners can't such invective shower.
SYPHAX: Can truth the tender ear of wheedlers injure so?
BOMILCAR: You like a reed yourself have wavered to and fro.
SYPHAX: With foreign troops my land I never have invaded.
MASINISSA: What good does losing time, and having harsh words
    traded?
Be quick, march Syphax off, and in a cell lock up.
SYPHAX: Yet Syphax's spirit's freedom none of this can stop.
MASINISSA: Bomilcar, quick, with guards the castle have
    surrounded:
To have, with no way out, whoever's in, impounded;
Besides Vermina now the haughty Queen do find
Who spawned this conflagration; in jail have her confined!
SOPHONISBA: Great prince, you, most serene! All-powerful
    campaigner,
Take pity on your drudge, become my brood's sustainer,
She's kneeling at your feet, and pleas for mercy bears.
MASINISSA: What? Is she a drudge who casque and breastplate
    wears?
SOPHONISBA: It's Sophonisba, spurned by gods, who're flighty like
    a feather,
Plaything of spurious luck, struck by misfortune's weather;
Erstwhile a queen, and now, she's nothing but a maid,
For whom her cruel fate all solace caused to face,
Except that she is now in Masinissa's power,
A wreck that landed on a rock, on which the tower
Of starry-shining virtue, the Pharus, stands erect.
Forgive a woman showing such reckless disrespect,
Who's nothing but your slave, that she your knees is touching,
That she falls at his feet, the master's, who is clutching
My death's and mercy's arrows, with claims to head and neck.
With kisses if I may your victor's hand bedeck,
My lord, as captive, if permitted is imploring,
I, Moorish woman, kneeling, my limpid tears outpouring,
I do implore by your crown's scintillating glow,
And by the grace of gods, whence all your triumphs flow,
I beg you by Numidia's name and reputation,

Which you and Syphax are, for no pacification,
Not for the sake of realm, crown, life, nor for freedom's sake.
No! Sophonisba craves her ties with life to break.
The wreaths that garnish us are dart heads many-pointed,
Transfixing our heart, they rip our head anointed.
Misfortune gnaws on us, good fortune makes us blind,
Because Moors sport, they say, two extra eyes behind.
A burden was my realm, the crown mere thorns did bear;
All pomp and office with ripe seed I now compare
Which luck strew for us, as to ruin it us lured.
The heavens are too black, our luck is too inured
That I for something sweet from it might venture hoping.
I swear, oh, mighty Prince, with joy for death I'm groping.
The aloe stench of sour life profoundly I resent,
To which not even fate could gentler sweetness lend.
From gourd seeds pomegranates one should not expect.

MASINISSA: Rise, splendid Queen, there is no need to genuflect.
What's crushing you reveal. Pray, what is your command?

SOPHONISBA: For utter joy, how can I make you understand
My soul-consuming woe! My liege, the Roman fetters
They so afflict my heart. But if your lordship shatters
Those haughty men's affront, such wolves' relentless claws,
I'm satisfied, made whole. As Syphax's Queen by law,
The King's, who shares your blood, I've many years now lived;
You too from Africa your essence have received.
This anchor of my hope and solace hails my soul.
You can't be as atrocious as alien Rome's control.
But if, great Prince, your might be torn from you and faded,
By me, your drudge and slave, yourself let be persuaded
To drive your splendid sword (I taste it with great zest)
Through my boys' bodies and through Sophonisba's breast.
Now bring our children here; by bowing and by scraping,
Rome's harsher servitude we hope to be escaping.
And, should I wish in vain, as priestess I would bring
To you their spurting blood, as holy offering.

MASINISSA: Serenest Sophonisba, your sorrow I am sharing,
With poison flows your mouth, and my heart, too, it's tearing.
Breathe freely now and give yourself some time to rest.
The storm may blow toward the port. My light, now test,
My help and troth, have your legitimate desire.

SOPHONISBA: Except for joy-fraught tears, to what can I aspire
  To bring my guardian god as thankful offering?
  My face which Syphax once had found quite ravishing
  Can only manage tears, my breasts' life-quickening treasure
  Which were two quivers once and wells of tender pleasure,
  Are just with sobbing rich. My soul, whose rattling ends,
  The incense now will light owed you as reverence.
  Oh, yes! Deign to accept my children's adoration.
  Don't spurn as did the god this trivial donation.
  Heart sets the offerings' price, not value of the hoard;
  Run, dearest boys, and fall upon the victor's sword!
ADHERBAL: Oh, mightiest Lord and Prince! We lie here in
    prostration,
  We're slaves of Masinissa's unending domination.
  Just do not lead us, wretches, beneath the Roman yoke.
HIERBA: We wish for death, and thousand torments we invoke,
  Before the hangman's block with laughter we'll go kneeling,
  With lions' dens and dragons' nests be gladly dealing,
  So long Your Grace does not send us to Rome as slaves.
MASINISSA: Rise, noble Princelings. From these buds there clearly
    waves
  The trunk's exquisiteness, the future fruits' perfection.
  Uncloud, oh, Most Serene, your heavenly complexion,
  Manastabal, now her, her loyal sons, attend,
  For quiet follows storm, as comfort woe will end.
MASINISSA, *alone:*
  Woe! And twice woe! Am I defeater or defeated?
  The tiger oft bags hunter, who him as quarry treated,
  But not a weakly doe. And Sophonisba throws
  Me into iron bands. We're winning, but she goes
  Off with the laurel wreaths. We cut and yet feel pain!
  We rule the castle, but she in our heart does reign!
  We're master of the realm, she, hangman of our zest!
  A tyrant in our soul, and viper in our breast!
  Knows Sophonisba, like Medea, to conjure?
  Shall I Creusa's flame and Creon's woe endure?
  Can she like basilisk with just a glance enchant?
  Will I go up in flames, because the tinder can't
  Be seen of such huge flames? I am consumed, I'm flaming!
  My idol, Sophonisba! Away! I am proclaiming

Myself your prisoner and your most abject pelf.
What's coming next? Now, Masinissa, curb yourself!
You'll have this spider to you honey sweetness giving?
You'll have this silkworm you your funeral habit weaving?
Like moths, intentionally, you'll charge into the glow?
The blood of Asdrubal, his snake you do not know?
Exhaling only poison, that only death sends flowing,
The flame by which Numidia now up in smoke is going?
The worm which Syphax's breast with zeal did sting, provoke,
Till from the realm he drove us, the pact with Rome then broke?
And Masinissa would be such a dragon wooing,
This maggot would embrace, with snakes for friendship suing?
This witch without delay into a dungeon throw;
Chase her from fold and breast. No, Masinissa, no!
Ambition's blinding you, in vulgar bounds you're racing
Spurred by revenge and lust: in thought yourself disgracing,
When you King Syphax's guilt let on her shoulders crash,
Whip innocence with envy's and dark suspicions' lash.
Supposing she, incensed at Rome, did him incite.
What lamb, when being hurt, its crippler wouldn't fight?
A snail, a beetle will, those teasing them, set at
With their weak horns. This Sophonisba sets instead
My soul on fire: that your beauty's rays aren't feigning
As precious common stones, nor shells no pearls containing.
You're Hasdrubal's own sprout, of his heroic tree,
Who'd built New Carthage, held of two seas mastery,
And, full of gallantry, stood always girt for battle;
Oh, on your lily breasts Alcides' heart did settle.
Oh, lightning sparks your eyes, and grace ensouls your build.
I burn! Oh, woe, twice woe! and yet, my heart is chilled,
Its thoughts when turned to Rome and toward Scipio's
    countenance.
Rash prurience deserves the sour fruit of penance.
What care should Masinissa for realm and scepter show?
Yes, true! One cannot just to any temple go
With lips unlocked and voice that nothing does conceal,
And Masinissa dare not say: I glow; but he must seal
His lips, when you, oh, sun, he wants to reverence,
His finger on his mouth. But no, such flame intense
Can't under ashes of a stifled fear lie blighted.

Rome may well show dismay, my scepter might be slighted,
And favor turn to hate. My scepter's luck and land,
My life thread, all hang now in Sophonisba's hand;
My pulse beats, as within her breast my heart is beating.
But will not Syphax then, with leering glances meeting
Our tender joys, her love's and favor's gift resist?
No! Syphax rightaway will perish by this fist!

The Scene Represents a Dungeon
Syphax. Sophonisba.

SYPHAX: You, vengeful gods! you're by the realm's loss
    disappointed?
You'd have Numidia's lord and royal head anointed,
Protector Africa's steeped in this dungeon's night,
Die in decay and rot? Be warned you, whom the bright
Glow of your purple blinds, on scepter reeds relying:
That who sits pilloried today, or is in fetters lying,
Was Croesus yesterday. Woe! What wanted Syphax's might?
The Moorish land's bright star, and now, a snuffed out light.
The nations' arbiter, of magnates mediator,
To thraldom now condemned, who, like a slavish traitor,
Wears heavy bonds now. Once did Rome and Carthage sue
For favors on my part. Of greatest heroes two,
The Roman Scipio, Moor Asdrubal the latter,
They curried my hand's favor, my ears did sweetly flatter,
And for my friendship both at once themselves bestirred.
Oh, that I, Scipio, you, evil-omen bird,
To kill with raging fists had then not found the daring,
When you and Hasdrubal the selfsame bed were sharing?
Make ready, Syphax, to restore what's gone awry.
It's not so terrible now grim death to descry,
When in the dark just barely mole's eyes one did possess.
Prepare yourself this knife into your breast to press!
SOPHONISBA: Stop, Syphax!
SYPHAX: Aren't we then to even perish free?
SOPHONISBA: Against yourself don't practice grisly tyranny!
SYPHAX: In tender youth had I but made this observation!
SOPHONISBA: In mishap brings impatience no gain, but hesitation.
SYPHAX: Can I in constant fear against more insults hold?

SOPHONISBA: When lightnings stop, the sun can turn to glowing
    gold.
SYPHAX: From men as well as gods for nothing more I'm hoping.
SOPHONISBA: Rough weather gone, the sun its beams on you is
    sloping.
SYPHAX: A sunbeam? but from whom?
SOPHONISBA: From me.
SYPHAX: Oh, spurious light!
    Oh, wretched sun! Quick, hither, knife!
SOPHONISBA: Indeed, you might
    Know Sophonisba better.
SYPHAX: Ye gods!
SOPHONISBA: Your sun's own splendor
    Which floods this night, the dungeon's anguish turns to tender
    Delight, my bonds, to freedom.
SYPHAX: But what dream is this?
    A specter, mocking me?
SOPHONISBA: No, prince, plain truth this is!
    What brought me to your chains was care for your well-being.
SYPHAX: It's Sophonisba's ghost?
SOPHONISBA: Your savior, me, you're seeing.
SYPHAX: I hear my sweetheart, but a man is whom I see.
SOPHONISBA: Behold here faith and need disguised in mummery.
SYPHAX: What? Is my angel now a Roman mercenary?
SOPHONISBA: Love, dearest love, does Proteus's imprint carry,
    It turns to anything, takes any color on
    Like a chameleon. Love urged me, dear, to don
    These clothes, assistance thus and aid to you assuring.
SYPHAX: What kind of help can such a danger be procuring?
SOPHONISBA: Exchange with me your clothes, do this with utmost
    haste.
SYPHAX: Ah, paragon of faith!
SOPHONISBA: Be quick, and time don't waste!
    The vigilance of guards will not allow debating.
SYPHAX: To free me, to the dragon herself she's immolating?
SOPHONISBA: Now then, secure your flight. I can take care of
    things.
SYPHAX: Who will unlock my bonds?
SOPHONISBA: Your Sophonisba brings
    The keys with her.

SYPHAX: My spirit before your faith must pall.
I'd rather hangmen should my body rudely haul
Across swords, lances, hooks, and axes, eyelids let
Be sliced away, my face against the sun have set;
I'd stand more pain than that by which we Regulus shattered,
Than, by my going free, I'd see in turn you fettered.
SOPHONISBA: This latter, dearest one, there's no one now can stop!
SYPHAX: I'd rather die!
SOPHONISBA: Dear angel, simply lock me up!
Rest easy, for thereby my welfare is unfolding.
SYPHAX: My spirit's heavy with lament and dark foreboding!
SOPHONISBA: Be off now, undeterred. There's no one I can tell
That would indict you. Since your tongue speaks Latin well,
With talk, if in a quandary, you might yourself yet save.
SYPHAX: For one last kiss of yours, my darling, I still crave!
SOPHONISBA: Let gods your guidance be and heaven your defense.
But what does Sophonisba glean from such a recompense?
Around me, whirring chains. Yet, through my still ears flitting
Rings Masinissa's word; its ring is unremitting.
He felt my grief. Who this can sense, there is no doubt,
Cannot but be in love. My Syphax, which way out?
When Masinissa's hand kept love seeds to us strewing,
Could I engage, my sweet, in our own love's undoing?
No, Sophonisba, heaven resents, and will chastise
Oath breakers, who this image, and then that idolize.
Oh, who could fathom Syphax's cursing us and damning?
And, wouldn't Masinissa, though passion be him fanning,
Once he'd repent his lust, like poison, spit us out?
For vice, upon the act, self-loathing brings about.
Yet, why should one oppose ascendant constellations?
My Syphax isn't struck by gods' harsh condemnations
That now one image, then another he'd adore.
Yes, what is it our time does teach us to explore?
For what's a need, a virtue must forge our understanding.
He sees me and the realm inclining to their ending,
He can by right no more his Sophonisba curse;
She breaks his chains, and round her neck, she makes them
    hers,
Chains, which for Masinissa I've been myself preparing
As tokens of my faith, in love's lure him ensnaring.

Masinissa. Sophonisba.

MASINISSA: Why in this solitude, himself disparaging,
　Does Syphax rave? Now, traitor, you hear your hour ring:
　Blow life and passion forth, released by lust for power,
　It's Masinissa's steel that probes your bowels this hour,
　Whose realm from him, peace breaker, you did expropriate.
　What sighs, what mumbles he? Let's hear you, what you prate!
SOPHONISBA: Yes, Masinissa, let revenge come to fruition,
　Your cause is not unjust, mine close is to perdition.
MASINISSA: Does his despair irk me to mete out punishment?
SOPHONISBA: Because my death alone recovery can grant.
MASINISSA: Since you condemn yourself, for wealth and power
　lusting,
　Receive now death and thrust.
SOPHONISBA: Yes, through these breasts start thrusting!
MASINISSA: Good heavens! I grow numb!
SOPHONISBA: 　　　　　　　　　What's this, the dagger droops?
MASINISSA: What? to a woman's guise the royal Syphax stoops?
　This work of wonder let's in its odd ways admire!
SOPHONISBA: Won't Sophonisba die by Masinissa's ire?
MASINISSA: Ye gods, is this a dream? Am I bereft of sense?
　Could this be Sophonisba? Syphax gone is hence?
SOPHONISBA: It's she, illustrious Prince, before your lordship
　kneeling.
MASINISSA: Is my Manastabel her in a keep concealing?
　Let brimstone be his pay, my fist his hangman be!
SOPHONISBA: Not so! It is my troth that here thus shackles me.
MASINISSA: Your troth? This strange event explaining does require.
SOPHONISBA: What metal doesn't melt love's all-consuming fire?
MASINISSA: Methinks that your account is sheer and empty dream.
SOPHONISBA: Forgive me, Prince, my crime too dastardly I deem
　To be revealed.
MASINISSA: 　　　　Speak out! What do you call transgression?
SOPHONISBA: I stammer when my tongue is struggling for
　expression.
MASINISSA: Your mouth goes numb before what heart and hand
　had tried?
SOPHONISBA: It's I who Syphax from this chasm loose have pried.

MASINISSA: And had yourself with chains on his account then
    braided?
SOPHONISBA: Quite so! because for him I gladly would have faded.
    Almighty lord and Prince! This stroke you mustn't stay;
    This breast with purple stain, in Syphax's place you may
    Take me as offering. I know my undertaking
    Is capital offense. As favor I'd be taking,
    If I, your foolish slave, who's kneeling at your feet,
    And hungers after death, her end could quickly meet
    At your, not Roman, hands.
MASINISSA: Serenest Sophonisbe,
    You make the tale come true of the most loyal Thisbe?
    Oh, adamantine troth! Oh, love, which outside you
    No equal model boasts. Your virtue does outdo
    Your beauty even. Why is Masinissa staring
    About the goddess prostrate at his feet not caring?
    It's time to break Andromeda's damned steel in two!
    Don't keep from her the fact that Sophonisba you
    As goddess, angel, your eye's apple, sun entices;
    And I, her abject slave and drudge.
SOPHONISBA: I know my vices.
    Don't desecrate your mouth with idle words of praise.
MASINISSA: Your virtue's light sets me with flame and heat ablaze.
    I'm burning, by the ray of beauty set on fire!
    How soon won't be undone who's triumph's multiplier?
    How's into fetters clapped who turns the others free?
    The ray of love with arrow-rapid course now see
    Like wax the fury melt, the victor frigid-hearted
    Like brimstone fire, how the craving's candle started
    Hate's smoke now to dispel! How Masinissa flames;
    Who, you, the victor, and himself, the vanquished names!
SOPHONISBA: Don't let your shimmer dim in such cave's
    obscuration.
    The tender soul's initial stirring trepidation
    Is far from being clouds, just on the heights faint haze,
    Soon quenched by sun and wits. So, too, my Prince, your gaze,
    Ere noontime has arrived, more clearly will be seeing.
MASINISSA: Not so! my flames from time and reason won't be
    fleeing!

Although I did attempt at first this lust to block,
Still, I fled like a doe, already arrow-struck.
From you with all my might my eyes I'd have averted,
Yet they were, like the eagle's, which soon I have asserted,
You, their own sun disk fair! If only did my pain
Vouchsafe me peace and sleep, if in the dream's domain
To me it seemed! I burn, my burnings unabated!
Thus ivy from its shrub can't quite be separated,
Nor I from you, and breathe. Yes, when we are apart,
I'm dead. Because I have, except for yours, no heart.
Before my Sophonisba you see myself prostrating;
My heat with dewy kisses start reciprocating!
Two drops of purest bliss do in my heart instill.
What's this I feel? Gods, help! Through such hot passion still
Death's steel and impotence into our hearts can slither?
My life wax melts, as my love candle starts to wither
With too much heat my veins' oil, blood it takes by storm.
If only my own soul in you I could transform!

SOPHONISBA: Prince, solace of my eyes! Although my soul is
    swimming
In these same flames which from your heart are overbrimming,
The heavens our passion with kindness do not greet,
To lamps their oil deny, pour water on love's heat.

MASINISSA: What brute does stars and heavens so darkly
    represent?

SOPHONISBA: By rights but on King Syphax my eyes their rays
    should slant.

MASINISSA: A hopeless cause you deem when Syphax's on the run?

SOPHONISBA: I'd stay his spouse, although his fortune were
    undone.

MASINISSA: Stratonice wooed, with Seleucus not extinguished.

SOPHONISBA: So Seleucus willingly her to his son relinquished.

MASINISSA: Not even Syphax now with jealousy should burn.

SOPHONISBA: Bad luck will not love's pillars into ashes turn.

MASINISSA: Yet Hasdrubal had me for you as groom selected.

SOPHONISBA: For him, not you, had Carthage as marriage broker
    acted.

MASINISSA: Can Kaccabe by law change parents' own design?

SOPHONISBA: The fatherland comes first, before it, all incline.

MASINISSA: The law of war dissolves your vows, my ward you
    making.
SOPHONISBA: Your welfare for my favors you're thinking of
    forsaking?
MASINISSA: A squinting eye does not an honest love deter.
SOPHONISBA: You know the verdict's rigor, when you Rome's
    wrath incur!
MASINISSA: Shall Rome then also laws for love to us decree?
SOPHONISBA: So Scipio's hostage I'll continue here to be.
MASINISSA: Did Masinissa not for Scipio Cyrtha take?
SOPHONISBA: The greatest magnates Rome into her tools will
    make.
MASINISSA: I'm not a slave of Rome, we are a federation.
SOPHONISBA: They always reap where others provided irrigation.
MASINISSA: They won't reap, Sophonisba, while Masinissa lives.
SOPHONISBA: To me, I fear, all this a shroud's foreboding gives!
MASINISSA: Before I break my oath to you, Rome's pact I sever.
SOPHONISBA: My guardian god to gainsay no longer I'll endeavor.
    The flame within me I can't any longer hide.
    My torrid kiss let now revive a mouth that died.
    For kissing is the core, the soul of love's sensation.
    Now joy will follow tears, and sunshine, obfuscation.
    I am beside myself, by joy and luck oppressed.
    I'm offering my heart, and dedicate my breast
    On hallowed ground.
MASINISSA: Good heavens! Has Sophonisba fainted?
SOPHONISBA: I draw the tonic from your mouth with coral
    painted.
MASINISSA: The night of double suns does strew its teary dew?
SOPHONISBA: My heat melts down my soul and flees from me to
    you!
MASINISSA: And mine thirsts after yours. You, prostrate, I'm
    adoring.
SOPHONISBA: Your realm with my own soul to you I am
    restoring.
MASINISSA: Its horn the unicorn, as token of its might,
    Thus lays in ladies' laps. Let's prudently, my light,
    Head for our nuptials, leave this casemate of detention.
    Once wed, we will impede Rome's easy intervention.

CHORUS TO ACT II

(In the setting of a temple, Love and Heaven—each citing rich mythological evidence—dispute which is the supreme divine principle. Love responds triumphantly to the invoked forces of Passion to rule, of Hell, Cruelty, Earth, Water, Honor, and Fame. The chorus concludes in a celebration of the imperial couple, Leopold and Margarite of Austria, whose marriage inaugurates a new golden age of Love, with which all cosmic powers are reconciled.)

ACT III

Masinissa, Bomilcar, Manastabal.

BOMILCAR: Is there a chance the King his plan might have revised?
MASINISSA: The nuptial rites will be here promptly finalized.
MANASTABAL: Rare are the rash resolve and leap that do not
  flounder.
MASINISSA: Where stands the cliff on which I am supposed to
  founder?
BOMILCAR: You can, serenest Prince, learn much from Syphax's
  story.
MASINISSA: He fell, too high ascending, on wings of blind
  vainglory.
MANASTABAL: As Sophonisba earlier goaded him to pride.
MASINISSA: As if an Icarus the sun can ever chide.
BOMILCAR: She is a bloodstained star, an imp, a comet rushing.
MASINISSA: For such a blasphemy your face ought to be blushing.
MANASTABAL: Our troth and oath have placed your welfare in our
  care.
MASINISSA: In Masinissa's, too, does Sophonisba share.
BOMILCAR: Who with her mother's milk on Punic poison suckled?
MASINISSA: For Rome, against great Carthage, have we not armor
  buckled?
MANASTABAL: Why felt the Prince compelled to join Rome's cause
  and claim?
MASINISSA: Unjustly you impute to her the city's blame.
BOMILCAR: This nest of wasps shares in the same deceit and
  cunning.

MASINISSA: That she's of Barcas's stem this I find quite becoming.
MANASTABAL: A poisonous shadow casts the yew, a pretty tree.
MASINISSA: You blame on Sophonisba what sort of roguery?
BOMILCAR: To break with Rome her spells King Syphax have seen
    swaying.
MASINISSA: This is a gnat against an enemy inveighing.
MANASTABAL: And in your ears the selfsame venom she will blow.
MASINISSA: I know for sure how far a wife's request may go.
BOMILCAR: What will be Scipio's and Laelius's position?
MASINISSA: To tie our hands should we as king give them
    permission?
MANASTABAL: You are their ally, she, their natural-born foe.
MASINISSA: Our nuptials a friendship between them will make
    grow.
BOMILCAR: Her homeland from her soul she surely can't erase!
MASINISSA: At Byrsa Rome cannot its bow forever brace.
MANASTABAL: Rome will not rest until it Kaccabe sees wrecked.
MASINISSA: This easier is planned than put into effect.
BOMILCAR: For Kaccabe his foremost pinions they did whittle.
MASINISSA: The greatest city in the world so far has suffered little.
MANASTABAL: We note a drop in men's and citizens' amount.
MASINISSA: It seven hundred times its thousands still can count.
BOMILCAR: The best have all been slain. Exhausted is its treasure.
MASINISSA: It gold from Africa, like from a well, can measure.
BOMILCAR: And which all Africa as leech does also curse.
MASINISSA: Whose aid to battle Rome seeks the entire earth.
BOMILCAR: What does the Prince intend? The bonds with Rome to
    sunder?
MASINISSA: So long as by such step our freedom won't go under.
MANASTABAL: Where such suspicion sprouts, all trust must needs
    decay.
MASINISSA: Mistrust has not a whit in me as yet gained sway.
BOMILCAR: I wish that woman were Your Lordship not
    misleading!
MASINISSA: Who firmly stands like us, no danger runs of skidding.
MANASTABAL: The love drive is a fish whose touch lames like a
    blow.
MASINISSA: You spiders, who your venom on purest lilies sow,
    Resemble boorish Moors, incapable of learning
    The boon of our sun; they, just because it's burning,

Spit shame and oaths at it. Indeed, your stupid light
Will always choose just shade, but sun itself will spite,
Not Sophonisba's sheen, but just her blotch and blemish,
That reason, time, and wits will surely cleanse, make vanish.
The long-considered business must go into effect.
I will not hear you argue nor brook that you object.

Sophonisba. Masinissa. Bogudes. Bomilcar. Manastabal. Himilco.
Micipsa. Adherbal. Hierba. The Queen's ladies-in-waiting.
Twelve naked Cupidines.

SOPHONISBA: Is this the golden night who will shame all the days?
    Who to Diana's horn its dew, like pearls, relays;
    Whom the enamored skies with thousand lamps bedeck,
    As fortune with a kinder ray our progress seems to track,
    Than when we first were by the glittering daylight greeted,
    As you, Numidia, the first time had us feted
    With sumptuous nuptial rites? There sets upon my breast
    And head the lust of love, my heart's by joy possessed,
    I am beside myself, on Masinissa's urging
    With him to be in everlasting nuptials merging.
MASINISSA: My tongue is by the bond of love with silence bound,
    My soul is by the sea of happy feelings drowned!
    You, mighty gods, help! help! Bless our flames, do tether
    And also clamp our hearts with your own hands together!
BOGUDES: The sky itself bless now this holy sacrament!
    Make firm your welfare, and your glory permanent!
    Let's for Astarte, who lights day and night her fire,
    Ignites all souls, and yet keeps moist the world entire,
    With myrtles brighten her eternal altar's flame.
    The incense, Children, pass, which bears our Saba's name.
    Strew roses all around, with scattered nuts starting playing,
    The juice of grapes upon the burning fire spraying.
    From civet musk and amber the fragrant vapors rouse.
    Use myrtle bloom and with this holy water douse
    Her loving bridal locks. And there my hand imposes
    A lance, her hair to part. And with the wreath of roses
    We'll flower both their brows, the locks catch in this veil
    Of finest golden mesh, then, shout to them: wassail!
ALL: Bless Masinissa, Sophonisba with good fortune!
    Let no black star, no poisonous glances them importune!

BOGUDES: Exchange the wedding rings, whose shining metal may
  Not more enduring be than your good fortune's ray!
  Now give the newlyweds the fire and the water!
  Together clamp the braided hands once more, and tauter!
  For Sophonisba now I tie her belt and cord,
  Which Masinissa's hand, by welcome rest restored,
  In bed will loosen. Then, by way of an ovation,
  The crowd will at their feet fall face down in prostration.
  You, nymphs, begin to strew love's blossoms all around.
  Enclose them, Children, in the torches' limpid round.
ALL: Bless Sophonisba, Masinissa with good fortune!
  Let no black star, no poisonous glances them importune!
BOGUDES: Now, Children, loose three snow white doves as
      offering,
  Onto the goddess's lap them gently lowering.
  Ah, Delephat, you, whom did salt and sea engender,
  Who older still than Ammon rate,
  These two help to initiate!
  To both the gift of love and luck in treaties tender.
  Bestow on them such fertile fruitfulness,
  As lends the scaly creature your largesse!
  Salambo, of the strongest salt of pleasure
  Strew on their bed and table a good measure,
  That, as our food with salt, more spiceful be our life!
  Let soul and mouth love's sugar fully savor;
  Do not cause Priapus to make her quaver!
  Command that time for both run fast, with laughter rife!
  Oh, heaven's lofty queen, Mylitta, joys conveying,
  Accept the offering's dough which your own image molds,
  And West Phoenicia for protective aegis holds,
  Protect the newlyweds, grant us for what we're yearning!
  Astarte, as our Earth's sun burning,
  Who, as no Atlas could, the earth globe, as she flares,
  Upon her shoulders bears,
  By whom days splendid turn, the nights to light are turning,
  Beloved Queen of our hearts,
  Phoenicians' sempiternal tutelary,
  Take what this offering imparts,
  The lovers' love to utter raptures carry!
  These doves' pure blood I sanctify,

My hands into their bowels I'm dipping,
Which on the hallowed flames are dripping,
Your holy heat to pacify.
Allow sweet candles of your charm and favor
To fill these wedded hearts with joys to savor!

ALL: Bless Sophonisba, Masinissa with good fortune,
Let no black star, no poisonous glances them importune!

BOGUDES: What's this? one dove seems to be shying from the heat?
The entrails let us scan to check if it is meet
This wedlock should be joined, and to Astarte's liking!
The absence of the bladder in itself is striking!
The liver's wrongly placed and shriveled to a ball.
But in the other one the heart is all too small.
The flames just flicker, aren't as pure as when ignited.
Soon some event I'm sure this marriage will have blighted.

SOPHONISBA: Oh, gods of virtuous wedlock, stand by, don't turn
    away!
This sunshine don't allow to turn a noxious ray!
But woe! my ice-cold limbs now numb have started waxing!
My heart boils over, quakes, I'm in a faint collapsing!

Laelius amidst a crowd of Roman soldiers, in addition to all characters from the previous scene.

LAELIUS: Good heavens! can this be? It's real or deceit?
Is Masinissa kneeling before Dercetes' feet?
He's pressing Sophonisba's suit with utmost vigor!

MASINISSA: Can our marriage then among world's wonders figure?

LAELIUS: To such thing happening would never Rome conform.

MASINISSA: Suppose it's done already! Shall I cut to your norm,
The robe I wear, from Rome her haughty nod beseeching?

LAELIUS: In things that might the precious pact with Rome be
    breaching.

MASINISSA: Which point is it that tears my marriage bonds in
    two?

LAELIUS: The points are legion, since our foe is joined to you.

MASINISSA: No longer she's a foe to Masinissa married.

LAELIUS: As spoils she was to be to Rome in triumph carried.

MASINISSA: Is Sophonisba not to be the victor's prize?

LAELIUS: With Roman arms you did Numidia comprise.

MASINISSA: To Masinissa Cyrtha, the capital, has ceded.

LAELIUS: First Hasdrubal's defeat by Scipio was needed!
MASINISSA: And by this arm the latter's camp was set aflame.
LAELIUS: The head was Scipio, you just his hand became.
MASINISSA: Where fought your Scipio, when Syphax we did take?
LAELIUS: Is there to Laelius no share you might forsake?
MASINISSA: You're giving credit only to the army's chief.
LAELIUS: That Laelius has been your slave is your belief?
MASINISSA: Have you been Masinissa for your servant taking?
LAELIUS: I'm shocked that toward Rome so bold you should be
    making.
MASINISSA: This Rome, for which I Africa's gates did open up?
LAELIUS: The course of Roman arms, what bolt did ever stop?
MASINISSA: The Moorish triumphs do the sun's own carriage ride.
LAELIUS: Your feats and triumphs longer than Rome's you claim
    will bide?
MASINISSA: We are Phoenicians, Tsor is our fatherland,
    The great Khna sired it, south, east its glory fanned.
    Wherever shadows fall, and stars the orb are gilding,
    There our mast had sailed, and our hand went building.
    And everywhere for edifice and law the base we laid.
    We taught you how in battle the ranks should be arrayed,
    How hand can into eye, eye into ears be rendered
    By script, which we invented. Wisdom was engendered
    In our home, and then, to Athens, Memphis brought.
    Ships, too, the very first, by our ax were wrought,
    The art of reckoning from our brain came hailing,
    We were the first who by the stars' sure lead went sailing;
    The pillars named for Hercules, where he'd once relaxed,
    Were for the world a path toward the ocean; next,
    The Red Sea broached, we Africa circumnavigated,
    Discovered Thule; Hanno's ships negotiated
    The course to Helios's bed and to a newfound world
    Which Kaccabe as secret keeps, not to be unfurled
    As freedom's port, for our, and the sun's protection,
    If Ammon should decree that Rome the world's subjection
    Be granted, and our land, whence Rome obtains its grain
    Be turned into a desert. Still, the dice remain
    Upon the table to be cast. From quivers poking
    See our arrows, which like clouds the air are choking.
    Numidia's darts are trained at Rome, and won't go wide,

When princes are prescribed whom they can take for bride.
Pride comes before the fall, to you be Regulus's lesson,
Disdain before prostration.

LAELIUS: Let love and gall not lessen
The grasp of reason, nor your peace and joy defy.

MASINISSA: What I am doing, right and wisdom justify.

LAELIUS: You'll rue it, once your lust and rage you fail to mind.

MASINISSA: You tear my heartstrings, and with heels my body
    grind.

LAELIUS: You've canceled our pact?

MASINISSA: Those terms that Rome injured.

LAELIUS: That Rome should break a pact is something never heard.

MASINISSA: I haven't in the least from Rome's pact deviated.

LAELIUS: Your nuptials have the pact completely abrogated.

MASINISSA: A slave, no king is forced his heart's choice to
    disclaim!

LAELIUS: To woo the foe will shift the federation's aim.

MASINISSA: Rome sees in women foes, in fear before them quivers?

LAELIUS: Her love's attractive charm with perjury pacts shivers.

MASINISSA: No! Masinissa is no flapping weather vane.

LAELIUS: King Syphax's breach of faith shows what she can obtain.

MASINISSA: She'll not associate with those who would seduce.

LAELIUS: By pruning boughs you can't the toxic root reduce.

MASINISSA: To Sophonisba innate poison you impute?

LAELIUS: For Rome, what is more poisoned than stems from
    Barcas's root?

MASINISSA: Like Masinissa she is troth and pact promoting.

LAELIUS: She's poisonous ground, though oil and sugar be her
    coating.

MASINISSA: Such wretched game with oaths plays no one but a
    fool.

LAELIUS: She's sworn to us before, on us her rage to cool.

MASINISSA: Blasphemers see the sun with spots and shade abated.

LAELIUS: We will not sanction what you have initiated.

MASINISSA: I likewise ask who'll change our mind and our intent.

LAELIUS: This instant Sophonisba from you I order rent.

MASINISSA: The first that touches her will sword and death be
    kissing.

LAELIUS: Comply with my command, his insolence dismissing!

MASINISSA: Up, noble Moors! Resist armed might with sterner
    might!

BOMILCAR: Think twice, you heroes!

MASINISSA: Up! death's chill let snuff our light,
Ere we serve Rome as slaves!

MASINISSA: With swords keep them besetting!

BOMILCAR: Stop, heroes, do not run! And if your swords need
whetting
To spill your gall and wrath, don't cool your heat and slash
Into your entrails, but, the blood of foes let splash,
Let's raze the nest that's Carthage, where new swords now they
whet.

MASINISSA: Whom, than who strikes our heart, as foe we'll more
regret?
Who with a murderous force besets us, calls us slave?

MANASTABAL: For now, let Laelius his claim to vengeance waive,
Until the heat of passion the heart can start to tame,
And Scipio comes himself. Rash eagerness will aim
At lashing out, which reason, sense, and mind regret.

LAELIUS: Are Laelius and Rome to quake before his threat?

MASINISSA: Should we stand by, while to a wolf our lamb we lose?

BOMILCAR: Take heed: there're things that let themselves be based
on screws
And stood up on their end, which neither wit nor sweat
Will manage to set straight, regardless how we fret.
Will Rome with Masinissa on her account now break?
His services misprize, his loyalty forsake?
Yet Carthage stands, although great Cyrtha has gone down.
It trusts in fortune's wheel, and Hannibal's renown.
In brief: if to this pact you're war and discord bringing,
Silk Masinissa won't, nor will Rome silk be spinning.

LAELIUS: The discord, I admit, might be as well delayed,
Till Scipio himself a ruling will have made,
If Syphax and his wife as prize rate your protection.

MASINISSA: He be the judge, with more restraint and
circumspection.

LAELIUS: Your hope cajoles you, for his sword will as swift slice
The bond in two, according to Laelius's advice.
Torquatus with the rest of captives I require
Without delay brought here!

HIMILCO: Have Laelius's desire
This instant satisfied. Torquatus, though, has been
Killed for the kingdom's good, as offering by the Queen.

Torquatus to deliver is not in our power.
LAELIUS: You, tigers, now like poisonous vermin do you cower?
A devilish misdeed, conceited craziness!
What? Brimstone hasn't rained, bright bolt of lightning has
Not struck the sacrifice which skin with gooseflesh crawling
And hair makes stand on end, and heaven finds apalling,
Which erstwhile Hystaspides as horrid for you banned;
You, who to your disgrace the power understand
Inherent in your heinous deeds, and your condition,
And that of your damned Moorish realm which faced perdition
By Agathocles' fist? The deities you find
As cruel as yourselves? You, who so dumb and blind
Do humans slaughter, for whose long life with prayers
Others ask as God's will? Your altars cover layers
Of sticky blood you spilled that stains the tainted sand?
What of the rituals which Gelo for you banned?
Fine! For your nobles shall the same law now obtain.
Fetch us those who as captives of ours yet remain
This instant here. Which priest, dross of humanity,
Inhumanly performed this gross atrocity?
Is it this slave of idols? His face's color pallid,
His trembling body are for me proof more than valid,
He held this blood court for hell's sake. And so I rule:
You'll feel yourself, if human blood the wrath of gods can cool,
How on idolatry the heavens hail are raining,
And those you curse are from on high laurel wreaths obtaining.

Laelius, Mamercus. Bogudes. Three prisoners. Among them
Syphax in disguise. Sophonisba, Masinissa, in addition to all char-
acters from the previous scene.

MAMERCUS: Oh, mighty hero, here, three Moors to you I've
      brought,
Whom I tonight in their disguise as Romans caught
As they were leaving town.
LAELIUS: Good timing! You're observant.
Torquatus's noble blood shall by blood of a servant
Be sprinkled and atoned. This instant let them be
Your offering.
BOGUDES: Sir, permission's not granted.
LAELIUS: Who dictates what you do?
BOGUDES: It's heaven's lofty ordinance.

LAELIUS: What madness, silly prattle this, that tests my sufferance!
 Why was Torquatus not protected on that score?
BOGUDES: Our gods' infernal wrath demands but foreign gore,
 Unless the parents wish their own child immolated.
LAELIUS: You desperate wretches, with what monstrous load
  you've weighted
 The altar of your gods? Does this not Atreus's board
 For your Thyestes lay? Has not the Titan poured
 His spangled light as at Mycene, back crablike crawling?
 Is nature not aghast at her own self? I'm calling
 You, murderer, to start the damned Moors' sacrifice;
 This, beginning with them, Rome more than justifies.
BOGUDES: Ere I should do this, rather my ghost I would exhale.
LAELIUS: You'd have yourself by hangmen, dense rogue, through
  torments trail?
BOGUDES: To feel the gods' revenge is worse than bearing this.
LAELIUS: Then soon will cool on you its fire the abyss,
 More than Busiris you by Furies will be harried.
 This instant to the stake this devil's priest be carried,
 The stake he with demonic murder oft defiled.
BOGUDES: Such death confirms the gods have on Bogudes smiled,
 The gods to whom himself Bogudes dedicated,
 Since as their altar's victim he thrives, and they are sated;
 I kiss their noble cross.
LAELIUS: Behold, what craziness!
 How this despairing wretch shows scorn and stubbornness!
 When he's nailed on, don't have his bosom perforated,
 Till he'll have seen these three black souls evacuated.
BOGUDES: There dwells in innocence a diamantine heart
 And eyes of porphyry that neither maudlin smart
 Nor wet gloom moves.
LAELIUS: The upshot will give instruction.
 How far stubbornness can ignore self-destruction.
 But is no Busir now in Cyrtha who'd agree
 Upon this murderous altar to sacrifice these three?
 This horror starts a strong disgust in me to fire;
 To see the Romans stained by it I don't desire.
 Is there among you, Moors, no one who'd put these three
 To death, avenging us, and through such deviltry
 Gain our favor, praise?
SOPHONISBA: May I with utmost daring

Through desperate means my way to welfare start preparing?
Here, Laelius, at your disposal stands a Queen
Who has no qualms about the threesome doing in,
To prove that Masinissa, the King that I did marry,
Rome made me see as friend, the Moors, as adversary,
And that a snow white heart behind brown breasts can dwell.

LAELIUS: Should I believe her words? So be it! See how well
She acts on what her mouth avers.

SOPHONISBA: I'll laugh, while pressing
The knife into their breasts. The three I'll start undressing.
Now pass the knife to me. Step closer to the light.
Good heavens! I am doomed! The knife I cannot quite
Hold onto. Mighty gods! My mouth and hands grow rigid!

LAELIUS: What? Can her fervid drive to kill so fast grow frigid?

SOPHONISBA: Woe! This . . .

LAELIUS: She daydreams?

SOPHONISBA: Is . . .

LAELIUS: Who?

SOPHONISBA: Syphax.

LAELIUS: Syphax?

SOPHONISBA: Yes!

BOMILCAR: She's in a trance?

SOPHONISBA: It's he!

BOMILCAR: Absurd!

SOPHONISBA: Beneath the dress,
About the sign his breast bears there can be no mistake!

MASINISSA: Who'd ever such a face as this for Syphax's take!

SOPHONISBA: Lift off his made-up face, the wig pull from his head.

SYPHAX: Alas, it's I. Don't be from your intent misled
By sheer coincidence, nor swayed by my high station.
To kings, much less than bonds, death causes aggravation,
Because their foes despise them, and friends, abominate,
As perjury they watch intriguers implicate.
Get going, Syphax, up! the dagger from her wrest,
Offense and love avenge!

MASINISSA: Stop, madman!

SYPHAX: I attest:
Far better that this knife pierce through her arteries' well,
Than to let prurient filth her breasts and lilies swell,
That her and my chilled blood, in black streaks fused, should
    slither,

Lest Masinissa's flames her glory cause to wither.

SOPHONISBA: My Syphax then a hangman for me here wants to be?

SYPHAX: Yes, in your blood this knife submerging merrily.

SOPHONISBA: My love in you such fierce revenge could have ignited?

SYPHAX: A wine-crazed dragon turns a love that has been slighted.

SOPHONISBA: What was it, sweet, I did, to cause you such disgrace?

SYPHAX: Unfaithful wretch! Behind him, you gave me second place!

SOPHONISBA: Us fate, not faithlessness, has from each other wrested.

SYPHAX: What is true love is by misfortune only tested.

SOPHONISBA: Forgive me, if your foot went slipping on this ice!

SYPHAX: Behold hypocrisy go slipping on its lies.

SOPHONISBA: The love for you within my bosom keeps on raving.

SYPHAX: How can the traitress still be for new nuptials craving?

SOPHONISBA: Because it grants me life, not harm and your defeat.

SYPHAX: How holds a heart that's pure a twofold love and heat?

SOPHONISBA: Harsh need made it a twofold seat in me acquire.

SYPHAX: You blind us both with suns of secondary fire.

SOPHONISBA: I swear you're both for me two suns entirely true,
My heart is dedicated and linked to both of you.
Remember, my sweet light, with what impassioned wooing
Until this day to keep your love I have been suing;
How I with searing heat, and you by lust possessed
Have melted in my lap, and languished on my breast;
How I breathed out my soul, your mouth with it infusing,
Your hand I would caress which, now my love refusing,
Turns murderous, slaying me. How oft your steadfast oath,
By fickleness forsworn, said neither death nor loath,
Time, fire, metal, stake, not even heavens' thunder
Would make you hate me, nor your jealousy us sunder.
Sooth, I believe that jealousy in you stirs vengeful rage.
Still, reason, what won't serve its purpose to engage,
With scorn casts to the wind. What joy's in it, my lover,
When your beloved, whose love you never can recover,
With you the storm destroys? and she can't swim away
Though fortune should a piece of board let drift her way?
True love no favor may to lovers true deny.
Besides, King Syphax might his enemy pacify,

If he to Masinissa will cede me willingly,
Whose prize by luck and virtue I have been meant to be.
If that's not done, what's lost too paltry is for giving.
But should it Syphax please to see my poor heart grieving,
And all my joy undone, I kneel here down for you;
With that suspended stroke now bravely carry through!

SYPHAX: Ye gods, have you as yet to play with me not tired?
My abject fall your wrath not cooling keeps, but fired?
Your rage is not snuffed out? Should love and jealousy
And lust and reason rack me? The yoke I now can see
With servitude the crowned neck beforehand sore besetting.
No, Masinissa, no, your axes, hooks start whetting,
Go, sharpen steel and sword, you won't with my consent
Rend from me Sophonisba. Or, changing my intent,
Shall I dispatch his bride with fame and profit added?
No! Certainly good works with feud cannot be wedded.
Damnation and disgrace upon the two I shed!
I wish on them decay, dread on their wedding bed,
Their throne in dust collapsed.

MASINISSA: The fool keep round here standing,
Until his rage abates, upon our mirth attending.
It's up to Laelius's discretion, for he knows
How best of Syphax and the town one should dispose.

SYPHAX: What perfidy! You dare before the public to infract
Troth, marriage vows, and oath? And with my foe compact
In front of me about my, not your, property?
Up, Syphax! With your fame's unscathed integrity,
With eyes that are not glazed, and heart that does not grieve,
Such horror you can't stand! Help ghastly pains relieve,
Her dagger use which she, to pierce my bosom, drew!

LAELIUS: Halt, Syphax! Wrest the knife from him! As captive, you
Can't choose the tomb and death. Yet it's not past conceiving
You'll see, before you think, your wife as widow leaving,
From Masinissa torn. Now lock these up for me.
Your judge and of the others Scipio will be.

CHORUS TO ACT III

(While Beauty and Conceit appear as mute figures in the background, Jealousy and Envy express consternation over their failure

to disrupt the marriage bond between Sophonisba and Masinissa.
Folly mocks and Reason rebukes the incomprehension of these
confused powers, while Despair closes the chorus with a grim
suggestion of the Queen's suicide.)

ACT IV

The setting is a royal hall.
Scipio. Laelius. Syphax. A crowd of Roman military commanders,
captains, and soldiers.

SCIPIO: The gods saw fit that we, upon the field of battle,
  Should Syphax's breach of peace victoriously settle.
  Your grateful debtors are posterity and Rome,
  And to the Capitol in triumph you'll be shown.
  And heaven, meanwhile, too, to us assistance rendered:
  For Utica and Tunis have also now surrendered,
  The right-hand wall of Carthage; the new town is thereby
  Already half-besieged. Their naval force did try
  With no success on our fewer ships descending.
  But now disclose what clever ruse you used, upending
  The great Numidian realm, that in the shortest span
  Came under our rule.
LAELIUS: When your courageous ken,
  Oh, most serene, grand hero, Hasdrubal had bested,
  And Masinissa on our side the foe invested,
  The forfeit realm devolved on him as rightful heir,
  From Syphax being stripped, who with no time to spare
  To raise another army in his realm was trying,
  Still bigger than the one at Utica, went flying
  Before your host's advance. With this new-gathered might
  My host and Masinissa's he engaged to fight.
  The enemy horse came, a rattling hail's profusion,
  Down on our vanguard; in the balance hung confusion
  And panicky retreat. The storm wind, though, did wane
  To everyone's surprise, when our footfolk came,
  And with closed columns Syphax's cavalry they scattered.
  As in the first assault their ardent zeal us battered,
  So lukewarm was their stand, so cowardly their flight.

And as their king with might and main to end their plight
Would range his fleeing host into a new position,
And in the forefront fights, he soon sees his ambition
His wounded horse bring down, and he, with those who fought
To rescue him, made captive, are before me brought,
Triumphant Scipio's foot to kiss here in submission,
While Masinissa with the cavalry division
To Cyrtha's walls proceeds to let them see the King,
With threats demands they start the town gates opening,
So instantly the fortress is his without a battle.

SCIPIO: The gods have made it clear that it's your hero's mettle
That sparks their influence, moves their celestial thrust,
Since easily our foe it humbles in the dust.
To show you that your virtue we properly esteem,
Your image etched in metal and marble bright will gleam,
As long as by the Tiber's current Rome is laved.
But, Syphax, into what will be your name engraved?
Where writ your evil fame and abject recollection?
You be the judge: whether against you to take action,
Rome has no cause to show? What could impel to this?
You stooped to perjury when you did breach the peace,
When you the bond dissolved that you to me attested.
Of shame, as earlier of troth, have you yourself divested?
You, perjurer, speak up, if Rome did give you cause
So wretchedly to breach the treaty's every clause?

SYPHAX: Almighty Scipio! I'm for my dereliction
So punished by the gods that no human conviction
Can make my woe more cruel in the least degree,
Even if ax and stake have been assigned to me;
I have been cast so deep, who once so high was living.
Both Rome and Carthage were one function to me giving—
That of their welfare's anchor—vied for my esteem;
With reverence they wafted me easy friendship's steam,
Like offerings to gods they brought their eager pledges.
This Asdrubal confirms, and Scipio alleges:
Each did his level best, they both did honor me,
To seem my special pet. The difference now you see!
Before me, Masinissa, in hedges hid, did live
But now scarce deigns I should his stirrup kisses give,
And as at dogs and henchmen Scipio snaps at me.

Learn how by gods' dread lightnings giants dwarfed can be!
Yet Syphax takes the blame! His foolish fury showing,
He raised this final storm, with empty bluster blowing,
As arms I would take up, and Rome I dared defy.
Because my raving craze the whole world could descry,
When I from Barcas's stem, snake of the Punic desert,
I did select a wife. It's there the heat was gathered,
The torch brought to my house, and plague sowed in my heart,
That's why now on my realm flames crack and brightly dart,
My welfare turns to ashes. And in my bed now lazes
The snake (I wish I never let upon her rest my gazes!)
Raised high, yes, to my lap, and to my breast held tight,
The worm who does in me the hate for Rome incite,
Medea, who Numidia's palaces ignited,
It's she who turned me gainst the fine guest I'd invited,
Like Busiris, in my hand the murder ax did thrust,
And me in mail she shod.

SCIPIO: Who flame and plague will trust,
And vipers on his breast, beneath his roof them carries,
Is not worth pitying. A prudent ruler buries
His ear and counsel deep, to women keeps them closed,
Like snakes, who in a circle the exorcist enclosed.

SYPHAX: There's no Ulysses who'd fend off this Circe's ruses.

SCIPIO: Who's foundered always will present such lame excuses.

SYPHAX: She is a scorpion, with poison always filled,
By death and frost in winter pretending to be stilled,
But when the sun and favor start stroking her and warming,
Her sting is worse than snakes', more fierce than bees when
    swarming,
She hides her sting behind her honeyed blandishment.

SCIPIO: Thus bee and scorpion entail their punishment.

SYPHAX: The former loses stinger, the latter, strength of stunning,
When we are stung by them. And still, the vilest cunning
Yet one vile instrument in fact to women gave,
In climbing to the top they use their husbands' grave
For their luck's cornerstone, their welfare thus renewing.
For though they have more poison than dragons fire-spewing,
Which lions locks in yokes, and eagles fells in flight,
The hollow stinger duct of scorpions is quite
More visible than those with women's poison baited.

What mischief hasn't yet my own wife instigated?
Numidia she topples, sets Kaccabe aflame,
Sees nothing but the brightest side, plays fortune's game,
Whose hand new wedding candles here already has lighted.

SCIPIO: Does Syphax rave by anger, fear, and woe excited?

SYPHAX: One thing brings solace, and my heartache fills with zest:
That my archfoe now kisses Sophonisba's breast;
And that this brute, this land's worst plague and infestation,
Infects his bed and house.

SCIPIO: Who in this conflagration
Partakes?

SYPHAX: It's Masinissa, whom her poisonous bite,
Which makes the looks of basilisks and newts seem slight,
Has more than me befuddled, and quicker set on fire,
Once she had gazed at him.

SCIPIO: Great gods! such mad desire
Can be residing in this hero's stalwart heart?

SYPHAX: Yes, since as spouse she holds in it the greater part.

SCIPIO: This foolishness resists a rational admission.

LAELIUS: What he has said is true. He brooked no opposition,
No earnest talk, no warning. He ran off in despair,
A stag in fullest rut, with killing, wrath did flare,
Burst into threats and oaths when I his plan tried thwarting.

SCIPIO: Alas, I wish you weren't such shame to me imparting!
Oh, more than noble hero! Whereto did drift your thoughts?
A woman for this town, which equals her to gods,
You chose to be its queen? You, lion of Numidians,
What evils would this worm not make into your minions?
The bites of scorpions sting most in the event
The sun's in Leo's house and Dog Star has ascent
As double harmfulness.

LAELIUS: Quite so. His spouse does stem
From Hanno, whom Carchedan severely did condemn
For walking a tamed lion with him upon a string.
Walks Sophonisba empty-handed? To one ring
Two lions she has tethered, two kings infatuated,
Who worships Ammon, Rome erstwhile had venerated,
The world in war enmeshed.

SYPHAX: She Syphax couldn't quite
Make tame, but I was hexed. I worshipped her eyes' light

More piously than Lybians the sun invoke.
My solace was her face, her sight did bliss provoke,
Her welfare was my wish, my god she was, in brief,
My heart, her shrine. And now, my shame she would as lief
Use as an oar of her well-being, wings of fortune,
Would with my bonds her tender gazes not importune,
She's kissing my old foe, laughs at my shackles' whir.
But, woe upon the bird by berries lured, who'd stir,
By love's allurement trapped. Rome will be realizing
Soon sand shoals, crags, where Sophonisba plays, are rising.
But if I see her punished for her perjury,
To go to Rome in heavy bonds gladly I'll agree.
CAPTAIN: Prince Masinissa's here and Scipio would greet.
SCIPIO: The Prince with open arms and greatest joy we meet.
    Into his room lead Syphax now without delay.

Masinissa. Scipio. Laelius. A crowd of Romans. A crowd of Masinissa's military commanders. A crowd of Numidian prisoners.

MASINISSA: Most fortunate Scipio! Propitious heavens may
    Send Africa in homage before your lordship stooping,
    Your fortune's wind soon down on Kaccabe come swooping!
    The fair and precious dust sweep into sea and fields!
    What Masinissa's hand and troth that never yields
    Has in Numidia begun that's salutary,
    The work is of our gods. Caught is our adversary,
    The capital as leaders reverences us.
    Here is the crown itself, if you disposed are thus,
    Dispatch it to the Capitol. Keys to Syphax's treasure
    And strongholds I present you; use them at your pleasure;
    The scepter, too, my people has to me returned,
    Now I tread native soil. Since Masinissa learned
    With little to make do: first, grace of heavens' regions,
    And then, Lord Scipio's favor, pluck of Roman legions,
    Regained my realm for me. And here's the standard, too,
    Of Syphax, which my arm, by custom and by due,
    Lays down before your feet. Besides, I bring you fettered
    The magnates of the realm, whose might has just been shattered;
    If Scipio accepts them as tokens of my plight,
    I claim no booty, nor the victor trophy's right.
SCIPIO: My brother and my friend with whom I have been sharing

My heart's half for some time: fame's candle brightly flaring
Which had his virtue lit in regions of the Moors
Glows over Abila. A friendship such as yours
According to its merit by Rome can't be requited.
This can't be even by a gold-cast statue righted
Of you, by Romulus's own, on shrine and market set.
For virtue is much more than that which artists fret;
And more than metal, ivory it should be rewarded.
Yet now the King and crown we take as was accorded,
And of Numidian captives take the teeming crowd,
The banners and the hoard, what once the foe endowed,
In terms of bonds, thus Rome with sundry thanks entwining;
It's there, to your great honor, today we're them consigning.
This instant Laelius these things will make secure.
But Masinissa offering us his keys to your
Realm's strongholds and his scepter at our feet submitting,
Shows great politeness. To reward him is befitting.
To be enriched by foes redounds to Rome's own fame.
He's our greatest friend, and these are his to claim.
Gods grant him that he may with all his kinsmen flower!
And Scipio with Rome will plead with all his power
That on his head should Africa still more crowns descry,
Whereon yet greater mountains will build up Rome and I.

MASINISSA: May gods Rome and their captain with their largesse
 sustain!
Upon their foes let lightning, hail, and brimstone rain!

Scipio. Masinissa.

SCIPIO: But wait, King Masinissa. A thought occurred to me.
 Where might be Sophonisba? For she must also be
 Of Rome most cherished prize. He's silent, he starts paling!
 He trembles!! What's his fear, what horror is assailing
 His aspect and his heart?
MASINISSA: Oh, friend!
SCIPIO: Speak up, man, speak!
MASINISSA: Oh, Sophonisba!
SCIPIO: Out with it!
MASINISSA: I am too weak
 To utter it!

SCIPIO: Is this a dream? Your mind and sense awaken!
MASINISSA: For Sophonisba is.
SCIPIO: Is what?
MASINISSA: To be forsaken?
SCIPIO: Quite right. To Rome today she will be taken hence.
MASINISSA: The thread that holds my life, luck's compass turns
     askance.
SCIPIO: What? Do your luck and pluck on our foe's life depend?
MASINISSA: Yes, Masinissa's spirit with hers he will expend.
SCIPIO: What kind of source is it whence such a madness burst?
MASINISSA: You'd better test the tree, ere you its fruits have cursed.
SCIPIO: Is it that Masinissa in love with her has fallen?
MASINISSA: Indeed! Because of her this joy has me befallen.
SCIPIO: Who yesterday was worse than spiders, snakes as foe?
MASINISSA: A gloomy grove oft turns into an altar's glow.
SCIPIO: Who with her mother's milk was hate and poison swilling?
MASINISSA: But dragons can through taming become a bit more
     willing.
SCIPIO: And Syphax through her willingness his realm has lost.
MASINISSA: The rose retains her worth though she a life had cost.
SCIPIO: A charming woman sets the wisest head atwitter.
MASINISSA: Love's sugar cannot faith and milk cause to go bitter.
SCIPIO: What does the hero's nerve in nasty bonds confine?
MASINISSA: Both virtue and her form, which are in her divine.
SCIPIO: In Rome and Africa don't some with her compete?
MASINISSA: No star in worth and glow the true sun can delete.
SCIPIO: Lust often sees a sun in paltry comet's mold.
MASINISSA: That grudge, that cannot smell a thing, should roses
     scold!
SCIPIO: Good looks are pretty poppies, not quickening life, but
     fazing.
MASINISSA: They wake the dead, whenever their pretty eyes are
     gazing.
SCIPIO: With reason you should kill the charm of full-blown
     curves.
MASINISSA: When ground and gable burn, a dousing hardly
     serves.
SCIPIO: Your love toward the top have you already carried?
MASINISSA: Of course, because I have the Queen already married.

SCIPIO: Oho! this craziness, is it to be believed?

MASINISSA: My good-luck star has wished it, gods' blessing it received.

SCIPIO: What men call fate may be their sin's dissimulation.

MASINISSA: Who can resist the lure of heavenly temptation?

SCIPIO: He's folly's victim whom voluptuousness ensnares.

MASINISSA: The Venus-worship thus its rites with ease prepares.

SCIPIO: God is, as spirit, chaste, chaste hearts' devotion heeding.

MASINISSA: The holy oil of pureness keeps marriage candles feeding.

SCIPIO: Not when blind instinct forces us on sheet ice to digress.

MASINISSA: Who stumbles isn't right away barred from leaves and grass.

SCIPIO: He does indulge in vice who's through his fingers peering.

MASINISSA: To what objective may your eagerness be steering?

SCIPIO: That Masinissa rend his marriage and his vow.

MASINISSA: This won't my conscience, nor will heaven this allow.

SCIPIO: Your matrimony's status as legal never rated.

MASINISSA: Can what the heavens forged be by man's law abated?

SCIPIO: By all the laws of war she's Rome's subservient slave.

MASINISSA: Perhaps, but my own claim to her I do not waive.

SCIPIO: One whom a poisonous wrath against Rome always fired.

MASINISSA: She is unjustly blamed for that which Syphax sired.

SCIPIO: You fight in vain for her, yourself you should subdue.

MASINISSA: By plaguing me and her, what good does Rome pursue?

SCIPIO: I pity you, my friend, to heart your sorrow taking.
My sensibility is in your woe partaking,
Your welfare is my care. So his advice don't cast
So grossly to the winds, whom proved has in the past
Experience as honest, who'd never thought of sparing
His blood for Masinissa. If you remember bearing
Me trust once on that day you came into my tent,
Where we a friendship pledge together did cement,
Whereafter to your hopes and fortune you conceded
To me free access, when to gain you have succeeded
This sought-for honesty, then don't imagine now
That Scipio at last to guile and crime will bow.
The virtues' magnet has supposedly attracted
You, as you vow, to me. Grand gifts by men affected

I never had but one which does enrich my might:
My heart finds far too meek love's ardent appetite.
To me is lewdness poison, lust always tartly tasted,
And, rest assured, that nothing so much as they has wasted
The spring of our times. No poisonous mildew saps,
No hoarfrost tender blooms in such huge numbers snaps
As does debauchery's heat. Against foul lechery's spell,
Grown men need stronger means than armies to repel,
For into snares for taming with sugared grains it lures,
Gives us angelic winks, and yet, pure hell assures.
This virtue Masinissa also must start learning,
To be just like I am, to see his name, too, burning
Among the stars upon sun's orb. Who tames debauchery,
Gains more than who ties foes to triumphs' panoply,
Nay, daunts all Syphaxes. No more Alcides tested
His heart and force, which giants, snake, and lion bested,
Than at the crossroads he avoided lechery.
You, stalwart hero, Syphax's realm crushed horribly,
Yet turn now milksop, let the cobwebs dull your senses?
Throw on the scale the vile and lewd luxuriances!
A handful of real honor twelve crates of lust outweighs.
Don't let your glory such a lurid stain disgrace.
A model let me be whose light is past dismissing.
Have you ever seen Scipio a woman kissing?
Have I Allucius's near-godlike gorgeous bride
With but a finger touched, into her gazes pried?
Yet Sophonisba couldn't to her a candle hold.
MASINISSA: Who'd dare on Scipio his own virtue mold?
SCIPIO: I am a man like you, but lust I did subdue.
MASINISSA: You sprang from Jupiter, divine blood flows in you.
    Your actions prove this. He (as snake, by passion fired,
    Who also on Olympia Alexander sired)
    About your mother's couch with that intent was seen.
SCIPIO: He is the gods' own son, who's dressed in virtue's sheen.
MASINISSA: I am from Lybia. In our towns won't flower
    A thing that isn't fiery. There sun and love do shower,
    More heat in wintertime, and with more force and might,
    Than when the Dog Star burns in your summer's glum
        midnight.
SCIPIO: Take Hannibal for model and mirror, there's none better,

Whose chastity serves love as its severest fetter.
At wine, he's always old, and ice, in beauty's face.
MASINISSA: Is he from Africa, yet heat his love won't brace?
SCIPIO: He's wise. Keep foes from seeing you shamed and red-
    faced turn.
And even stubborn Kaccabe your ears with laugh will burn;
The council summons home who, with petulant hand,
The olive branch do offer, to save their fatherland
Plant kisses on our feet, to Mother Earth keep praying,
With tears to peace they hope the Romans to be swaying.
Your tenth campaign allows you also your tenth ring,
Which you would game away as if a paltry thing,
Since you have not the will from lethargy to break.
I don't decide, since over what for Rome we take
By sword, Rome has first right. If Rome then shares allows,
She may grant you a portion. Hence Syphax and his spouse,
His realm, wealth, nation are, in fact, all Roman booty.
In brief, today to go to Rome now the Queen's first duty.
This is my final word. Decide what makes more sense:
Rome's favor, or the smoke of steamy prurience.
MASINISSA: Ah, Scipio, indeed! I've to and fro been rushing,
My face with blood suffused, most shamefully I'm blushing;
From eye and heart the tear of woe is breaking through!
Almighty warlord! I here do submit to you!
Dispose of Masinissa at will and at discretion.
But where may I consolement find and intercession
For what torments my soul, my conscience robs of peace,
Since I by hand and mouth to her have promised this:
That into foreign hands she'd never be delivered?
SCIPIO: This promise Masinissa's discretion, which has shivered
Far greater foes than plans of crazed lasciviousness,
Will wisely set aside. Your prudence now address.

Masinissa, alone.

MASINISSA: Ah! Sophonisba is to pine in Roman bondage?
This bitter core then hides inside the golden leafage;
Such spurious favors you, foul Romans, make us see,
You build up our hopes, fool our simplicity!
Your name to speak, like Saturn's, has me aggravated.
Numidia from Ceuta you deem best separated,

So that our feud may give you gold and blood as prize.
The breakup of our marriage such great boon signifies?
The eye-thorn Carthage you don't think can be uprooted,
World dominance fought out, the peoples' riches looted,
For which on every nation Rome gangrene foams and gall,
Unless Queen Sophonisba from our world you haul?
It's Hannibal, not Sophonisba, who your light effaces,
And now that threat good fortune through her erases.
She, next to me, has blocked his wheel and wings pulled out,
Unfeathered, he can't fly from Rome and from his rout.
How high Rome's climbed since I have joined them, made them
    stronger!
Carchedon's Juno won't ride lions any longer,
Her scepter and her bolt she dropped from either hand.
To be Alcides' scion Carthage can't contend.
Why should from force and thanklessness Masinissa smart?
Should Sophonisba go, must Sophonisba part?
Won't my eyes lose their light the moment she is gone?
The eagle's will go blind not sharpened by the sun.
Oh, rock-hard Scipio, whom had a tiger Caspian,
The Niger's basilisk, a she-wolf Arimaspian
On blood and venom nursed! Hyrcania's, Zemlya's ice
He's feeding in his heart; him, though hotly I'd entice
And wheedle him, in spite of love's consuming fire
Which from my breast broke forth, engulfing him entire,
Him pity does not melt. You'd think that virtue might
And troth deserve much more. My eyes' sole solace, light,
My idol Sophonisba, you're to be from me riven?
What gain for such a loss could possibly be given?
Gold mountains, heavy scepters they are promising.
Oh, simpleton! A circle wealth is that peace cannot bring,
A slave house of the soul, the dolt's false idolizing,
A golden mask which greed and worry is disguising,
Which poorer makes the poor, the hungry hasn't fed,
Which searched for is with sweat, is held with fright and dread,
And lost with heartache. Washed-out diamonds' bright sparkling
Pales next to Sophonisba. Ivory turns darkling,
When near her skin. Her mouth's two rubies outrank those
Of Taprobanes. What there in the Tagus flows,
One single hair from Sophonisba's head outprizes.

What are, then, crown and realm? Who's there that realizes
That every crown's a yoke, its gold, the weight of lead,
Each diamond on it, a feather grass instead,
The pearls are salt of tears, the rubies richly glowing
Are spilled-out princely blood, the purple's mellow flowing
Serves evil, for the fawners a swarm nest, there to play
The spade as trump, the royal jack blowing thus away?
No, Sophonisba! Realm, crowns, purple, scepters vying
With you are so much foam, bean husks, and bubbles flying.
Insatiable Rome! Numidia take and occupy,
As long as my Queen's lord is no one else but I!
Stop, Masinissa, at what shoals, what Scyllas steering
Are you your desperate ship? Your will you, wildly veering,
And masked desire let become your guiding light?
Don't forfeit staff and helm to lechery's delight.
With your Numidia you from the start had mated,
The kingdom is your spouse. To it you're dedicated,
Except for breach of vows, you can't endanger it.
For lordship is your god, an altar is your wit.
Yourself you would be putting out your eye of reason
And worse than Hannibal commit on luck high treason,
Who did at Croton Juno's golden statue mock.
Decide if of well-being or woman you take stock.
The clockwork of our acts, to reason's impulse ceding,
The eye must be their hand. Who, jack-o'-lanterns heeding,
Lust's pretense follows, in morass inevitably sinks.
A foolish love's eye only at passion's tinder winks.
For beauty's fraud, as vulture preys upon the tenderhearted,
As shark, the predator of boon. It's time you started
The lights of sober reason which Scipio has lit
To follow to the port! What would your blind rush hit
As goal for Sophonisba? Three nights of lusty bundling,
And lips so often kissed, breasts roused by prior fondling,
In brief, a wench estranged from shame and void of troth,
A Helen with a swanlike body full of loath,
And with a raven's heart. Should you such woman marry
Who, whom today she hugs, tomorrow tries to bury,
Who kisses Masinissa, while Syphax lives, who sets
Out traps for him, and weaves a mesh of tricky nets?
No, Masinissa, no, your lechery start damning,

She is a poisonous branch from Barcas's yew tree stemming,
Who those, beneath her rest and slumber gathering,
By shading them destroys, decay apportioning,
With poisonous dower poised; for her, pure love's not fitting.
Hers is the crocodile's way: when human flesh he's eating,
He's seized by sullen grief; yet she can't wet an eye,
Should Syphax in the ominous crocodile's jaws die.
But, wait! is there no hope her ways she might be mending?
For oft misfortune's foot, to punishment's block bending,
Learns wisdom at long last. But no, old vices bear
No clean uprooting. Not the wind, time, water, air,
The putrid stench from reeking vessels can be slaking.
Off, Sophonisba! of your coffin measure they are taking,
And sealed has been your fall. But, woe, what agony
This sentence causes us. My heart floats in the sea!
I wade in sand and dread! Can there be no backtracking?
Who'd have luck, fame, and laurels flourish, never slacking,
His name among the stars in votive temples etched,
Away from wavering senses' crazed path he must be snatched.

Masinissa. Disalces.

MASINISSA: Your coming is well-timed, Disalces.
DISALCES: Ready, Sire,
   For your commands!
MASINISSA: Today, my nuptials did conspire
   Skies, reason, accident, to split in two as rot.
   Now bring me glass and wine and venom on the spot!
DISALCES: Good heavens! Why the venom?
MASINISSA: Comply with what we're saying
   But, oh, what quick tattoo my heartbeat I feel playing!
   Against my mind are warring sagacity and lust,
   As one, and then the other at each other thrust.
   And yet the knot of doubt is open, loosely trailing,
   As love has missed, but reason scored, its goal not failing.
DISALCES: The things he asked for, here I'm bringing to the King.
MASINISSA: What wretches, we! In poison and death still
      glittering!
   To throttle us, a rope from silk and purple's plaited.
   Does it hurt less, when aloes wood is indicated
   To burn us at the stake, or when with emeralds set

Are daggers which for our throats they keenly whet?
In jasper and in crystal the venom comes. What wonder!
For this is justified: like glass we fly asunder.
But how: should I myself her such a prize present?
Why not? What I'm forced to do she can't resent!
Her dream, aside from me, who's able of enlightening?
No! Jupiter's not present, when he hurls his lightning!
With you to Sophonisba I this poison send:
Announce to her I'm still her husband and her friend,
My double promise I have not forgotten ever.
But, since the mighty ones now our marriage sever,
And to remain her cherished spouse heaven won't allow,
Assure her I won't break what was my second vow:
That into Roman hands she will not fall while living;
For which as surest remedy this cup to her I'm giving.

DISALCES: Woe! How will Sophonisba take this awful blow!
MASINISSA: If bravely, it will be her greatest honor's show!
DISALCES: Which shuts her in her grave?
MASINISSA: But plucks her from confinement.
DISALCES: Oh, were I spared to act on this adjust assignment!
    With horror crawls my skin. The death of kin her land
    Makes known by heralds only if, to death condemned,
    They in the dungeon lie, soon to be executed.
MASINISSA: She should take heart that her own line's in Belus
        rooted,
    That she is Hasdrubal's, the mighty suffete's, child,
    Elissa's grandchild, who by flames had been beguiled,
    Born in Chaedreanech, the clan's home by tradition;
    That worms do not appear in graves that are Phoenician,
    And that Hamilcar's head, with all those who can rival
    With him in virtue, is adored; and should recall
    That two crowned heads, once in the past, for her hand did
        woo,
    So that this gift as lesson, solace she might view.
DISALCES: What of your nuptials, and your faith, what of your
        oath?
MASINISSA: The scepter when's at stake, such vanities I loathe.
DISALCES: Her sweetheart you can't be, but does she merit killing?
MASINISSA: Indeed. It's thus her welfare I shall be fulfilling.
DISALCES: A Roman could with greater fame perform this deed.

MASINISSA: Such man would do his best her killing to impede.
DISALCES: Why deal with her, oh, Prince, with such unusual rigor?
MASINISSA: So that in Rome she doesn't in the triumph figure.
DISALCES: Her death should bring the Prince some favor and some gain?
MASINISSA: Be quiet, go, Disalces, my patience do not strain!
But, halt! I feel I'm done for, going numb, and trembling.
Go on! No time to doubt. Suspense I'm not dissembling.
Forgive! Oh, look, my heart and eye both break!
Go on, on! for the end no other course can take.

CHORUS TO ACT IV

(The chorus enacts the topos of Hercules at the crossroads, facing the choice between the rival disputants, Voluptuousness and Virtue. Hercules takes the path of Virtue which conducts to a hero's laurels and eternal life, and extols Leopold, the victor over the Ottoman empire, the modern analogue to Carthage.)

ACT V

The setting is within the Temple of the Sun and the Moon.

Sophonisba. The Priestess Elagabal. The Ghost of Dido.

SOPHONISBA: Is this the sanctuary where from two stars do learn
Blind mortals signs whereon their future yet will turn?
ELAGABAL. It is. Because those eyes on earth see everything,
And day and night give light, their spirit laboring
The dismal intellect of mankind to enlighten,
Thus those who knowledge of things future yearn to heighten
And here the sun and moon invoke with reverence,
Their wish see granted. Sophonisba, in this sense
Can here herself elect the way that she would learn
Of what her future holds. On earth stars' spirits burn,
Within the Theraphim: here, Thammuz's image soars,
And here our Hecate's. Her prompting is the source
In souls wherefrom love's mutual passion starts to brood.
Thus hearts must either open or they must occlude;

This wheel's each turn controls them, each loosening of this
   band.
Here is a firstborn's head, which by a high priest's hand
Was torn off from its neck, in brine and spices salted,
When its erratic course that comet would have vaulted.
Who on this golden tablet Moloch's name will write,
A candle for him lights, and stays throughout the night,
Before the altar kneeling, gains answer to petition.
This gold and silver altar did Dido once commission
That into it the sun's and moon's own force might flow.
Hence what concerns our future it can help us know,
Things that no soothsayer is likely to disclose,
But only certain days may you it questions pose:
When Hada enters Cancer, Adad, the Lion's house.
But clearer could no oracle to us espouse
The truth than that great spirit who in Dido's grave hovers;
This rock did hollow out her cult's devoted lovers,
Like that which Dido's fame at Kaccabe presents.
SOPHONISBA: Elissa's spirit stirs what kind of reverence?
ELAGABAL: You must take off your shoes; Elissa's form embracing,
   Send blood off from your arm into the fire racing.
   Behold this white wool cap: your hair with it you top,
   Throw incense on the altar, a myrtle branch pick up.
   Next, Dido's grave must be with apples consecrated,
   Whose culture Derceto at Cyprus innovated.
   You'll sleep on Dido's grave, once all these rites are done.
SOPHONISBA: When will my plea be heard by her and by the sun?
ELAGABAL: As soon as at first light the sunrise rays start surging
   Upon Elissa's image, a vision starts emerging,
   That to the sleepers here their destiny will show.
SOPHONISBA: A vision? and therewith the sun ignites its flow!
ELAGABAL: Yes, Dido will appear, a purple habit wearing,
   With emeralds in her hair, a Carchédon bow bearing,
   That's slung across her back, the arrows are of gold;
   Her features and her charm the same as those of old.
SOPHONISBA: How do the spirits then their oracle convey?
ELAGABAL: The Earth Spirit at Delphi the priestesses will sway
   Our future to disclose. Dodona's fane of oak
   Speaks through two doves, at times, through oaken boughs it
     spoke,
   Or through a brassy dragon Asclepius has spoken,

And Hammon's horn-topped head did vouched-for truths
  betoken.
Yet through her mouth and belly Elissa can alone
Divulge more clearly all that there is to be known.
Now, sleep! the time is near, the smaller stars have faded.
SOPHONISBA: Ere dawn to answer she then cannot be persuaded,
  Since normally all spirits do favor best the dark?
ELAGABAL: Yes, who of Hecate and Moth display the mark.
  Elissa's ghost alone bright daylight does enliven
  As sun child of great Baal. And other ways are given
  To quicken Theraphim thanks to the world's main eye.
  Its light is full of spirit. It takes one ray to fly
  To Memnon's stony image, whose lifeless lips send rolling
  A pleasurable sound. When light starts cliffs ensouling,
  Then Apis's column to the sun its face will turn
  As heliotropes do. No sunrise will there burn,
  Unless a kiss it on Serapis's statue throws,
  And sweetest milk from hundred breasts outpouring flows
  Of Isis the abundant, as soon as by her hand
  The lights are lit. Osiris, by this holy brand
  Spurts out the wine that from the altar runs in trickles.
SOPHONISBA: Assailed by sleepiness, I feel sweat's tingling prickles.
ELAGABAL: Upon the hollowed altar a ray falls from the sky.
  The tutelary deity begins to prophesy.
DIDO'S GHOST: You, our world's both heart and eye,
  Which quickens earth and sea, the stars with glow endowing,
  Elysian fields you too must ply,
  And to the sun our shade is still devoutly bowing.
  Elissa, though her life she's rendered,
  Her manly heart has not surrendered,
  Her shade about her tomb still errs, more busy, deft,
  Than erstwhile in the world, ere she'd her body left.
  She's still sun's priestess after her demise;
  Her ghost was, like Sicharba's devoted to the sun,
  She still burns laurel wood, her blood she's spraying on
  The altar's flames, as sun's due sacrifice.
  Comforting her husband's ghost, whom his brother's ax did
    tumble,
  With the balm of loyal loving, from her wounds, which trickling
    drained,
  By herself the oil of living from her arteries she strained,

As Hiarbes into snares hoped to see her honor stumble.
This is why my Carthage does my name as goddess reverence,
And my soulless shade can therefore future things tell in
    advance.
But, oh! my Carthage, woe! what sky-high city you!
In flame and fire I can see your glitter crumbling,
Behind a plow the oxen draw furrows, slowly lumbering,
Where once my oxhide such far-reaching borders drew.
Where images of brass and marble now are standing,
There moss and grass will be and soot,
And sprawling beech trees taking root,
For forage sheep on walls and towers will be fending
Which more than forty yards aloft are jutting,
Where now are elephants and people strutting.
Since Rome to fret about security is prone,
It would see Carthage now to carrion transmuted,
To rubble have forthwith reduced its every stone,
For even so could Rome be ravaged and uprooted.
A prelude has been Cyrtha's and Numidia's fall
Reflecting faithfully what Carthage might befall.
Oh, wretched Sophonisba! Your downfall has me crying!
Your Syphax bears the yoke, by fate's decrees you're dying!
Yet not unjustly judged at all.
You're pouring oil on flames, wood brings he to the fire.
The Moor will be the Romans' thrall.
What pity you weren't fathered by Elissa's sire!
But if you find one whit that we may have in common,
Regard the downfall which your woe is spicing up,
See Hasdrubal lose nerve, his spouse her courage summon;
As he crawls into bonds, she'll in the fire drop.
Hence save in time what fame and honor is concerning.
In Masinissa's breast there hardly dwells more trust
Than in Hiárbes' heart. Their purpose lewd is lust,
A lesson from my woodpile and theirs you should be learning.
It is the greatest boon to ashes to be turned,
Ere realm and scepter has the deities' lightning burned.
But do not start in women's fashion weeping,
For he who to the winds pledged troth and oaths has cast,
To Carthage wood and brimstone brings for her fiery blast,
Unlikely silk and gold as profit will be reaping.

So Masinissa, whom the town
Carchédon nurtured to renown,
Will crowns indeed, but as a slave, be wearing.
Rome, which the world's enslavement holds
For fate, which heaven's will unfolds,
For Masinissa's race the irons is preparing.
A yoke I see his grandson drag along.
Yet palms, triumphs, and fortune's flower
Not always will to Rome belong.
This war once over, safety's dubious dower
Will rock Rome into sleep and laziness.
The plebes, wealth, power with pride the nobles cause to swell,
And pluck, become the servant of voluptuousness,
Will Rome's course downwards with growing speed impel.
The Gothic deluge, Wendish swarms and thunder
Will wrest away from Roman hands their plunder.
But these brigands' might quite mortal fails in our earthly orb,
Just like Carthage, of whose horror Tunis is the hub becoming,
For the Arabs' race accursed, rage of God, Earth's plague, is
    coming,
Like a deluge, both our kingdoms to take over and absorb.
Yes, the Saracens' wild current, which no sluices are restraining,
Glow of Musa's banners, in the Iber, Boetis mirroring,
And in fair Garumna's course, till the mighty clan that's reigning
Down in princely Austria, earth and orb comes rescuing.
Turk, Moor, crescent pale at golden wedding candles being
    lighted,
When Prince Philip weds the noblest blood that sprang from
    Ferdinand,
And Granada, their last nest, with his heart is reunited.
Clearly it's the last disclosèd treasure which rich nature's hand
Will unveil, a world that's new, for the old one was too small
For the House of Austria, mighty heroes, one and all.
Atlas and Alcides managed just one single sphere to shoulder,
Alexander just one world had been able to ensnare,
And yet Austria's own brood in such giants' tales is bolder:
On each shoulder not too heavy feel two worlds they carry there.
They must rescue Africa from her tyranny and fetters,
Which by Omar were imposed, but their vanquishing sword
    shatters.

King Charles, of that name the fifth, with flags that crush
   resistance,
Which Tunis, Tripoli, Bizerte, Aphrodis
Will view with trembling, points to triumphs in the distance,
And teaches he's much left to win apart from these.
Amidas kisses on the Second Philip's foot impresses,
While Suleiman as King of Tunis him addresses.
But all these feats we rightly dub
Mere prelude to what is rehearsing
Now Leopold, the lion cub,
Who schemes more deeds, more force is nursing.
And the Ister, Neutra, Rab Saracen blood will be staining;
Eagles facing, Mohammed his pale crescent will roll up,
Nor will Africa's vast beaches Austrian conquests ever stop.
Cyrtha, Carthage you will see laurels on his forehead raining
And his sword, with triumph dripping, Muhmed's bands will
   cut in two,
When the lion brings the Spanish lioness for him to woo.
With the crocodile and dragon there behold the eagle playing,
As if they were hares or bats, or a doe, whom fear is swaying,
And now Europe's bird imperial flashes thunderbolts and rays,
When the tutelary beast of Africa its fiery brimstone sprays.
Thus Africa and Carthage are in ruin lying.
Up, Sophonisba, this is a good day for dying.

Sophonisba. Elagabal. Adherbal. Hierba. Himilco.

SOPHONISBA: Oh, wretched Africa! Gods lightweight like a
   feather,
Why would you pour on us this doom and bad-luck weather?
Oh, wretched Sophonisba, oh, sorry fatherland!
But, courage! Let's not be seized by the enemy's hand!
Not Masinissa's vice, nor Roman fulmination,
Nor perfidy let's feel. A soothing consolation
For those cast in despair, the foe thus to forestall.
My intimate priestess friend, bring hither from the hall
My dearest children; for eternal glory vying,
Will Sophonisba prove Elissa's peer in dying.
Their vanished spirit do accept, their oath and pledge:
You, no one else I wish to kiss on life's last edge.
This very night in close embrace with you I will be huddling.

It's clear mere thick haze our mind had been befuddling
Back when my Syphax's mouth and Masinissa's lip
Were sucking on my breast. My heartache's cutting deep,
My inmost soul is bleeding. Now, darling children, hurry
To hug me; to the claws of our adversary
You're bound to be consigned. But if you have the nerve
Your blood, like mine, allow as offering to serve,
Ere you'd see Africa by other nations plundered,
The Moors' nobility like outcasts' offal squandered,
Yourselves weighed down with chains!

ADHERBAL, HIERBA: We opt for death and fame,
Make clear your wish. We'll flee from servitude and shame.
Whatever you command, will be by us abided.

SOPHONISBA: Let's then, since our fall the gods have decided,
And heavens sanctioned, let's now staunchly Dido's crown
Of martyrdom achieve, and castle, temple, town
Burn down, as victims high by ourselves elected.
Posterity no grander crypt could have for us erected,
Than being by the ashes of Africa concealed,
And in the temples' dread as dust and corpses sealed!
A grave site from the foe are we then to solicit?
No balm can save us from decay's and maggots' visit,
Indeed, what spares the worm, the Romans will not spare
Who corpses search for gold, all sepulchers strip bare.
Flames won't conserve for them husks even as our traces,
Which they could desecrate. The flame that us embraces
Must every man honor who brings god offerings.
Besides, it is this flame that serves the soul as wings,
When to the stars it soars. By fire invigorated
Are earth and sea. By earthly glow impersonated,
It does sun's beauty spread, sun's holy effigy.
No beast needs fire, save man, whose essence flutters free
From stars. It cleanses all that is contaminated,
As spirit of the world, by it all's animated,
It is inception and incineration, too.
How fortunate the grave which fire makes us woo:
Be off at once and seize the altar's torches, fire
The castle and the fane. Oh, more than blessed pyre!
Where, integrated, Queen and realm their dust confound,
On fresh-lit flames her blood will make a hissing sound.

ELAGABAL: Your children, Sophonisba? What end are you
  pursuing?

ADHERBAL, HIERBA: Let us!

ELAGABAL: What? Make you burn?

SOPHONISBA: Yes, yes!

ELAGABAL: Think what you're doing!
  The ire of the gods with flames you'd aggravate?

SOPHONISBA: The gods themselves such service should appreciate.

ELAGABAL: When temples, effigies with crackling flames fierce
  burn?

SOPHONISBA: Ere into foreign idols them the foe can turn.
  That Rome, which calls a rock, not our gods, divine,
  Which stripped the olive tree at Gades' holy shrine,
  The emerald fruit it bore on golden branches ravaged,
  While in Pygmalion's shrine Alcides' bones disparaged,
  Won't spare this shrine, to Romulus will it consecrate,
  The killer in him, and the she-wolf celebrate.
  The whore called Flora will begin the moon abating,
  With fear and pallors Rome will Febris be placating.

ELAGABAL: Yet incense Rome, too, brings the sun as sacrifice.

SOPHONISBA: The sun itself its own profaning prophesies.
  You, Children, go, ignite all, for the sun loves fire.

ELAGABAL: Your children and yourself claim sun and gods as sire?
  Wait! do not rush at them, your house and home let stand.

HIMILCO: Serenest, there's a messenger to whom you must attend.

SOPHONISBA: We fear ill tidings.

HIMILCO: It's King Masinissa's message.

SOPHONISBA: This, too, bodes ill. What now? Should I deny him
  passage?
  Yes, yes! but no! I will upon him here attend.
  Misfortune's aloe taste, though bitter, won't offend
  Her, who has gall upon her mother's bosom savored.
  Have courage! Ruin's outwaited whoever's wavered.

*Disalces. Sophonisba. Adherbal, Hierbal. Himilco. Micipsa. Elag-
abal. Ladies-in-waiting.*

DISALCES: Serenest Queen, whose spirit with heroic grace
  And firm resolve can stare into misfortune's face,
  It is your rock-hard heart which, fortune's impacts braving,
  Stays anvil-like inert, the path for me is paving,

My fearfulness gives dare that I should make so bold
(The gods perceive the feelings which do my heart enfold!).
You, worthy one,—would that on roses you were treading,—
I bear but sigh-fraught news, heartrending tidings spreading.

SOPHONISBA: Since I don't fall by chance, you needn't hide from
    me
The cruel facts of statecraft's shrouded perfidy,
That coffins sows with tulips, lets tears on murder hover.
Who's planning our death without delay discover!

DISALCES: The gods I do invoke as truthful witnesses
That Masinissa with hellfire's dread distress
Me in this wrought-up state, disturbed, half-dead is sending.

SOPHONISBA: The foes rejoice when one is in the harbor landing.

DISALCES: He calls for death himself, at friends and light he
    swears,
Himself he's cursing, and the times, because he cares
About his marriage oath, by him as holy cherished,
Which he can't keep, and her, whom hope alone had nourished,
On whom his very soul, with ardor still aglow,
And his own blood, as food he'd pledge he would bestow.
He would all for her welfare to poisonous worms deliver
With readiness, which both their limpid bosoms shiver;
Yes, by his screaming flesh both troth and oath he'd seal,
If this did servitude and death with solace heal.
Ah, how he does deplore the Romans' grim, hard rigor
He tried in vain to change with unabating vigor.
Harsh Scipio splits wedlock and the law in two.
He says: Rome will as slave Queen Sophonisba view;
In Rome his pomp and triumph she must beautify.
She'll feel what storms in Masinissa's heart must vie,
And how his soul must hurt, since now, no effort, care,
His blood's last drop will manage his lovely Queen to tear
Out of the tiger's maw, the lion's clawed detention.
The life of his beloved could save no intervention;
His loyalty and oath hence poison bring and death.
Her birth, wit, dignity, the state of her distress,
And fatherland will lead her to the right decision,
If dying she prefers to fetters' rough attrition.

SOPHONISBA: Hail, welcome drink, which I so happily receive,
Since Masinissa has no better gift to give.

Sought-after freedom juice, desired marriage portion!
Disalces, surely no apple can apportion
Me more delightful balm, no grapevine sweeter wine
Than Masinissa's drink, its poison making mine.
Advise him, friend, who now as Queen I am dismissing
That we with pleasure are this drinking vessel kissing,
And that our mouth will gladly soon this nectar sup.
May Masinissa live, recalling, through this cup,
A pleasant night him wishes the one who here expires.
Go, tell him what concerning the two of us transpires:
The body's cleft, not love. We're sorry thoroughly
For having sinned against our fame through vanity,
That for the second time untimely we've remarried,
While fate bade us a grave to dig, and to be buried.
But dying with resolve will every stain efface,
And fame and laurels our virtue's dread and ashes grace.

*Sophonisba. Adherbal. Hierba. Tychaeus. Hiempsal. Himilcc
Micipsa. Ladies-in-waiting.*

SOPHONISBA: My intimate friend, the golden day at last is dawnin
Of luck, of vanity, on whom all souls are fawning,
The yoke to shuffle off, the mask to tear away
Of empty specters who with fear would us belay.
Dull eyes alone themselves in death's dark shadow fritter.
To pampered lips alone the aloe's taste is bitter.
Like civet balm and amber preserved inside the jar,
So is heroic spirit. What things inside it are,
Absorb the fragrance. And the gravest irritation
By patience is made sweet.
HIMILCO: Our time's odd deviation!
Is our kingdom's sun inclining to its tomb?
SOPHONISBA: The suns grow splendid when they golden hue
assume.
MICIPSA: What kind of sin with so much woe are we redressing?
SOPHONISBA: More than the heavens punish we have been
transgressing.
HIMILCO: The sin of Masinissa and perfidy are spared.
SOPHONISBA: In time his perfidy my own's pay will have shared.
A sin is for a sin a tool of equal measure.
Diuspitar whets his bolt when napping at his leisure.

And with this brimstone earth and world does terrorize,
Which to the stars did earlier from earth as vapor rise.
Unfaithfulness struck back which Syphax had affected
Whom earlier I betrayed. It's high time that I acted
On Masinissa's deed and what the fates exact!
Come, truthful freedom juice, my fetters disconnect!

MICIPSA: Serenest Queen, what's this? for him you so much care
Who has no fonder wish than that you should despair,
It's to his gruesome joy you blood and spirit vow?

SOPHONISBA: This offering does me more good than Masinissa
now.

TYCHAEUS: When he, like Saturn, his own flesh is devouring?

SOPHONISBA: Though I am hurt by him, he by the overpowering
Harsh Scipio is hurt.

TYCHAEUS: He bows to Roman might?

SOPHONISBA: Triumphant violence makes all injustice right.

TYCHAEUS: If he can't free you, he should not arrange your killing.

SOPHONISBA: In freedom's dire straits death is my wish fulfilling.

TYCHAEUS: It's nature's freak, ambition's, and revenge's child.

SOPHONISBA: Believe me, in this venom the oil of love runs wild.

HIMILCO: Upon your fleshless bones your spouse his luck's
erecting.

SOPHONISBA: Inside the crypt we are most precious stones
detecting.

MICIPSA: The body's searing pain, for friends, most abject woe.

SOPHONISBA: The pain is cured by death, the woe with time will
go.

HIMILCO: Not from all consolation the gods you yet restrain.

SOPHONISBA: But Romans in steel collars begin us to enchain.

MICIPSA: And heaven can from bond and iron loosen you.

SOPHONISBA: If you yourself your lifeline bravely cut in two.

HIMILCO: Rome for such noble blood won't seek such harsh
solution.

SOPHONISBA: For Regulus in Sophonisba Rome seeks retribution.

MICIPSA: Does Rome by right the Queen another's fault impute?

SOPHONISBA: The right lies where one triumphs, impatience
breeds to boot.
Don't set upon me now, my spirit stop assailing,
This is the time to die. The poisonous cup's regaling
Our bounty is indeed, to goddess raising me.

Did not Hamilcar, too, become a god, as he
Withdrew from Gelo's hand, his life span quickly shivered,
Himself as his own victim to the flame delivered?
I'm dying; you, Elissa, playmate I'll be true.
Though, Melcarthos, no firstfruits I'll sacrifice for you,
Do not reject my corpse; Tychaeus, not my pleading.
Your welfare bear in mind; from Cyrtha's huts receding,
Shall now your hero's arm from Rome Carchédon save.

TYCHAEUS: Dear Queen, I'll stand by you, your priest I'm to the
    grave.

SOPHONISBA: I die in ecstasy. My life so fraught with sorrow
    For me holds no more joy. No bounties holds tomorrow.
With my King Syphax rose my own good fortune's sun,
And now with him it sets; and so its rapid run
Heads for misfortune's sea, which is but vapors loosing
And thunderbolts above, and in eyes tears producing.
If heart more blood now than the ocean water cries,
It's not that heavens just black stars show to my eyes,
It's not that pearl and gold are from our head now straying,
It's not that we've quit purple, in shrouds ourselves arraying,
No! But our children's fall, our friends' laments and pain,
Are what assails my breast, cuts heart and soul in twain.
Oh, would that my own bonds your freedom still could buy,
My blood your savior be! We'd welcome that we die,
With joy would Roman yoke on our shoulders lay!
But, oh! what meager solace! Beside death, aught else may
Be freedom's anchor, or as sorrow's harbor serve.
Dear friends, do spare your grief, your worried winks reserve.
Steep cliff and spirit won't from storm and fate collapse.
The oak resists the wind which flimsy poplars snaps.
My children, heart's delight, hug me with all your passion,
Vouchsafe me your last kiss. May gods show you compassion,
Since I, as friend, must leave you, helpless, unconsoled.
Come here, and with a kiss give blessings hundredfold.
Himilco, here the ring with our seal you're taking,
As a remembrance and, yourself a mirror making,
Show how there is no seal misfortune's hand won't smite;
One moment often can snuff out our luck and light.
Micipsa, as a sweet remembrance you are getting
Queen Sophonisba's portrait. The stones which are its setting

With star-bright sheen about her face they this assert:
A diamond may even into a quartz convert!
Orynthia, this jewel is yours, and Elenisse's
This necklace, Agatha's, this ring, and all the kisses
As this now dying mouth may unto you bestow.

ORYNTHIA: Cold turns my heart in me, my limbs all icy grow.

SOPHONISBA: My pearls, and these Elissa's earrings start removing.
Keep these, Elgada, thus my love for you I'm proving.
My now so ruinous station to you should illustrate
Why pierced ears are a sign of those of highborn state.

ELGADA: In heaven you will see your boon itself completing.

SOPHONISBA: Quite so. I know I will. With wreaths let us cease
feting,
Which earthly are and dry, a withering delight.
And so we wish the earth and shadow a good night.
Elissa "You are freeborn!" keeps reiterating.
My guardian spirit on my pierced ears keeps on grating,
He says: thus every slave is branded now in Rome.
Eternal life can earn as solid right alone
Stoutheartedness in death.

ELGADA: Our corpses hereabout lying
Your holy vanguard be!

ELENISSE: Let us precede in dying
The queen, ere she, unflinching, her life will sacrifice.

SOPHONISBA: No, dearest children, no, curb your resentment's
cries,
Revive your soul and spirit. You are not so resented
By Rome the way I am.

ELENISSE: Our brows we've then consented
To bow to fate's grim rage which giants reeling sends,
And strikes crown-bearing heads? The bolt that trunks upends
Weak branches too must splinter.

SOPHONISBA: Low hedges it does skirt,
When cedars it strikes down. Your minds from fear avert,
Don't bog down in despair. Seek cheer, encouragement
From heavens' grace and favor, which hold me in contempt.
But what, dear children, can against your woe as aid,
Your mother leave, whom gods' decree condemned to fade;
Whom fate already had of her estate deprived,
Ere death the right to its inheritance revived?

Throne, purple, crown, and realm have to the foe been handed.
Two swords remain: to Syphax's hip this one appended,
That one the doughty fist of Hasdrubal bedecked.
That's your bequest. Your soul if ever should affect
The nimble spark of virtue, our fathers' glorious image,
And if your veins contain a drop of that grand lineage
Which Barcas's stem has nursed, in time you will see steel
Avenge us. One last time come closer, if you will,
To have these swords to you by Mother once more handed.
Yet, what's this stir about? By Lybians are tended
No dragons that are wilder than are our foes.
When Rome a head lops off, the victim's child, too, goes
Upon the chopping block. For you, too, will send dying
This lioness's rage. With corpses all 'round lying
Will Rome amuse itself, strike us with direst pain.
But those should perish who a shameful life disdain!
Away! Let us the drink of Masinissa favor!
This poison doesn't poison: in this glass I savor
The mix of boon and freedom. With it, you I toast.

ADHERBAL: You see me favorably to your pledge disposed.

HIERBA: I crave this nectar which beyond all else is sweeter.

SOPHONISBA: It's sweet since need and nerve the drink do make
    less bitter.

HIERBA: To me, then, dearest mother, this drink you'll have to
    pass.

SOPHONISBA: Help drain dry our sorrow's barrel with this glass.

HIMILCO: Micipsa, shall we then the princes' lives see shattered?

HIERBA: You don't prefer to see us dead, than basely fettered?

MICIPSA: There nothing yet divine assistance to forestall.

HIEMPSAL: Who won't go willingly will violently fall,
    When fate a blow delivers. The glass pass me, dear brother,
    In which to leave enough for me I must you bother.

SOPHONISBA: Who dies unfazed, he truly laughs at fate, time, and
    foes,
    Gains peace and fame for vanity and terror's needless throes.
    Come for the parting kiss, oh, Children worth adoring,
    As you here dying lie, my heart on you's outpouring.
    My eyes are turning dim, they're staring into space,
    My limbs are growing cold.

HIEMPSAL: Now me and her embrace,

My brother: here our bodies nothing can divide,
Our souls, too, undivided, thus ever shall abide.
HIERBA: One heaven girds the souls, three bodies in one vault.
SOPHONISBA: Should as a funeral bier your cradle, too, be palled?
ORYNTHIA: Help, heavens! They decline, now on the earth they're
   lying,
SOPHONISBA: And as we fade (good night!) our fears and woes are
   dying.
ELENISSE: Our bad-luck star must rise, their suns plunge to their
   doom.
HIMILCO: The Roman anger storm at us alone will boom?
   Micipsa, let us to a doughty death aspire,
   Flee jail and shame, but peace, and honor, face, acquire!
MICIPSA: Micipsa hails the thought. Allow our noble sword,
   Before a servile knife through our throats has bored;
   With fearless fight and wounds with fancy purple glowing,
   To princes whom we fealty till our death are owing,
   We sacrifice ourselves. A thrall grasps highest good,
   Who troth and fame achieves and whose spurting blood would
   Anoint his master's corpse.
AGATHE: Gods, lightweight like a feather,
   Why do you pour on us such fulminating weather?
   Now Africa herself with her own steel condemns.
   The heroes' fist the sword into own bowels rams.
   They're falling; heavens help! The kingdom's stays are falling.
   To journey to redemption, dear sisters, let's stop stalling,
   Our breasts' untainted milk turn purple by this sword.

Masinissa. Orynthia. Elenisse. Menalippe.

MASINISSA: Halt, Sophonisba! what? what basilisk has poured
   Its deadly gaze's poison for its own undoing?
   Can now your madness be your own demise pursuing?
   Woe! Sophonisba, what? already dead and cold?
   Confounded menials! Not one of you was bold
   Enough to have by force the poison from her wrested?
ORYNTHIA: Are handmaids to prevent what victors grim
   requested?
MASINISSA: When to a wrong decision despair has turned the
   mind.

ELENISSE: When fear and impotence themselves our hands do
  bind.
MASINISSA: Quick, save her, if a breath in her may still be fleeting.
  Bring balsam, oil, and wine, if there's a pulse still beating.
  I murdered her! I must myself of her take hold.
  My brightly burning heart will on her corpse grow cold.
  Oh, woe! she's gone. With her for me the roses perished
  Which for my pining soul a bower were most cherished.
  Her breath evaporated, whom once my lust caressed.
  And yet, there's still a glimmer inside her cooling breast
  Of her unquenchable balm, and brimstone of my passion;
  The vacant stare is luring in a tender fashion
  The ardor of my heart; with all my soul I strive
  To catch the scent I know upon her lips must thrive.
  I, Masinissa, her my idol am addressing,
  Upon her frigid mouth the very last kiss pressing!
  Love's sugar even now once more instill in me.
  More than a funeral bier your corpse will for me be,
  But, as did Periander, I'll keep you as my treasure,
  And even with your shade I'll ply both love and pleasure.
  But, Masinissa, woe, what crazy aim is this?
  You killed her and you'd dare disturb her spirit's peace?
  As earlier her body, her corpse you would bemire?
  Her specter can you see yourself affright with fire?
  Serenest Queen, your rage against me now assuage,
  Because I have resolved to pay my error's gauge.
  Alas, of what misdeeds have I become the debtor?
  Alas, why haven't me the heavens deigned to shatter?
  Alas, why hasn't yet engulfed me the abyss?
  And why her ranting shade Megaeras didn't please
  To send for my demise with well-earned torments flocking?
  I see it: now the underground caverns are unlocking.
  Her face hurls bolts, her arms with flaming heat assail.
  Up, Masinissa, on your sword yourself impale!
  So that one coffin and one day both of us see buried.
  Now placate with your blood and with your specter lurid
  Her irritated shade!

Masinissa. Scipio. Laelius. Syphax. Juba. Mamercus. Bogudes. A crowd of Roman Army officers and soldiers.

SCIPIO: Enough! are you insane?
MASINISSA: Good heavens! who would such a rightful blow
    restrain?
SCIPIO: For what despair and rut your senses you've forsaken?
    Make sure the sword is from his hands this minute taken.
MASINISSA: Am I to be deprived of death as final peace?
SCIPIO: It's proper, if you can't decide what proper is.
MASINISSA: This heinous murder more than dreadful death did
    merit.
SCIPIO: Reveal to us who's been by your injustice harried.
MASINISSA: By my insidious poison my spouse here dead you see.
SCIPIO: But was the choice not hers? Your hint was no decree.
MASINISSA: A counsel that betrays is no less crime's expression.
SCIPIO: She bore too little pain for what was her transgression.
MASINISSA: Against me she did not transgress, against her, I.
SCIPIO: Both Rome and heaven wished discretion you apply.
MASINISSA: The gods for my transgression are seeking retribution.
SCIPIO: Yet they condemn with scorn the self's own execution
    And disfavor those who at themselves would rage,
    Who mar both right and nature. This foolish fit assuage,
    Don't let it drive you mad, this lecherous woman's dying,
    For you are lucky, and cease this self-denying
    Of your own health and fame. This counsel don't disdain:
    Your heart by lust was clouded, and by a dream, your brain.
    You'll rue your vile decision, with shamefaced redness smart,
    As soon as reason's light the haze will cause to part.
    Revive now with more fame your spirit's daring nerve,
    Ere time and foe as critics of your folly serve,
    While your devoted friend says this as just a warning.
    Your foe now even, Syphax, once cursing you and scorning,
    Begins to love you due to Sophonisba's fall,
    Since her disloyalty could any man but gall.
    Consider: if by right her fate should have you harassed,
    Who in one day to love two men was not embarrassed,
    And who by destiny's own clock her love would set,
    Who bawdy swapping did as fun and gain abet.
MASINISSA: I shall, oh, mighty chief, my sorrow try to master,
    And for my injuries will seek some salve and plaster.

But since my heart's one-half in her here buried lies,
And since to her and me the favor Rome denies
That first her corpse to Rome won't after all be carried,
Since Rome has thus ensnared the way she should be buried,
Allow me not alive such wrenching woe to view.
SCIPIO: You're asking for what Rome cannot deny to you.
Upon my triumph's glow I need no corpse to bask.
Whatever Masinissa in pomp and show may ask
For properly interring the Queen who's now deceased,
To let him freely choose both Rome and I are pleased.
Whence Masinissa should today start realizing
That now toward the starry vault is virtue rising,
That Rome leaves loyal service and noble bravery,
Blood spilled for fame, though by a stranger's gallantry,
By no means unrewarded, nor treason unrequited.
This, then, will be the verdict, as by me it's cited:
Prince Syphax lost his realm, his freedom, scepter, throne
Which forfeit are to Rome. You, Laelius, on your own
The captive take to Rome, the fastest transport finding.
Who severs troth and oath, him fetters will be binding.
But let the spoils a foretaste of triumph only be,
For Carthage turned to ashes will seal our victory.
LAELIUS: To crown with triumph Rome and you the gods must
    mean,
As on you do her lords, the counsels, burghers lean.
To all of these much more my evidence will show
What fortune had decreed so many years ago:
It's by the Scipios that Juno's town will perish.
SCIPIO: Rome will you, Masinissa, as ally always cherish.
Thus Syphax's realm devolves into your care through me.
Accept the crown and scepter. In turn you'll henceforth be
As Rome's most loyal ally to die forever striving.
ALL: Rome, Scipio, and Masinissa, let them go on thriving!

Translated by M. John Hanak

Johann Elias Schlegel

THE DUMB BEAUTY

CHARACTERS

RICHARD, *a rich old landed gentleman*
YOUNGWIT, *a young well-to-do landed gentleman*
JACOB, *Youngwit's servant*
LACONIUS, *a philosopher*
MRS. LOVETOTALK, *a widow, middle-class*
CHARLOTTE, *presumed to be Richard's daughter*
LEONORE, *presumed to be Mrs. Lovetotalk's daughter*
CATHERINE, *Mrs. Lovetotalk's servant*

Scene 1

The scene is set in Mrs. Lovetotalk's house.

Catherine. Jacob.

JACOB: Well, is there no one here a man can hear or see?
　Must my masters wait outside for all eternity?
　Not the slightest sign of life. Service! No one to see.
CATHERINE *(off)*: Hoho, who's that talking? Patience, we're having
　tea.
JACOB: You have visitors.
CATHERINE *(off)*:　　　　No one ever comes to call in this place.
　If you want to call on us come back on New Year's Day.
　Must my lady always walk around in her finery?
　And if she's in negligee she doesn't want people to see.
　　　　　　　　　(Enter Catherine.)
　All right, my friend, and whose servant are you, pray tell?
　I'll tell my mistress, even though she's not feeling well.
JACOB: I was hoping we could see the young lady at least.
CATHERINE: What, young ladies receiving men? I'll tell the priest,
　By God I will.

JACOB: And why would that be such a crime?
Surely she could spare her own father a little time.

CATHERINE: What, is Sir Richard here, our young mistress's daddy?

JACOB: Yes, and there's someone else with him she might want to see.
Young ladies don't cry, "God save us" when they set eyes on him.

CATHERINE: Is that so? Who is he then?

JACOB: What? More questions?
Are you dim?

CATHERINE: If the gentlemen would be so good as to step inside?
My mistress is well enough and will no longer hide.

Scene 2

Richard. Youngwit.

RICHARD: It's twenty years ago I brought my daughter here
From the country. That was when I had become a widower
For I didn't know the woman who lives here before.
She has done all she could to bring her up, and more.
I'll see her at last. Only through letters did I know of her.
She's an angelic child. To know her is to love her.
My heart beats faster for sheer joy, my dear sir son.

YOUNGWIT: And mine for sheer impatience. I think I am undone.

RICHARD: Her face is beautiful, with eyes that burn like fire.

YOUNGWIT: She could have got none other from her loving sire.

RICHARD: Flattery. But seriously, they say she looks like me.

YOUNGWIT: If she looked better still, how happy I would be.

RICHARD: Also, she is the best in all that women do.
My dear Youngwit she will make marvelous soups for you.

YOUNGWIT: I would not want her to make them with her own hand.

RICHARD: And those letters she writes, tell me, are they not grand?
Whenever I read one it's full of words of wisdom,
And in zoology she knows prostomium.

YOUNGWIT: Did she learn much?

RICHARD: Much indeed. Enough in any case.
They make young girls almost too smart, you know, these days.
They have to cram their heads with all kinds of things, right or wrong.

Would you have guessed she also speaks three foreign tongues?

YOUNGWIT: But is she lively too? And does she speak with all?

RICHARD: Of course she does. She speaks three languages, you
    recall?

YOUNGWIT: Does she speak with common sense?

RICHARD: That I don't know too well,
    But she holds her own in the world, as far as people tell.
    She's good at makeup and at cards, knows to walk tall
    And plays a fair jingle on the piano withal.

YOUNGWIT: Oh, how pleased I am. I must conclude from all of this
    That she's all I want and will ensure my happiness.
    Diligence should not be as woman's main duty weighed;
    I take her for company, I do not need a maid.
    Many woo, it's true, as if a maid was all their yearning
    And choose a wife who will just keep the home fires burning,
    Who is held accountable for all that may befall
    And will do all our bidding at our beck and call.
    But I . . .

RICHARD: You young people love to ape words wise men say
    And yet you were all born today or yesterday.
    If only you have a wife that takes good care of you,
    Company is of little use; it will not feed you too.
    Compliments are like hot air; leave them to the high and mighty,
    Wives, husbands acting ignorant who their spouses be.
    Though they may like such things, for us they are not right;
    We have our money, so they are welcome to their might.
    We get the better deal. What use does the countryside
    Have for a smart, companionable, witty bride?

YOUNGWIT: I am no great lord, but I would like to think all the
    same
    That companionship was not meant to be beyond my aim
    And that no rank will restrict the freedom to enjoy
    For a man who has a wife who can her wit employ.
    All men must feel a secret sadness when they have
    To join others in mocking their own heart's better half,
    And the good wife he only shows off against his will,
    Shames him when she speaks and irritates him when she keeps
    still;
    When alone with her all he can do is kiss or yawn
    And if he seeks amusement he must long to be gone

From the house, and lest he must hear her tell her housemaids'
dreams
When she thinks she can at last her silences redeem.
RICHARD: Words, words, talk on. We shall see, my dearest sir and
son
That I'm the smarter man. But that will come anon.

Scene 3

Youngwit. Richard. Charlotte, who keeps bowing.

RICHARD: Who comes here?
YOUNGWIT: She's beautiful, Sir Richard, may I kiss her?
Richard *(bows deeply to Charlotte):*
Quiet!
YOUNGWIT: Is it her? . . . Is it not her?
RICHARD: How should I know, sir?
If she was my daughter she could speak to me, or something.
YOUNGWIT: I beg your pardon, I wonder if I might be so bold
To ask. Sir Richard's daughter, could I see her? I was told . . .
RICHARD: When will Mrs. Lovetotalk be with us?
CHARLOTTE *(bows):* Soon.
RICHARD: I'm glad.
And will my daughter be with us soon too?
CHARLOTTE: Yes, Dad.
RICHARD: I'm beginning to think it's her. Is that you, Charlotte?
Speak!
She doesn't know us yet, sir son, that's why she looks bleak.
YOUNGWIT *(aside to Richard):*
You said just now she speaks three languages, and well.
The one we speak may not be right for her. Who can tell?
RICHARD: You speak German, don't you, my child? Am I
welcome?
I brought some company to your vivarium.
You must talk to him. A little courage, girl, I say.
I guarantee he won't harm you in any way.

Scene 4

Youngwit. Richard. Charlotte. Mrs. Lovetotalk.

MRS. LOVETOTALK: I hope your dear child meets with your
approval, sir.

I see she's talking well. That art's best known to her.

RICHARD: Is it? So this is Charlotte then?

MRS. LOVETOTALK: It is indeed.

RICHARD: She didn't tell me anything.

MRS. LOVETOTALK: There was no need.
Sir Richard, what makes you think of asking questions like that?
If she wasn't yours, do you think I'd say you were her dad?
Charlotte, my child, why don't you kiss your daddy's hand?
Believe me, this child's brains would make angels look bland.

RICHARD: I didn't notice.

MRS. LOVETOTALK: More than I would like, most of the time.
I know that praising her too loudly is a crime.
Young ladies tend to let their thoughts run wild, forsooth,
But then again, is it always a crime to tell the truth?
I myself am often amazed—I tell you on my honor—
At the wise words I hear in this house, coming from her.

RICHARD: But only in the house.

MRS. LOVETOTALK: Where else? We don't go out
Much, and in this house strangers are not often about.
People think up things all the time. We live our quiet way,
But even so, who gives widows the time of day?

RICHARD: Mrs. Lovetotalk, if evil attacks even you
Then I must truly ask: what is this world coming to?

MRS. LOVETOTALK: Sir, you don't know how things are done in big
    cities:
A woman can hardly walk out of her front door in peace,
There are so many people with so little to do
They mock the world and take your peace away from you;
And I don't want to get too social after all,
For if you are time passes you by with idle talk,
And that's not what I want. Young people especially
Learn nothing there but pure and utter vanity.
I also liked to be among people before
When I was very young and managed to mean more.
The greatest lady was often left standing alone;
They all ran to me wherever I let myself be shown.

YOUNGWIT: That I can see.

MRS. LOVETOTALK: Why else avoid society?
Why should I want other women to envy me?

RICHARD: You should be safe from all that now my dear, I guess.
MRS. LOVETOTALK: For years I've lived a life of lonely politesse.
  My own daughter has had to leave my house withal
  So that I could give yours the very best of all:
  The poor girl spends her days with my sister in her house
  And doesn't see much that is good there. A flittermouse
  She'll be and little more. I didn't want to keep
  Them together because my hatred of chitchat runs deep.
  Two girls talk only of makeup and of cosmetics
  And fill each other's heads with idle homiletics.
  I hope you gentlemen will not be unkind to me;
  I'm almost ashamed these days when people come to see
  Us here. You see we're both dressed most improperly.
  We were not feeling too well, the poor dear girl and me.
RICHARD: Not dressed properly? Six flowers in the capillaries
  And skirts more like a tent for seven Janissaries?
  All that is nothing?
MRS. LOVETOTALK: It's just my daily negligee,
  And not much makeup. I don't see people anyway.
  "Let yourself be carried, dear," my sister says to me,
  To the concert hall or else to watch a comedy.
  From all such vanity, sir, I stay well away:
  People go there only to put themselves on display.
YOUNGWIT: But to think: "If I were there people would look at
  me"—
  Mrs. Lovetotalk, can that be done without vanity?
MRS. LOVETOTALK: No! Don't offer to take me there, young man,
  ever.
  I never went, and would I ever go? Never!
  Charlotte doesn't ask for that kind of thing much either
  Nor does she think there is a side to life called lighter.
  She was a clever child, even when she was small.
  She would make it big one day. That was soon obvious to all.
  She was so quiet, so devout, a joy to keep.
  Many's the day I did not hear even a peep.
RICHARD: Mrs. Lovetotalk, listen, and speak to me alone.
  Youngwit will speak to my daughter in a merry tone.
  Young ladies who often seem to speak against their will
  Must afterwards be begged at greater length to keep still.

Scene 5

Charlotte. Youngwit.

YOUNGWIT: One can be lonely in town too, I didn't know.
CHARLOTTE: Oh yes!
YOUNGWIT: Doesn't the time grow long for you?
CHARLOTTE: Oh no!
YOUNGWIT: Maybe you shorten time by reading books, my lady?
CHARLOTTE: Oh no!
YOUNGWIT: The weather hasn't been very good lately.
CHARLOTTE: I don't know.
YOUNGWIT: Of course it's never really bad for you;
   You don't go out much, do you?
CHARLOTTE: No, you're right there too.
YOUNGWIT: We had very bad roads on our trip here, your dad
   And I, you know.
CHARLOTTE: Is that so?
YOUNGWIT: The ice was very bad.
CHARLOTTE: As bad as that?
YOUNGWIT: But the desire to set eyes on you
   Sooner gave us no rest: we just had to get through.
CHARLOTTE: Is that true?
YOUNGWIT: And you must want to get to know your dad?
CHARLOTTE: I'm glad.
YOUNGWIT: He kept talking about you like mad.
   No other word was spoken, he made such a fuss
   About you the whole trip.
CHARLOTTE: When are you leaving us?
YOUNGWIT: Why ask about our leaving already, mademoiselle?
   I think that kind of question doesn't bode too well.
CHARLOTTE: Why not?
YOUNGWIT: You can be sure of it, just wait and see.
   We want to take you back with us. Do you agree?
CHARLOTTE: If it has to be, if I get Mrs. Lovetotalk's fiat.
YOUNGWIT: But you like the countryside?
CHARLOTTE: I don't, it's much too quiet.
YOUNGWIT: But you must like that if you live here by yourself
   alone.
CHARLOTTE: Yes, it's better in the city after all.
YOUNGWIT: Pardon,

I'm all for the city if you want company,
But if I want solitude the city's not for me.
CHARLOTTE: Really?
YOUNGWIT: Although in cities you hear a thing or two
That makes you laugh and sets your tongue a-wagging too.
CHARLOTTE: You do?
YOUNGWIT: A lot. So tell me quickly, what's the news?
CHARLOTTE: We had a woman here, I think, and she would muse
About coffee going up, and not much to be got,
And tea the same.
YOUNGWIT *(mops up the perspiration on his forehead)*: Excuse
me, I think it's very hot.
CHARLOTTE: No, no.
YOUNGWIT: Yes, I feel so hot . . . and so, oh my,
So strange; the fear, you see, excuse me, oh well, good-bye.
CHARLOTTE: Are you going so soon? Won't you play a game of
square?
YOUNGWIT: Excuse me, I must go and get myself a little fresh air.

Scene 6

Charlotte sits down and fiddles with her fan. Jacob. Catherine.

JACOB: Sweet Jesus! This is no place for country bumpkinses:
They treat their servants here as they would treat their princes!
You servant girls serve coffee and tea just like high-class dames
And then you always put a "sir" before our names.
In big cities a lackey comes into his own;
They give the noble liveries a blissful home.
CATHERINE: Well, well, our country lackey seems to like our way.
JACOB: Yes, I must say I'm pleased with my status today
But the true perfection of my bliss I shall not see
Until little Catherine goes for a walk with me.
CATHERINE: No sir, that will not be.
JACOB: Oh yes, I'll be your guide.
CATHERINE: It's the walking, don't you see? Here when we walk
we ride.
JACOB: What, me? And ride? Well, Catherine, anything you say.
What do I care? But will there be a lot to pay?
CATHERINE: A tightwad too.

JACOB: A year's wages to the last cent
  I'd pay for this. I hope she won't think I don't want to spend
  Money on her. Let's ride, so what. If she comes with me
  To the countryside I'd get to know her more easily.
CATHERINE: But the first question is: do I want to stoop down
  Like that? Here I only know first-class lackeys and frown
  On those who do not serve a knight. I won't let them near me.
  And, Sir Jacob, you are a pitiful sight to see.
JACOB: Sht, sht, who sits here and has heard our every word?
CATHERINE: No need to worry about her, speak undeterred.
  It's only the young mistress.
JACOB: Sir Youngwit's spouse to be?
CATHERINE: Who else?
JACOB: Indeed. You know each other well, I see.
CATHERINE: Why not? We feel and think alike, my mistress and I.
  What do I get if I praise your master to the sky?
JACOB: You must have raised her then.
CATHERINE: I did, I'm glad to say.
JACOB: I'm off.
CATHERINE: Wait a minute, why do you run away?
JACOB: My master will be here soon.
CATHERINE: So what? Let masters be.
JACOB: It wouldn't be a pretty sight if he came looking for me.

Scene 7

Catherine. Charlotte.

CATHERINE: Stupid! He runs as if the devil were on his heels.
  I wanted to ask him more questions. Who knows what he
    conceals?
  Well now, my lady, sitting by yourself quietly in the wings—
  You wouldn't really be thinking of important things?
CHARLOTTE: Oh no, you know I like to sit in peace when I can
  And quietly play "open" and "closed" with my old fan.
CATHERINE: I wouldn't say no to that myself: nothing to do
  Nothing to think, and you hardly know if you are you.
  It wouldn't be so bad to be a stone, I think,
  That cannot move, say yes or no or anything.
  But is your gentleman caller gone? How did you like him?

CHARLOTTE: He seemed all right to me, not too bright and not too dim.

He'd like to say a lot, but his words don't want to flow.

CATHERINE: Do you answer him?

CHARLOTTE: A word or two, at times, as words go.

CATHERINE: No more?

CHARLOTTE: Why? Isn't he old enough to speak alone?

Does he expect me to interrupt him with moan and groan?

CATHERINE: Yes, of course. Even the devil finds small consolation

When one always speaks and the other listens in conversation.

Unless you are a fool who wants to hear himself all day

You will soon find yourself without too much to say.

CHARLOTTE: Really? And what do you think I should be telling him then?

CATHERINE: Whatever you think.

CHARLOTTE: Oh no, don't ever say that again.

CATHERINE: Why not?

CHARLOTTE: It's not seemly.

CATHERINE: Not even in this room?

CHARLOTTE: I think of the gifts a bride can expect from a groom.

CATHERINE: You'll get a lot of stuff, more than you ever hoped for.

The countess I served before I came to you got more

Than she wanted.

CHARLOTTE: Well, I would want to put her to shame.

If they don't give me lots I don't want to take their name.

CATHERINE: First came a big basket with ribbons and flowers.

See? So.

CHARLOTTE: Lace too?

CATHERINE: What do you think?

CHARLOTTE: As big as this hand I show?

CATHERINE: Well, that wouldn't be small.

CHARLOTTE: And that's how big I want mine.

CATHERINE: Of course. Underneath the best jewels sparkled with a bright shine.

CHARLOTTE: I want those too.

CATHERINE: And with them came a watch also,

And boxes.

CHARLOTTE: No case?

CATHERINE: No.

CHARLOTTE: I want two, or else no go.

CATHERINE: Later on we found a cloth with many-colored flowers.
CHARLOTTE: If my cloth isn't as big as a garden I'll be sour.
CATHERINE: And a nightstand finally, pure silver.
CHARLOTTE: No, I want gold,
  And nothing else. I hope it doesn't seem too bold
  Of me to want my bridegroom to know this in advance
  But I don't want to tell him myself—there's the nuance.
CATHERINE: There's help for that. I'll have a word with his servant.
CHARLOTTE: Good, go! If you talk to him I'm sure he'll
  understand.

Scene 8

Mrs. Lovetotalk. Charlotte.

MRS. LOVETOTALK: So these are the thanks I get for all my pains,
  Charlotte.
  They think I don't know how to raise a child, by God.
  I hear you're not good enough for that agrarian
  Philosopher, Youngwit, smart-ass vulgarian.
  Do you know he ran to your father with some tale to tell?
  You must have said something that didn't sit too well
  With him. He grasped Sir Richard's hand, overcome with
    sorrow,
  And whispered in his ear: "If only she weren't so low
  On wit." What's the matter with the clown? Why does he hold
  You in such contempt? What did you do? Why is he so bold
  To think all wit is his alone? What did you say?
CHARLOTTE: Nothing.
MRS. LOVETOTALK: There must be something that makes him
  talk this way, Charlotte.
CHARLOTTE: Nothing, really.
MRS. LOVETOTALK: You can tell me, you know.
  Maybe you're not dressed well enough. Come on girl, show,
  Come on, turn around . . . It's well cut and worn with elegance.
  Why does the idiot say you lack intelligence?
  How do you bear yourself? Show me. The head's too high,
  Too far back. But who could fail to see the wit in your eye?
  Take a few more steps. Walk over to me. Now take a bow.
  That's it: that's wrong. Look here: this way. You can bow now.

I don't find anything. That Youngwit is a bore.
She's intelligent enough, and more.

Scene 9

Mrs. Lovetotalk. Charlotte. Leonore.

MRS. LOVETOTALK: What's this? Leonore?
  What do you want?
LEONORE: What do I want? I want nothing
  Except the happiness being with you will bring.
MRS. LOVETOTALK: You drop in all the time.
LEONORE: It may seem often to you
  But it seems rarely to me. Anyway, if it were true
  That I came every day, would that be a good reason
  To reprimand me?
MRS. LOVETOTALK: You waste your time walking in season
  And out.
LEONORE: But when I see you time passes pleasantly.
MRS. LOVETOTALK: "When I see you," my foot. If only you came
  to see me.
  I know your kind: you only come because you're curious,
  Because you heard people had come to visit us.
LEONORE: My dearest mother, do . . .
MRS. LOVETOTALK: Dearest?
LEONORE: Well then, Mama.
MRS. LOVETOTALK: You don't know that yet. You don't do me
  much honor, do you?
LEONORE: I didn't know "Mother" was an official title too.
MRS. LOVETOTALK: I don't know why my sister raises you so
  badly.
  Young girls who meet so many people must end sadly.
  It has gone far enough: I'm going to tell her now
  She shouldn't live with you like that, all thee and thou.
  Look at you. The way you stand. All that is much too free.
  You don't blush and you're not shy when there are people to
  see.
  You speak to everyone. Young ladies must keep quiet.
  And every day you show yourself off and run riot
  In polite society. You only come here to be seen.
  It's uncouth and unbecoming: young ladies shouldn't preen.

LEONORE: I can go away again. It only takes a word from you.
  I'll be sure to pick a better time for my next venue.
MRS. LOVETOTALK: You're so intelligent I only have to say
  A word you don't like and there you go, running away.
  Since you know everything and pick people apart
  Tell me what's wrong with Charlotte, since you're well versed in
    the art
  Of pleasing. We have a young fool here, fresh from the provinces.
  Her father brought him along. I don't think she convinces
  Him of her charms. He talks as if he's the only one
  Who knows she's lacking in intelligence. So stun
  Me with yours, be good enough to tell me what to do,
  Tell me what's wrong with her. I don't see it. Do you?
LEONORE: I don't.
MRS. LOVETOTALK: You should.
LEONORE: You might not like what I have to say.
MRS. LOVETOTALK: Nonsense. Tell me.
LEONORE: No, Mama.
MRS. LOVETOTALK: Come on girl, *au fait.*
LEONORE: She doesn't say much.
MRS. LOVETOTALK: As long as you can blab, my young
  fly-by-night,
  You think you have it made. She doesn't say much, that's right.
  That proves she's wiser than you are. Sweet words that charm
  Do young girls little good and bring them grievous harm.
LEONORE: If that was a general rule it would be a good thing
    indeed,
  But, as it is, not many men would stand for it.
MRS. LOVETOTALK: Many men, you say? And how on earth would
    you know that?
  Many men indeed. And you know who they want, or what?
  That's what you get for talking and joking with men.
  Many men—and who made you so smart? Tell me again.
LEONORE: Come, come, there is no shame in knowing that we
    must talk
  Politely with men when they see us. I would never balk at that.
MRS. LOVETOTALK: I'm almost beginning to believe that there are
    many
  Clowns who'd rather have a blabbermouth than any

Young girl of intelligence and wit. Listen, you must
Teach Charlotte how to talk. Right now. You hear? I trust . . .
LEONORE: You think I could?
MRS. LOVETOTALK: You can. I don't want your excuses.
Tell her what she should tell Youngwit. Teach her your ruses.
I'm off, I'm going to give him a piece of my mind.
You go as soon as she can speak. Don't stay behind
To show yourself to strangers.

Scene 10

Leonore. Charlotte.

LEONORE: What does my mother say?
I don't understand.
CHARLOTTE: I don't want to learn from you. Go away.
LEONORE: I would not presume to teach you anything, Charlotte.
Nature teaches you. You think you've need of me. You have not.
To speak in this world you only need self-confidence,
That's half the battle. You need no other experience.
CHARLOTTE: Yes, you do.
LEONORE: Don't worry your pretty little head about
it all.
A mouth like yours is allowed to speak as luck will befall.
Not all the girls who please are held in high esteem
Because they say nothing beyond the words they scheme
Together in their heads. The boldness to say a stupid thing
Often passes for wit. The art is in daring.
Give it a try. You're pretty and you're young, and such
Young ladies, when they open their mouths, are admired much.
CHARLOTTE: I see you're mocking me. I'm going to tell on you.
LEONORE: No! If I weren't serious I'd have better things to do.
CHARLOTTE: All right.
LEONORE: But to suddenly shine in what you have to
say,
Believe me, what I just told you is the only way,
For to say yes or no with true intelligence
And not to seem to treat small things with negligence,
To joke at the right time and to speak at every throw

With everyone only about the things they know
And to guide the speech of others in the direction you
Want it to go needs time, skill, and some thinking too.

CHARLOTTE: That's enough!

LEONORE: Now what? You're crying.

CHARLOTTE: You keep
    mocking me, Leonore,
You speak to me only in barbed words that make me sore.

LEONORE: Me? That's how you see what I'm doing out of
    affection?
My advice is: go on, just speak, just try a little reflection.
That counts for much in the beginning.

CHARLOTTE: There comes my papa.

*They both want to leave. Charlotte runs off but Leonore turns
        back because she notices she has been noticed.*

Scene 11

Richard. Youngwit. Leonore.

RICHARD: Girls, no, don't run away. Charlotte, stay there, girls! Ah
    Charlotte, where are you going? Charlotte, listen, I say,
    When your father calls.

LEONORE: Sir, I'm afraid she thinks she may
    Upset you.

RICHARD: You must love her well to speak for her like this.

LEONORE: As a daughter of this household I know what my duty
    is.
Allow me to fetch her back for you. She must still be near.

RICHARD: No.

LEONORE: I take my leave.

RICHARD: No, no, not straightaway. Stay here.

LEONORE: Your dearest daughter . . .

RICHARD: Don't worry, I see her
    often enough.

LEONORE: But the same's not true for her.

RICHARD: The young lady speaks
    sense, off the cuff.

YOUNGWIT: You have only shown yourself and you're leaving us
    again?

LEONORE: Please, sir.

RICHARD: No. Please. Shall we never get to know you
    then?
LEONORE: It's only to my loss when people get to know me.
RICHARD: And our loss is great indeed when she leaves so
    suddenly.
LEONORE: Very well. I shall leave you like this. Ignorance is bliss.
RICHARD: But as a daughter of the household you owe me a kiss.
LEONORE: That honor should be your daughter's only, that I know.
RICHARD: Come, come, don't run away. You little fool. Don't go.

Scene 12

Richard. Youngwit. Charlotte with a deck of cards.

RICHARD: Charlotte, are you coming now? You didn't wait for me
    When I called you before. Cards? What's this I see?
    What am I to do with them?
CHARLOTTE: Play with me.
RICHARD: You must be mad.
    Do you think I waste my time playing cards? Not me, too bad.
    What's in it for you if I relieve you of your money?
CHARLOTTE: No, I want to win enough to buy myself a bunny
    Dress.
RICHARD: Here's your money, now go.
CHARLOTTE: And a jacket too, gray.
    And a skirt that I could put on every day.
RICHARD: Leave me alone with your cards. You're taking this to
    excess;
    I see you need a mouth only to ask for another dress.
CHARLOTTE: Come play with me.
RICHARD: Leave me alone, I tell you, be gone!

Scene 13

Richard. Youngwit.

RICHARD: My God, the difference between her and the other one!
    If my daughter could only be even half as nice!
YOUNGWIT: Indeed. I would like that.
RICHARD: So would I, at any price.
    When I see a young lady who's naturally fair,

Not decked out with clothes or always walking as if on air,
It makes my heart laugh in my body and that makes it hard
For me to keep playing the eternal widower's part.

YOUNGWIT: Sir, may I say I delight in seeing you like this?

RICHARD: Why's that?

YOUNGWIT: Charlotte is pretty indeed, don't take me amiss.

RICHARD: She is.

YOUNGWIT: She would be an angel with a bit more wit.

RICHARD: Did you say wit? Don't make me laugh or think of it.
If only she were not a thing that walks as if pulled by a thread,
Only makes compliments and only wants to spread
Her skirt. She thinks clothes, is clothes, and only clothes ail her.
She hardly loves her father more than she loves her tailor.
She can hardly move her lips for all her good breeding
And thinks a yes or no are all she'll ever be needing,
And as long as she knows the kind of cards she should be giving
She imagines she has indeed mastered the art of living.
If she were pretty without constraint, and of good cheer,
If she would talk—not all the time—if she wouldn't veer
Too close to wit, if she were useful at home and knew
Right from wrong, I wouldn't ask what intelligence can do.

YOUNGWIT: Well sir, we would agree if only she had wit.

RICHARD: Wit? No, my good sir, I've frankly had my fill of it.
Don't talk to me about women's intelligence:
Those who have experienced it treat it with negligence.
When a power-hungry wife makes a child out of a man
And laughs in his face when he doesn't think all that she can,
Punishes him whenever he speaks without her advice,
Is a pest when they are at home but in company very nice,
And if he doesn't want what she wants she makes herself ill
With great chagrin and rants and raves until her will
Is done, she calls that intelligence. If I had one
Like that I'd be a fool if I didn't sleep alone.

YOUNGWIT: I find total agreement between us in that case.

RICHARD: If we agree, why then, we have a common base.

YOUNGWIT: But would one word decrease the friendship you feel
for me?

RICHARD: What? A fool's quarrel? What damage could it do to us?
I can't see . . .

YOUNGWIT: No, sir, I mean the word I'm still about to say.
RICHARD: Say it.
YOUNGWIT: But I know . . .
RICHARD: Well then, just put the word away.
YOUNGWIT: It must come out. I think it's best if I speak now.
RICHARD: Of course! Speak, sir. Go on. It will come out somehow.
YOUNGWIT: I did accept your proposal with great pleasure, sir,
    And looked forward to be your daughter's husband, if her
    Person would please me too, since that was the condition.
RICHARD: Yes, I think I see. Go on, conclude, would be my
    petition.
YOUNGWIT: Maybe her face will still attract a thousand eyes,
    Who knows she may still please of those who pass her by,
    She can still boast of her beauty and her bags of gold . . .
RICHARD: But you, Sir Youngwit?
YOUNGWIT: I spoke with her; my story's told.
RICHARD: I've heard enough. I think I know what's going on
    And I think you're not far wrong, my son.
YOUNGWIT: No more your son.
RICHARD: Come, come, I want to break that evil custom with
    good grace:
    No more my son, all right, but I still want your embrace:
    We will stay friends after all.
YOUNGWIT: That would please me.
RICHARD: The more so
    Since once you're family you often see your friendship go.
    But that damned woman who has deceived me so and thinks
    She raised a miracle for me, her I would jinx
    If I . . .

Scene 14

Youngwit. Richard. Mrs. Lovetotalk.

MRS. LOVETOTALK: If you what? What did you want to do with
    me?
    Here I am.
YOUNGWIT: We're not talking about you, ma'am.
MRS. LOVETOTALK: I see.
    If I . . .

YOUNGWIT: Don't gird your loins for a fight just yet, madam,
  The man who wants to harm you has not yet been born from
    Adam.
MRS. LOVETOTALK: But you, Sir Richard, I must say you are the
    type of man
  Who lets everybody tell him whatever tale they can.
  What's wrong with Charlotte? I think I know—God be
    praised—
  How young ladies who live in cities should be raised:
  I've been one myself and not all that long ago.
RICHARD: But I
  Also know right from wrong.
MRS. LOVETOTALK: But fashions change, sir; why,
  Your daughter has been raised in the most modern way.
RICHARD: You mean the Chinese way I think: she sits still and will
    not say
  A word.
MRS. LOVETOTALK: Well, tell me then what else you'd have me do.
RICHARD: She could say a word or two.
MRS. LOVETOTALK: Indeed, a word or two.
  He wants to make young ladies talk, do you hear that?
  Is that what you want, too? Shouldn't you be laughing, or what?
RICHARD: Why should I?
MRS. LOVETOTALK: Why not?
RICHARD: Tell me why.
MRS. LOVETOTALK: Young ladies
  soon change their tune:
  Women do many things differently after their honeymoon.
YOUNGWIT: But then they speak all the more.
MRS. LOVETOTALK: I am speaking right
  now.
YOUNGWIT: But they also gain intelligence.
MRS. LOVETOTALK: As I did, somehow.
  I didn't say a word when I was young.
RICHARD: Are you sure of that?
YOUNGWIT: Perhaps that's why becoming a woman made you
    more glad.
MRS. LOVETOTALK: No! If we taught our daughters to speak when
    they are young
  Who would gladly listen to us women for long?

YOUNGWIT: I see, is that the reason?

MRS. LOVETOTALK: Let's stop this hide-and-seek.
   Talk to her one last time, Sir Youngwit, let her prove that she
      can speak
   After all, Charlotte, and if he feels she's lacking
   In intelligence, so be it; then he can send her packing.

RICHARD: What do you say to that?

YOUNGWIT: I agree, just one more time.

MRS. LOVETOTALK: I bet she'll be a real oracle, truly sublime.

RICHARD: I must leave you here, Sir Youngwit; I think I'd better go
   To talk a little sense into my daughter, you know.

Scene 15

Youngwit. Jacob.

JACOB: At last I find the right moment to speak with you
   And what I say will be to your advantage too.

YOUNGWIT: Well?

JACOB: Well, I know you're wooing Sir Richard's daughter.
   They gave me something I think might help you to support her.

YOUNGWIT: What's that?

JACOB: A small present is sure to win a heart.
   It is the fashion: gifts must be given, if you're smart.
   With watches and with cases and with trifles of that kind
   I wanted to seduce many a simple child purblind.
   I thought. . . . Maybe you'd like to see a little sample?
   Something like this?

YOUNGWIT *(hits him):* Get lost, you fool, that's more than ample.

JACOB: Is this what I get for my advice? What's wrong with you?
   If a groom needs help, my God, even hangmen will do.
   People's heads are always full of whims. You never know
   What to do, or leave undone, or when to come, or go.

Scene 16

Youngwit. Jacob. Catherine.

JACOB: That's Catherine coming. My master is giving presents now.
   If only I could help her to a little something, but how?
   Listen, if he doesn't give you anything as well
   I'll share with you whatever me gives to me, *ma belle.*

CATHERINE: If you say so. . . . There's a man here, I think he's
    looking for you.
YOUNGWIT: Aren't you sure?
CATHERINE: No.
YOUNGWIT *(to Jacob):*   Ask him, then.
JACOB: I don't mind if I do.
CATHERINE: I asked him already and I still don't know.
YOUNGWIT: How come?
CATHERINE: He didn't say anything.
YOUNGWIT: Why on earth not?
CATHERINE: He's dumb.
  He made me understand that much with signs just now.
  I think he wanted to march into the room somehow.
JACOB: Here he is himself. I'll be damned if I know what he wants.

Scene 17

Youngwit. Laconius.

YOUNGWIT: Is it you, Laconius, my dear old friend? Your hands!
  You old philosopher! Welcome, sit down with me.
  You are still in good health . . . and think of me, I see.
  You love me still, after all . . . I am grateful to you.
  How is the algebra? . . . I hope you are well too.
  People who have money also have time for thought.
  In my case money matters have left me all distraught.
LACONIUS: I hear you want to get married. Don't do it, I say.
YOUNGWIT: It's still too soon to talk about it, anyway.
  Sir Richard wanted to show his daughter to me here
  And so that made me travel with him. He's a dear,
  The father, I like him, but my love for the daughter's far to seek.
  She doesn't say a word.
LACONIUS: Take her because she doesn't speak.
YOUNGWIT: You would like that. You don't like to hear even an
    inkling
  Of conversation for fear it would disturb your thinking.
  Listen, what's in it for me? I'll make the girl love you.
  She's good-looking. What do you think? Are you laughing, too?
  Even you would have the heart to take a woman still
  If there were one who would be silent at your will.

Listen, how old are you? Sixty? Not yet, or what?
Fifty anyway.

LACONIUS: Forty.

YOUNGWIT: Philosophy made that,
Those wrinkles on your forehead? My God, you're old and gray.
I never thought thinking could take a man's youth away.

Scene 18

Youngwit. Laconius. Catherine.

CATHERINE: Sir Youngwit, Sir Richard wants to see you urgently.
YOUNGWIT: Excuse me, old friend, I must leave you instantly.

Scene 19

Laconius. Catherine.

CATHERINE: There, off he goes. How shall I get rid of this old
    compeer?
Sir, are you thinking of spending the evening with us here?
Would you like to see some of the other rooms, maybe?
You make a sign? Such language is unknown to me.
                (Laconius gives her money.)
What's this? Two, three, and four. I must be dreaming; my God,
The man could be an angel! They don't speak either, they just
    nod.
He wants something all right, that I hear clear as day.
But what do you want, with whom? With my mistress, you say?
With my young lady then? Not her either. With me?
Maybe I'll understand if you tell me differently.
What do you want, dear sir? Come on!

LACONIUS: See Richard's daughter.
I want to see her without her seeing me.

CATHERINE: Old snorter,
That I don't get at all. Your other tongue was much clearer.
What, she should not see you when I take you near her?
What does that mean? Do you want to see her in the dark?
Or what?

LACONIUS: Hide me.

CATHERINE: And then? Tell me the rest of the lark.
LACONIUS: I want to hear her.
CATHERINE: What, as if she was a real professor?
   She was not made for listening to.
LACONIUS: At last. God bless her.
CATHERINE: I hear somebody coming. The young lady, I guess.
   Quick, sir, get yourself into this room. Go on. That's it. Yes.

Scene 20

Mrs. Lovetotalk. Charlotte. Catherine.

MRS. LOVETOTALK: Who's in that room?
CATHERINE *(aside):*   What now? Did she get wind of him?
   (to Mrs. Lovetotalk): Did you want to go inside?
MRS. LOVETOTALK: No.
CATHERINE: No sign of life or limb.
MRS. LOVETOTALK: Leave us alone.

Scene 21

Mrs. Lovetotalk. Charlotte.

MRS. LOVETOTALK: Come here, Charlotte, give me a kiss,
   And know by this you are my daughter.
CHARLOTTE: Your daughter? By this?
MRS. LOVETOTALK: Yes you, my dearest child, I am the mother
   who bore
   You and out of love for you I exchanged you for Leonore.
   Sir Richard gave her to me when she was not yet a year
   Old and looked just like you in size and age. My dear,
   No one else knows of the exchange, whom I took and whom I
     gave,
   Except for a serving woman, and she's already in her grave.
   Sir Richard, who entrusted his only child to me,
   Gets you, my daughter, instead of his daughter, you see?
   He thinks you're his, and on the day the Lord will call
   Him his daughter will get nothing and you'll inherit all.
   That's how my scheming did ensure your happiness.
CHARLOTTE: It did?
MRS. LOVETOTALK: But to keep all this you have to do as he says,

Just once. You have to be what he wants you to be,
Then you can become a woman of great ability
And walk in beautiful clothes to spite the others, you know,
And slowly get to the place in life where you want to go.
I beg you: don't let this happiness run through your hands.
Once you are Youngwit's wife—a wife does what she wants.
But I'll not rest before I know you're taken care of.
Sir Richard isn't dumb, and when push comes to shove
He may find out. One slight suspicion and it's all gone.
Once he suspects he'll know how to check on his suspicion.
His real daughter brought a birthmark into this world with her.
If he knows of it you and I can say, "Good night, kind sir."
So do your level best to get Youngwit out of here.
I've been thinking of a way to fool the poor old dear.
He complains that you don't think and that you never speak
So give the fool what he wants, don't give him cause to seek
Elsewhere. Even Leonore will have to help get you
What was meant for her without knowing she is. What a coup!
                    (She rings.)
Just don't tell anyone. It's for your own good, child.
                    (Enter Catherine)
Send Leonore to me, will you?
                    (Exit Catherine)
                              My good name would be defiled
If anyone found out. So be a good girl now
And learn to keep your mouth shut. Just let me show you how.

Scene 22

Mrs. Lovetotalk. Charlotte. Leonore.

MRS. LOVETOTALK: Come, Leonore, come, I need your help. I have
     a plan.
     You must obey me, and now I'll find out if you can.
     Remember, I brought you into this world with great pain.
     Child, show me now my suffering was not in vain.
LEONORE: Tell me what you want, Mama. What do you want from
     me?
MRS. LOVETOTALK: People laugh at Charlotte and criticize me in
     her, you see,
     And even though I brought her up as best I could,

A girl has to behave as a man thinks she should.
But they're not all of the same opinion. A girl who is
Too quiet for one is too free for another's happiness.
If I were a young man I'd get me a dumb girl for sure,
But Youngwit wants her to speak like an oracle, demure.
The stupid bore doesn't go for a pretty face that will
Not say much but still have many wishes to fulfill.
He was almost of a mind to bring it to an end.
It wasn't easy to convince him to speak to her again,
And if the poor girl doesn't speak like a book this time
We shall be through for good. No wedding bells will chime.
She will sit here and look; you will be hiding there.
No one will see you. Her dress will cover you everywhere.
Help her to say what she has to say, tell her word for word.
He thinks he's so smart; I think it's time his pride got hurt.

LEONORE: What did you say? Mama, you're not serious, are you?

MRS. LOVETOTALK: Serious? Of course, I am, it's a simple thing to do.

LEONORE: Let's say the plan succeeds. Do you think you should encourage . . .

MRS. LOVETOTALK: Are you trying to tell me how to arrange a marriage?

LEONORE: Don't you think he'll see through it at once?

MRS. LOVETOTALK: My own kith and kin!
Can you tell me why the egg thinks it's smarter than the chicken?

LEONORE: And what if you and I come to shame because of it?

MRS. LOVETOTALK: Just do it, girl, don't you see the beauty of the gambit?
I want obedience from you, and don't try to bore
Me with your advice. Don't do it and you're not my child anymore.
Charlotte, sit down. And you, go stand behind her, you hear!
Go on! Don't drag your feet! I think he must be near.
That's it. Help your sister a little bit. Don't move. Just stay
Where you are and I'll soon throw old Sir Richard your way.

Scene 23

Youngwit. Charlotte. Leonore, unseen.

YOUNGWIT: There is coldness in your manner and contempt, I see.
I think you are angry.
CHARLOTTE: The fault lies not with me.
YOUNGWIT: I only want to see that I've been wrong, that's all.
CHARLOTTE: The gift . . . to see that . . . is a rare . . . gift indeed
. . . and not small.
YOUNGWIT: Well said! But you didn't speak like that before, with
such grace.
Tell me, where was your wit then? I only saw your face.
CHARLOTTE: What else . . . is there . . . to show . . . to a young
gentleman?
They love . . . to do the talking . . . You only need a . . . rose.
YOUNGWIT: A rose? What for? What rose?
CHARLOTTE: People often . . . find wit
In the kind . . . of people . . . they never thought . . . capable of
it.
YOUNGWIT: That sounded as if I just heard two voices speak.
There's an echo in here.
CHARLOTTE: It will only . . . make you . . . weak.
YOUNGWIT: The echo . . .
CHARLOTTE: Stay away from me! You're getting much too near.
YOUNGWIT: Now the echo speaks first. What a strange thing to
hear.
Who's there? Come out. I can never forgive you for this.
(Leonore appears.)
You have wit to spare. You even rent it out. Don't you, miss?
(To Charlotte)
And you, oh no, don't be ashamed, my prettiest;
I must admit you'd be a good ventriloquist.
CHARLOTTE: No sir, not me.
LEONORE: Go on, mock me, sir, you have the right.
My friendship for Charlotte does in no way excuse my plight.
YOUNGWIT: Who came up with this ruse? Not bad, I must admit.
LEONORE: But not too good. That's why you can forgive us for it.
It doesn't do any harm and yet it is proof enough
That one doesn't want to lose a man like you in love.
YOUNGWIT: At least the ruse tells me this much, my pretty maid:
Pulling the wool over people's eyes is not your trade.
I think you show yourself from your better side when you
Apologize for yourself than when you try to do
Me in.

LEONORE: People apologize badly when they see
  They're in the wrong.
YOUNGWIT: In the wrong, you say? Most definitely.
  You couldn't find anything better to do, and so
  You played this game, just to see what it takes to make me blow
  My top.
LEONORE: You credit me with too much inventiveness.
  I don't aim that high in all I do; I settle for less.
YOUNGWIT: But you achieve much more than you ever wanted to.
LEONORE: My dear sir, I am finished with the role I played for you.
  You know I was only here in a supporting part.
  Here's the main character. You'd better try your art
  On her.
YOUNGWIT: Oh no. Please stay. I want to speak with you.
  You helped them with their ruse, now help me with my revenge.
  Please do!
  No, they will not get away with this piece of treachery.
  They will pay dearly for the joke they tried to play on me.
  To find the intelligence they told me to hope for,
  I shall have to ally myself with her who has it, and more.
LEONORE: You think I tried to pull the wool over your eyes.
  But sir, the right by which you condemn me applies
  To you as well. And your flattery won't work anymore.
  You don't give your trust to a man you tried to fool before.

Scene 24

Richard. Mrs. Lovetotalk. Charlotte. Leonore. Youngwit.

RICHARD: What's going on?
MRS. LOVETOTALK: Going on? I don't know where my head's at.
YOUNGWIT: Mrs. Lovetotalk's a woman of her word, I'll say that.
  You have earned my undying gratitude with this conversation:
  This time I found intelligence and imagination:
  I heard a child that speaks as angels speak above,
  Sir Richard, but alas, it's not your daughter I'm speaking of.
MRS. LOVETOTALK: What's that? Not his daughter? That's neither
  here nor there.
YOUNGWIT: Because she's yours, madam.
MRS. LOVETOTALK: No, no, she's not, I swear.
YOUNGWIT: Yes, your daughter, Mrs. Lovetotalk, is the one I
  adore.

I fell in love with her after a few words, no more.
Beauty can touch a heart all right, but not persuade it,
And wit can be truly conquered only by wit.
What good is the richest woman with little intelligence?
Gold left in a fool's hand is spent with negligence.
It only gives her the means to make a greater fool
Of herself, and find a thousand roads to ridicule.
Sir Richard, do you think . . .

RICHARD: Me? It's up to you to court her.

YOUNGWIT: Mrs. Lovetotalk.

MRS. LOVETOTALK: No, you're promised to Sir Richard's
daughter.

Or did you really think I would be such a cur
That I would take poor Charlotte's groom away from her?

YOUNGWIT: It's up to me . . .

Scene 25

The above. Laconius.

LACONIUS: Here, this is Sir Richard's daughter.

MRS. LOVETOTALK:

Who?

That's a lie! Who ever said a thing like that?

LACONIUS: You.

YOUNGWIT: The man's telling the truth.

RICHARD: Then I have been lied to.

LACONIUS: She said so. That's how it is.

LEONORE: Then I've been lied to, too.

RICHARD: Come, show me your arm, just let me take a look.

CHARLOTTE: Mother!

RICHARD: No, it's not her. It's you. I see it. You and no other.

MRS. LOVETOTALK: Good, take her with you then if you know
better, sir.

RICHARD: I'd gladly exchange a part of my estate for her.

MRS. LOVETOTALK: Then someone must have mixed them up at
birth. My God, this is wild!

YOUNGWIT: It's amazing how people tend to pick up the wrong
child.

MRS. LOVETOTALK: You'd be surprised.

RICHARD: I'm very pleased with the mistake;
Otherwise she might have raised my child herself, the snake.

My child! As soon as I saw you I felt love for you.
Well, Youngwit, you'll be my son still, isn't that true?

YOUNGWIT: If Leonore accepts my being called so from now on,
I am, Father, and this time I enjoy being your son.

LEONORE: I'm sorry about Charlotte. What shall we do with her?

RICHARD: Nothing.

LACONIUS: She can be my wife. Quiet is what I prefer.

YOUNGWIT: He thinks she won't be much trouble because she
doesn't speak,
A woman who keeps silent. No need for him to seek
Further.

RICHARD: But they don't keep silent all the time, it's true.
The quiet ones often speak when you least want them to.

YOUNGWIT: They make a happy pair. Hold hands, don't worry,
you mustn't.
He doesn't speak because he thinks, and she because she
doesn't.

RICHARD: But who'll teach the kids to speak, later?

MRS. LOVETOTALK: I will.

RICHARD: I see.
The wedding's settled. Now let's have fun.

LACONIUS: Will you have me?

(Charlotte bows)

Translated by André Lefevere

THE GERMAN LIBRARY
in 100 Volumes

Wolfram von Eschenbach
Parzival
Edited by André Lefevere

Gottfried von Strassburg
Tristan and Isolde
Edited and Revised by Francis G. Gentry
Foreword by C. Stephen Jaeger

German Mystical Writings
Edited by Karen J. Campbell
Foreword by Carol Zaleski

German Medieval Tales
Edited by Francis G. Gentry
Foreword by Thomas Berger

German Humanism and Reformation
Edited by Reinhard P. Becker
Foreword by Roland Bainton

Gotthold Ephraim Lessing
*Nathan the Wise, Minna von Barnhelm,
and other Plays and Writings*
Edited by Peter Demetz
Foreword by Hannah Arendt

Immanuel Kant
Philosophical Writings
Edited by Ernst Behler
Foreword by René Wellek

Friedrich Schiller
Plays: Intrigue and Love and Don Carlos
Edited by Walter Hinderer
Foreword by Gordon Craig

Friedrich Schiller
Wallenstein and Mary Stuart
Edited by Walter Hinderer

Johann Wolfgang von Goethe
The Sufferings of Young Werther
and *Elective Affinities*
Edited by Victor Lange
Forewords by Thomas Mann

German Romantic Criticism
Edited by A. Leslie Willson
Foreword by Ernst Behler

Friedrich Hölderlin
Hyperion and Selected Poems
Edited by Eric L. Santner

Philosophy of German Idealism
Edited by Ernst Behler

G. W. F. Hegel
*Encyclopedia of the Philosophical Sciences in Outline
and Critical Writings*
Edited by Ernst Behler

Heinrich von Kleist
Plays
Edited by Walter Hinderer
Foreword by E. L. Doctorow

E. T. A. Hoffmann
Tales
Edited by Victor Lange

Georg Büchner
Complete Works and Letters
Edited by Walter Hinderer and Henry J. Schmidt

German Fairy Tales
Edited by Helmut Brackert and Volkmar Sander
Foreword by Bruno Bettelheim

German Literary Fairy Tales
Edited by Frank G. Ryder and Robert M. Browning
Introduction by Gordon Birrell
Foreword by John Gardner

F. Grillparzer, J. H. Nestroy, F. Hebbel
Nineteenth Century German Plays
Edited by Egon Schwarz in collaboration with
Hannelore M. Spence

Heinrich Heine
Poetry and Prose
Edited by Jost Hermand and Robert C. Holub
Foreword by Alfred Kazin

Heinrich Heine
The Romantic School and other Essays
Edited by Jost Hermand and Robert C. Holub

Heinrich von Kleist and Jean Paul
German Romantic Novellas
Edited by Frank G. Ryder and Robert M. Browning
Foreword by John Simon

German Romantic Stories
Edited by Frank G. Ryder
Introduction by Gordon Birrell

German Poetry from 1750 to 1900
Edited by Robert M. Browning
Foreword by Michael Hamburger

Karl Marx, Friedrich Engels, August Bebel, and others
German Essays on Socialism in the Nineteenth Century
Edited by Frank Mecklenburg and Manfred Stassen

Gottfried Keller
Stories
Edited by Frank G. Ryder
Foreword by Max Frisch

Wilhelm Raabe
Novels
Edited by Volkmar Sander
Foreword by Joel Agee

Theodor Fontane
Short Novels and Other Writings
Edited by Peter Demetz
Foreword by Peter Gay

Theodor Fontane
Delusions, Confusions and The Poggenpuhl Family
Edited by Peter Demetz
Foreword by J. P. Stern
Introduction by William L. Zwiebel

Wilhelm Busch and Others
German Satirical Writings
Edited by Dieter P. Lotze and Volkmar Sander
Foreword by John Simon

Writings of German Composers
Edited by Jost Hermand and James Steakley

German Lieder
Edited by Philip Lieson Miller
Foreword by Hermann Hesse

Arthur Schnitzler
Plays and Stories
Edited by Egon Schwarz
Foreword by Stanley Elkin

Rainer Maria Rilke
Prose and Poetry
Edited by Egon Schwarz
Foreword by Howard Nemerov

Robert Musil
Selected Writings
Edited by Burton Pike
Foreword by Joel Agee

Essays on German Theater
Edited by Margaret Herzfeld-Sander
Foreword by Martin Esslin

German Novellas of Realism I and II
Edited by Jeffrey L. Sammons

Friedrich Dürrenmatt
Plays and Essays
Edited by Volkmar Sander
Foreword by Martin Esslin

Max Frisch
Novels, Plays, Essays
Edited by Rolf Kieser
Foreword by Peter Demetz

Gottfried Benn
Prose, Essays, Poems
Edited by Volkmar Sander
Foreword by E. B. Ashton
Introduction by Reinhard Paul Becker

German Essays on Art History
Edited by Gert Schiff

German Radio Plays
Edited by Everett Frost and Margaret Herzfeld-Sander

Hans Magnus Enzensberger
Critical Essays
Edited by Reinhold Grimm and Bruce Armstrong
Foreword by John Simon

All volumes available in hardcover and paperback editions at your bookstore or from the publisher. For more information on The German Library write to: The Continuum Publishing Company, 370 Lexington Avenue, New York, NY 10017.